Just War on Terror?
A Christian and Muslim Response

Edited by

DAVID FISHER
King's College, London

BRIAN WICKER
Council on Christian Approaches to Defence and Disarmament

ASHGATE

Published by
Ashgate Publishing Limited
Wey Court East
Union Road
Farnham
Surrey, GU9 7PT
England

Ashgate Publishing Company
Suite 420
101 Cherry Street
Burlington
VT 05401–4405
USA

www.ashgate.com

British Library Cataloguing in Publication Data
Just war on terror? : a Christian and Muslim response. 1. Just war doctrine.
2. War on Terrorism, 2001–2009 – Religious aspects – Christianity.
3. War on Terrorism, 2001–2009 – Religious aspects – Islam. 4. Terrorism –
Religious aspects – Islam. 5. Terrorism – Religious aspects—Christianity.
6. United States – Military policy – Moral and ethical aspects.
I. Fisher, David. II. Wicker, Brian, 1929– 363.3'2516–dc22

Library of Congress Cataloging–in–Publication Data
Just war on terror? : a Christian and Muslim response /
[edited by] David Fisher and Brian Wicker.
p. cm. Includes bibliographical references and index. ISBN 978-1-4094-0807-9
(alk. paper)—ISBN 978-1-4094-0808-6 (pbk. : alk.paper)—
ISBN 978-1-4094-0809-3 (ebk.) 1. Terrorism—Prevention—
Moral and ethical aspects. 2. War on Terrorism, 2001–2009. 3. Just war doctrine.
4. War—Religious aspects—Christianity. 5. War—Religious aspects—Islam.
I. Fisher, David, 1947– II. Wicker, Brian, 1929–
HV6431.J87 2010
241'.6242—dc22

2010008293

ISBN: 9781409408079 (hbk)
ISBN: 9781409408086 (pbk)
ISBN: 9781409408093 (ebk)

Mixed Sources
Product group from well-managed
forests and other controlled sources
www.fsc.org Cert no. SA-COC-1565
© 1996 Forest Stewardship Council
FSC

Printed and bound in Great Britain by
MPG Books Group, UK

Contents

PART THREE   NEW WAYS TO COUNTER THE THREAT

PART FOUR   AFTERWORD: CONCLUDING REFLECTIONS

Notes On Contributors

AHMAD ACHTAR is a lecturer in Islamic Studies at Heythrop College, University of London, where he works on Muslim/Christian relations, ethics and sacred texts. Research interests include the classical theory of *jihad*.

GENERAL SIR HUGH BEACH served as an officer in the British Army from the closing stages of World War Two to the climax of the Cold War in 1981 when he was Master General of the Ordnance, responsible for procurement. He has since been active in the management of several NGOs and has written, lectured and broadcast on arms control, disarmament and the ethics of peace and war.

PROFESSOR PHILIP BOBBITT is Herbert Wechsler Professor of Federal Jurisprudence and Director of the Center for National Security at Columbia University. He is also a fellow at the University of Texas and a member of a task force on law and terrorism at Hoover Institution, Stanford University. He has served as senior adviser at the White House, the Senate and the State Department in both Democratic and Republican administrations, and has held senior posts at the National Security Council. He is the author of a major work on combating terrorism, *Terror and Consent –The Wars for the Twenty-First Century*.

SHENAZ BUNGLAWALA is undertaking doctoral research on Religion in Turkish Politics in the Government Department at the London School of Economics.

ROSEMARY DURWARD is Senior Lecturer in Defence and International Affairs at the Royal Military Academy, Sandhust, and is now training for the Anglican priesthood. Her most recent publication is as co-editor of and contributor to *Religion, Conflict and Military Intervention* (Ashgate, December 2009).

DR DAVID FISHER was a senior official in the Ministry of Defence and Defence Adviser to the Prime Minister in the Cabinet Office. He is now undertaking research in the Department of War Studies at King's College, London. He is co-Chairman of the Council on Christian Approaches to Defence and Disarmament. He regularly contributes to books and journals on defence and ethical issues and is the author of *Morality and the Bomb*, written when he was a research fellow at Nuffield College, Oxford. His forthcoming book is *Morality and War – Can War Be Just in the 21st Century?*

PROFESSOR LORD HARRIES OF PENTREGARTH is the Gresham Professor of Divinity and President of the Council on Christian Approaches to Defence and

Disarmament. He was previously Bishop of Oxford and is an Honorary Professor of Theology at King's College, London. He regularly broadcasts and writes on religious and ethical issues.

PROFESSOR SIR MICHAEL HOWARD OM established the Department of War Studies at King's College, London, before taking up history chairs, first at Oxford, then at Yale universities. He helped found the International Institute for Strategic Studies of which he is now President and is a Vice President of the Council on Christian Approaches to Defence and Disarmament. In addition to his historical work, he has published prolifically on defence, disarmament and arms control.

DR RICHARD LOCK-PULLAN is a Senior Lecturer in the Department of Political Science and International Studies at the University of Birmingham and was previously a senior lecturer at the Defence Academy. He is the author of *US Intervention and Army Innovation: From Vietnam to Iraq* and has written a number of articles, latterly on the role of religion in politics.

SIR DAVID OMAND was Security and Intelligence Coordinator and Permanent Secretary at the Cabinet Office and Permanent Secretary at the Home Office, having served previously as Director of GCHQ and Policy Director in the Ministry of Defence. He is currently a visiting Professor at King's College, London.

NICK RITCHIE is a Research Fellow in the Department of Peace Studies at the University of Bradford and has published a number of articles on disarmament and nuclear policy issues.

PAUL SCHULTE is a Senior Associate of the Carnegie Endowment and a Senior Visiting Fellow at Kings College, LSE, SOAS and the Defence Academy. He was formerly a senior official in the Ministry of Defence and Department for International Development, working primarily on arms control and was founding Head of the UK's interdepartmental Post-Conflict Reconstruction Unit.

BRIAN WICKER was Principal of Fircroft College of Adult Education, Birmingham, having previously lectured in the Department of Adult Education in Birmingham University. He has been concerned with the ethics of war and nuclear deterrence for many years and has been Chairman/Vice President of *Pax Christi* since the 1970s. He was Chairman of the Council of Christian Approaches to Defence and Disarmament for whom he has edited and contributed to several books.

TIM WINTER lectures in Islamic Studies at Cambridge University and is Director of Studies in Theology at Wolfson College. He is an imam at the Cambridge Mosque, and is the director of the Muslim Academic Trust. He has written numerous articles on Islamic subjects and has edited the Cambridge Companion to Classical Islamic Theology (2008).

Foreword

Richard Harries

After 9/11 the phrase 'War on Terror' became a key element in the rhetoric of George Bush. But as too few noticed at the time, this was immediately to misconceive and misstate the nature of the conflict that the world now faces. Only belatedly are politicians acknowledging that the conflict is first and foremost a struggle for the allegiance of hearts and minds. Those who knew anything about the guerrilla wars and liberation movements after World War II should have realised that the strategies adopted then to counter them, and which need to be adopted now, are not totally dissimilar. Terrorists cannot win great military victories. But they can stay in existence long enough, and create enough mayhem, to achieve their political goals. They will only do this, however, if they can win and retain the support of those in whose name they commit terrorist acts. The extremists at present operating claim to be operating on behalf of the Muslim world against the West, and against Islamic governments corrupted by their association with the West. But does the wider Muslim community recognise the validity of this claim? In so far as they do the terrorists are being successful. In so far as they are not, the terrorists are failing. A rational counter terrorist strategy must ensure that they do not.

Of course military force will need to be used at some points as part of this strategy, but it must be subservient to this wider understanding of what is really at stake. Philip Bobbitt, one of the most distinguished analysts of the use of force today, has argued that force remains crucial. Although he lives in England for some of the year, and is an anglophile, it is probably true to say that he is representative of an American view on this issue. Is there a distinctively different European response? That is one of the interesting issues around which this book is shaped.

The book has been initiated by the Council on Christian Approaches to Defence and Disarmament, and many of the contributors write from a Christian standpoint, with its familiar Just War tradition. The book seeks, however, to explore common ground between traditions and Tim Winter and Ahmad Achtar – both Muslims – explore attitudes to war and violence in Islam. This raises the question about whether the traditional Just War criteria can be applied to a counter-terrorist strategy, or whether terrorism is at once so different and so threatening that they are no longer applicable.

Terrorism is the major threat facing many countries in the world and it is vital that we think clearly about the best way in which it can be countered, not just from a practical but a moral point of view. I believe these chapters, by distinguished contributors, drawing on a wide range of experience and expertise, help us greatly in this task.

Chapter 1

Introduction: A Clash of Civilisations?

David Fisher and Brian Wicker

Very occasionally there are events of such dramatic, world-wide impact that nearly everyone can remember where they were when the news broke. One such event was the terrorist attack on New York and Washington on 11 September 2001 that killed nearly three thousand civilians.

Why was the event so memorable? In part, because we all saw the riveting TV images of the two, apparently slow and cumbersome, civilian airliners crashing into the Twin Towers, in what was thought initially to be an accident. It soon became clear that this was no accident but a devastating attack by a terrorist group, whose name – Al-Qaʿida – would soon echo chillingly around the world.

Terrorism and terrorist attacks killing many innocent civilians are not new phenomena. But there were a number of disturbing novel features in this new brand of terrorism.

It came as a terrible shock to Americans that their country was once more under direct attack, the first time since Pearl Harbor. With the ending of the Cold War, it had been fondly supposed that such threats had gone away. It was thought that, if military forces were to have continuing utility, it would be to fight distant wars in support of broader national and even humanitarian interests, such as the 1999 NATO operation to protect the Muslim inhabitants of Kosovo from Serbian ethnic cleansing. The 9/11 attack – as it quickly became known – once more put self-defence at the top of the security agenda. It underlined, with stark clarity, the duty of a Government to defend its citizens – innocent civilians – from such hostile attack.

Attacking civilians is not a new terrorist tactic. But what was disturbing about the 9/11 assault was that it had been aimed at maximising civilian deaths, with apparent disregard for how this might adversely affect support for the terrorists' cause. It had also been perpetrated by people willing to lose their own lives in the process. Against such unrestrained and suicidal attacks it was difficult to offer direct defence, as the 9/11 assault itself dramatically illustrated. But nor did it seem likely that such terrorists could be deterred by the threat of force, however great the threat posed. Indeed, the terrorists might merely welcome the chance of self-immolating martyrdom. In the Cold War we had relied for our protection upon deterrence through the threat of reprisal and direct defence. But neither now appeared effective against the new terrorist threat.

A further worrying feature was that the attack had been mounted in the USA from far afield, in Afghanistan. It demonstrated that the terrorists had a global reach and capacity. This was achieved by a novel approach of outsourcing their operations through local operatives, both local groups and individuals. It also soon became clear that the terrorists were very adept at exploiting new technology, as illustrated by the way they used the internet to recruit and train their operatives, as well as to publicise their grisly exploits.

But for many in the West what was the most disturbing feature of the new terrorism was its overtly ideological and religious origin and objectives. This was made clear by Osama bin Laden in a variety of pronouncements and *fatwas*. In these he declared that, 'to kill the Americans and their allies – civilians and military – is an individual duty for every Muslim who can do it in any country in which it is possible.'[1] Such assaults were to be mounted not just in support of specific objectives, such as the withdrawal of US forces from Saudi Arabia, but also to achieve much broader aims, such as the abolition of democracy and the establishment of a universal Islamic caliphate and *sharia* law. Moreover, while the 9/11 attack had not employed weapons of mass destruction, bin Laden, when asked about acquiring chemical or nuclear weapons, had declared that, 'acquiring such weapons for the defence of Muslims is a religious duty.'[2] The devastation that could be wrought by such determined terrorists, if armed with weapons of mass destruction, presented a chilling prospect.

The diffusion of aims of the new terrorists was doubly disturbing. It was disturbing because such broad aims appeared beyond the reach of political negotiation. Terrorist campaigns often end in some form of political negotiation. But how could one negotiate with terrorists who apparently wanted to plunge Western society back to a pre-Reformation, pre-democratic past?

It was also very disturbing that this declaration of war on behalf of Islam against the Christian West seemed to betoken a new religious crusade. But this time the crusade was in reverse, from East to West. It seemed to signal the opening shots in the very 'clash of civilisations' and 'war between civilisations' against which Bernard Lewis and Samuel Huntington had prophetically warned at the start of the previous decade.[3] Muslim and Christian scholars, including the present editors, had devoted much time and effort trying to disprove Huntington's thesis and affirming the substantial overlap between the Muslim and Christian traditions. Indeed, the concluding words of a 1998 book by such scholars had been that, 'The

---

[1]   World Islamic Front Statement, 22 February 1998. The text is quoted in full in the Appendix to Chapter 4, 'Arguments Concerning Resistance in Contemporary Islam' by John Kelsay in Richard Sorabji and David Rodin (eds.), *The Ethics of War* (Aldershot, 2006) pp. 89–91.

[2]   Osama bin Laden, 'Conversation with Terror,' interview by Rahimilla Yusufzai, *Time,* (11 January 1999), p. 39.

[3]   'A clash of civilisations' was forecast by Bernard Lewis, 'The roots of Muslim rage,' *Atlantic Monthly,* 266, (September 1990), p. 60. It was taken up by Samuel Huntington who warned against 'a war between civilisations' in Samuel Huntington, 'The clash of civilisations?' *Foreign Affairs,* 72 (3) (Summer 1993), pp. 22–49.

much vaunted clash between Islamic and Christian cultures is thus a myth.'[4] But had Huntington been right all along? The 9/11 attack seemed to suggest that, far from a myth, the war between civilisations had already begun.

Faced with a new and deadly terrorist threat, Western Governments have been uncertain how it should be countered. President Bush promptly declared war not just on the terrorists who had attacked America but on Terror itself. With the election of President Obama, the rhetoric of war has been softened and some policies adjusted. But the problems and challenges to liberal democracy posed by terrorism still remain. Obama may talk less of war but he has substantially increased the US commitment to the war being waged against terrorists in Afghanistan. The need for liberal democracies to wage war on terror has also recently been robustly defended by Philip Bobbitt, a distinguished US academic and former Democrat adviser, in his widely acclaimed book, *Terror and Consent.*[5] His views are critically examined by a number of contributors.

Is a war against terror the right way to proceed? The American public mostly rallied behind the flag of a 'war on terror.' It is argued that only war will mobilise the resources and effort needed to defeat the new enemy. But many Europeans have expressed doubt whether a war against an abstract noun and a policy that appeared to prejudge the appropriate response always in favour of military action was the right way to proceed. Such doubts have been most clearly articulated by the British military historian Michael Howard who explains and develops his concerns in Chapter 5. Philip Bobbitt offers a response to these and other criticisms in the Afterword.

But, even if it is conceded that war is, at least sometimes, an appropriate response, there is still confusion on what grounds and how that war is to be conducted. Force can be used to protect a democratic society from attack. But can force be used to promote the spread of democratic values as a way of countering the spread of terrorism? If defence and deterrence are no longer effective against the new terrorist threat, how is a Government to fulfil its duty to protect its citizens? To counter the new threat it was argued that a new strategy was required, based on a doctrine of pre-emption – attacking the terrorist enemy before he can attack our country and people. This doctrine may offer a way to protect innocent civilians from attack but faces its own challenges and is difficult to reconcile with just war thinking, as David Fisher explains in Chapter 7. There are concerns over the legitimacy of using force not just to protect democracy but to promote democratic values, as Shenaz Bunglawala, Rosemary Durward and Paul Schulte examine in Chapter 9. There are also concerns whether Western Governments have given sufficient attention to non-military options for countering the proliferation of

---

[4]   Harfiyah Haleem, Oliver Ramsbotham, Saba Risaluddin, Brian Wicker (eds.), *The Crescent and the Cross – Muslim and Christian Approaches to War and Peace* (Basingstoke and New York, 1998), p. 214.

[5]   Philip Bobbitt, *Terror and Consent –The Wars for the Twenty-First Century* (London and New York, 2008).

weapons of mass destruction. The risks of nuclear terrorism and options to counter this by non-military means are explored by Nick Ritchie in Chapter 12.

A further challenge is how to acquire intelligence about the activities of the terrorists. In the Cold War intelligence had been acquired primarily by technical means, including satellites tracking the movement of men and materiel. But such operations are of little assistance against the new threat. There is no massing of armies and armaments to observe. Locally recruited terrorist operatives can hide themselves amongst the civilian population. Their weapons, though few and secret, can be deadly. Information about forthcoming attacks is in the terrorist's head, not visible from military manoeuvres on the ground. So how is life-saving information to be acquired? It was argued that new intelligence-gathering techniques, including new interrogation methods, were required. Pre-emptive intelligence can save lives. But, as David Omand explores in Chapter 8, if public trust is to be maintained, the methods employed to acquire such intelligence have to be morally acceptable. A delicate and difficult balance has to be struck, not between public security and human rights, but rather between an individual's right to security and his or her right to privacy and liberty.

The confusion amongst Governments has been not only about the right strategy and tactics to counter the new terrorist threat. There is also moral confusion. We are living in extreme times, so extreme measures have to be considered. In such dangerous times old-fashioned ethical constraints, it was suggested, are no longer relevant. Just war teaching might help guide our thinking about conventional, industrial inter-state, war. But could it help with this new kind of war and the many and multifarious responses that might be required to counter the new terrorist threat?

Paul Schulte explores some of these difficulties, including those presented by the battlefield application of new technology and tactics – the so-called Fourth Generation Warfare – in Chapter 11. These doubts are real and insistent. But we believe that the challenges they present to ethical thought can and must be overcome. In responding to a terrorist threat – however new and deadly it may seem and by whatever means are required – a liberal democracy must still exercise ethical restraint. For, otherwise, we risk compromising the very values we are seeking to defend. Moreover, whatever its imperfections, there is no better source for ethical guidance than the just war thinking that has developed since the times of St Augustine.

That tradition, as it has developed, insists that a military operation will only be just if undertaken with competent authority, for a just cause, with a right intention, as a last resort, and if the harm judged likely to result is not disproportionate to the good to be achieved, taking into account the probability of success; while in its conduct the principles of proportion and the immunity of innocents from direct attack should be complied with; and the operation should end in the establishment of a just peace.

These just war counsels, while couched in the language of war, apply to any use of military force. Their teaching is not tied to a particular mode of warfare, such as industrial inter-state warfare. Indeed, the tradition, dating back to St Augustine in the fifth century AD, long predates the nineteenth- and twentieth-century model of industrial inter-state war.

So, just war teaching, suitably refashioned, can still help guide our thinking about the new terrorist threat. Just war principles underpin our moral appraisal of the actions of terrorists. The 9/11 attack, aimed at maximising civilian casualties, is condemned because it was in clear breach of both the principles of proportion and the immunity of innocents from direct attack. The principles also furnish the ethical constraints that should guide how we, in turn, respond to terrorist attacks. We explore this in more detail in subsequent chapters. In Chapter 11 Hugh Beach traces how just war thinking has helped shape the development of a new US counterinsurgency doctrine, now being implemented in current operations in Afghanistan.

The just war principles, while most fully developed within a tradition of Christian thinking about war, are not, nor were ever intended to be, principles of appeal only to Christians. Indeed, the principles were developed by Aquinas and others within the natural law tradition of the church and were intended to be of appeal to men and women of reason anywhere. Most importantly, these ethical constraints are also reflected within Islamic thinking about war and peace, as the chapters by Tim Winter and Ahmad Achtar make clear. Islamic teaching sets tight limits to defensive *jihad*. The slaughter of innocents is as roundly condemned in mainstream Islamic teaching as it is in mainstream Christian thought, as well as in enlightened secular thinking.

So did 9/11 signal the start of a war between civilisations? Our answer is that it did not. Nor should it be allowed to be presented as if it did. Within both Christian and Islamic traditions there are extremist fringes, whether right-wing Christian fundamentalists in America, whose views Richard Lock-Pullan examines in Chapter 4, or the Salafist/Islamist extremists within Islam, whose influence Ahmad Achtar traces in Chapter 3. Al-Qa'ida – Achtar concludes – is a new, unique and fringe phenomenon within the Islamic scene. Such extremist fringes should not be confused with the central core of believers. Nor should their exaggeration of differences be allowed to obscure the common ground shared by both traditions. For Christians, as Brian Wicker explores in Chapter 5, there is an alternative vision of how mankind could be organised, as a community of diverse peoples, each with its own culture and history, but united in love for the common good of all.

Concern for the common good is central to the three Abrahamic faiths. Islam and Christianity are religions 'of the book', sharing, along with Judaism, a prophetic tradition, sacred literature and moral code. Our histories and cultures have been intertwined, each drawing from the other and both drawing from secular, particularly ancient Greek and Roman philosophy, that itself inspired the just war tradition. There always was, is and will remain an immense overlap between the traditions. The Al-Qa'ida extremists are thus as much at war with mainstream Islamic thinking as with mainstream Christian thinking and enlightened secular thought. The clash of Islamic and Christian cultures was a myth when Huntington first proclaimed it in 1993. It is still a myth.

PART ONE
The Role of Religion in Shaping Terrorism and the Responses to it

Chapter 2
Terrorism and Islamic Theologies of Religiously-Sanctioned War

Tim Winter

The Theological Matrix: a World in Perpetual Conflict?

Although Abraham famously greeted strangers with the word 'Peace',[1] the three religions which trace their pedigrees back to him have found numerous ways of sacralising the warrior's calling. In the Middle Ages this regularly produced fratricide and intransigence, and in our time the idea of an ancient sibling rivalry between his two sons, Isaac and Ishmael, is still invoked to explain current tensions between Islam and the West.[2] Monotheism, many believe, is intrinsically conflictual.[3]

At its best, however, thinking about war in the Abrahamic religions has supplied rich traditions of ethical reflection. Abraham's story in Genesis and the Koran lies at the deep origin of theologies which reject ethnocentrism and selfishness in favour of obedience to an objective higher justice. Each community, each 'people for God', is encouraged to vaunt its self-defence as valid only insofar as it is a defence of God's plan. In the developed theologies of war in Judaism, Christianity and Islam, to take up arms is not simply to protect oneself or one's ethnic group, it is to defend the precious principle that there should be justice in creation. The typical mark of monotheistic theologies of war, therefore, is that self-defence is not to be a defence of the self.

This militant possibility nonetheless coexists with a strong preference for peace. The 'Semitic religions' speak of the *darkhei shalom*, the *subul al-salām*: the ways of peace. Where the choice exists, peace must be chosen; such was clearly the consistent urging of the Prophets. Mercy must always preponderate, because humans are called to be custodians of a cosmic system which, despite its frequent harshness, is seen as a faded memory of the war-less harmony which prevailed before the Fall. For Islam, 'the Peace' becomes one of the names of God, in whom we were wholly brethren, *in illo tempore*. A frequently-quoted Koranic verse

---

[1]   Koran, 51:25. Cf. Genesis 18:1–5.

[2]   See for instance the cover story of *Time* magazine, 30 September 2002.

[3]   Jan Assman, *Moses the Egyptian: the memory of Egypt in Western monotheism* (Cambridge and London, 1997).

speaks of a time when all human souls, before conception and enfleshment in the world, were united in the confession of God's unity:

> And remember when thy Lord brought forth from the Children of Adam, their seed, and made them testify of themselves: 'Am I not your Lord?' 'Yes,' they said, 'We testify!' That was lest you should say on the Day of Resurrection: 'Of this we were unaware.'[4]

For theologians, the awareness of human unity before God thus seems grounded in more than the cliché of a shared Adamic ancestry, a pedigree which would in itself imply no necessary consequences given its rapid collapse, in the next generation, into fratricide. Instead, the scripture is understood to propose the restoration of harmony among human beings as the retrieval of an ancient shared moment, experienced as an all-encompassing human covenant.

There is something of this 'meta-nostalgia' in the Prophet's well-known prayer: 'Lord God, You are Peace, and from You is peace, and to You shall peace return, greet us therefore in peace, and bring us to the Garden in peace, O Lord of Majesty and Grace.'[5] 'Peace', *salām*, is to be the mutual greeting of the blessed in Heaven.[6] Paradise is itself *dār al-salām*, the abode of peace,[7] and as such straddles history with two indefinite periods of *salām*. The world which briefly supervenes is understood as an interval in which trials, determined by God's *jalāl* and *jamāl*, 'Majesty and Beauty', determine the human right to end as humans began, in a state of peace, a place of reconciliation before the face of God.[8]

Yet historic Muslim theology has also taught that the duty to work for peace on earth, for a proleptic anticipation of the infinitely hospitable Kingdom, often requires, as perhaps the most painful paradox of the 'fallen' human condition, the forcible disciplining of the lower possibilities of the self and of human institutions. The ways of peace may lead through conflict.[9] Contemporary Muslim thinkers, reacting to evangelical comparativists such as Kenneth Cragg, often hold that

---

[4]   Koran, 7:172. For this 'covenant' see Wadad al-Qadi, 'The Primordial Covenant and Human History in the Qur'ān', *Proceedings of the American Philosophical Society* 147 (2003), pp. 332–8.

[5]   Muslim, Masājid, 135. The name *al-Salām* for God originates in Koran 59:23, and in the hadith literature: Bukhārī, Adhān, p. 148.

[6]   Aḥmad ibn Ḥanbal, *al-Musnad* (Cairo, 1313AH), IV, 381; cf. Koran, 7:46; 50:34.

[7]   Koran, 6:127.

[8]   Jane Idleman Smith and Yvonne Yazbeck Haddad, *The Islamic Understanding of Death and Resurrection* (Albany, 1981), 63–98. For the salvation of non-Muslims see T. Winter, 'The last trump card: Islam and the supersession of other faiths', *Studies in Interreligious Dialogue* 9 (1999), 133–55.

[9]   'Sunni theorists understood force to be a possible and useful means of extending the territory of Islam and thus a tool in the quest for peace.' John Kelsay, *Islam and war: a study in comparative ethics* (Westminster, 1993), p. 35.

the Gospel strategy of non-resistance, with which the Koran's teaching is often contrasted, has seemed at once too optimistic and too pessimistic: optimistic because of its claim that passive witness, exampled in Christ and the martyrs, can reliably melt obdurate human hearts; and pessimistic because of its seeming conviction that the Fall renders any recourse to political or other structural action in society a self-defeating exercise. Cragg queries the Exodus model, and the Prophet's *Hijra* as well, as betraying an undue 'Semitic' hopefulness about the ability of a political liberation to deliver religiously. For him, the Promised Land all too easily entails spiritual defeat, as the soul is rotted by the need to vanquish Canaanites or the Quraysh. Our travails in Egypt, or Mecca, must be interrupted only by death or the day of the Lord. 'Liberation theology', that is to say, a political and even militant style of action against oppressive structures, risks enmeshing us in spiritual bondage.[10]

Islam, as articulated by apologists such as Shabbir Akhtar, tends to regard this as a disastrous misreading of the intentions of Jesus and the prophets. The insistence on waiting in Egypt seems morally unambitious. A due regard for the caliphal potential which God set in man at the time of the primordial covenant, a regard which, Muslims will claim, is surely a better support to humanism than a miserable stress on human sinfulness, persuades us that martyrdom is not the only future. Martyrdom, as a selfless witnessing (*shahāda*) to truth and justice, is of course a possible result, and the 'Semitic' move hardly underestimates it. Yet it is not the only virtue. As Akhtar puts it, earthly failure is not the only mode of religious success.[11]

Muslims might want to reduce this dichotomy by recalling that early Christianity was *understandably* pacifist. For Paul's communities, the *parousia* was imminent, and living in Christ offered the only prospect of peace and deliverance in a world where the Roman imperium seemed built to withstand any shock other than a battle led by God himself. By Augustine's time chiliastic expectations had weakened, and the Church found itself obliged to develop theories of statesmanship and just war which, as several recent authors have shown, do not depart fundamentally from the principles enunciated by the prophetic religions.[12]

The Ishmaelites, when they came into their inheritance, did not question this; and although they sometimes developed theologies of pragmatic non-violence,

---

[10]   Kenneth Cragg, *The Lively Credentials of God* (London, 1995), 15; for his idea of 'Semitism' see Kenneth Cragg, *Semitism: The Whence and the Where. 'How Dear Are your Counsels'* (Brighton and Portland, 2005).

[11]   Shabbir Akhtar, *The Final Imperative: an Islamic theology of liberation* (London, 1992).

[12]   John Kelsay and James Turner Johnson (eds), *Just War and Jihad: Historical and Theoretical Perspectives on War and Peace in Western and Islamic Traditions* (New York, Westport and London, 1991), and more recently, John Kelsay, *Arguing the Just War in Islam* (Harvard, 2007); cf. Norman Solomon, 'The Ethics of War in Judaism', in Richard Sorabji and David Rodin (eds), *The Ethics of War* (Aldershot, 2006), pp. 108–37.

Islamic pacifisms are rare.[13] The universalism of the Ishmaelite's calling has inclined Muslim political theorists to believe that Islam bears the key responsibility in restoring the primordial peace of the first prologue in heaven. In the middle ages, as though in emulation of the first universal prophet, Adam, the Ishmaelites felt that although the world may be a wilderness, they were called to make a garden within it. Like Muhammad, the believing community should move from a symbolic Mecca, capital of the wilderness and emblem of human hubris, to an oasis city, which becomes a new enclosed garden for the monotheistic truth. Later, Persian and Ottoman mirrors for princes repeat this image of the Muslim realm as a garden surrounded by deserts and fabulous beasts. Outside the House of Islam, the *dār al-Islām*, there is not peace, there is only war and predation; and unless one is militarily prepared, that House of War will surely invade and destroy the believing realm. In this way, classical Muslim theorists adopted a somewhat Hobbesian view of the world as strongly tending to chaos and aggression, and honoured the believing warrior as the indispensable earthly guarantor of tranquillity and justice.[14]

The Caliph's task was thus often compared to that of a gardener. If the weeds are left to flourish, and if wild beasts from beyond the pale intrude, the garden will do no honour to its owner. As the caliph preaches from the pulpit, he rests his hands on a sword. He has been authorised to bear it by the Koran itself, which, in a passage traditionally thought to be the first to authorise the use of force, announces: 'But for God's repelling some people by means of others, cloisters and churches and oratories and mosques, wherein the name of God is often mentioned, would surely have been thrown down' (22:40).

The Sufi poet Jalāl al-Dīn Rūmī (d.1273) put it this way:

> Knowledge and wealth and office and rank and fortune are a mischief in the hands of the evil-natured.
> Therefore the Jihad was made obligatory on true believers for this purpose, namely, that they might take the spear-point from the hand of the madman.[15]

The duty of custodianship falls only on caliphal shoulders. That is to say, upon the shoulders of the one who, like Adam, has been 'taught all the names' (Koran 2:31). Only a prophet, or a prophet-like figure, may slay without murdering. For Rūmī, and for the bulk of the Muslim tradition, the Prophet is a 'Perfect Man' because he represents not only God's names of beauty, but His names of majesty.

[13] Mohammed Abu-Nimer, 'A Framework for Nonviolence and Peacebuilding in Islam,' in *Journal of Law and Religion* 15 (2000–01), 217–265, p. 228 for a bibliography of Muslim works on non-violence.

[14] For the theology of this kind of pessimism, see for instance Ayman Shihadeh, *The Teleological Ethics of Fakhr al-Dīn al-Rāzī* (Leiden, 2006), p. 174.

[15] See the entire section in Jalāl al-Dīn Rūmī, *Mathnawī*, edited and translated by R.A. Nicholson, (London, 1925–40), V, 3734–3828.

Perfection unites the *mysterium tremendum et fascinans*. Hence: God forgives, and the Prophet forgives. God judges, and so does His Prophet. This is lawful only because the ego is disengaged.

As caliph, the Prophet, or his deputy, is merely the passive tool of God in restoring the balance of creation. A hadith tells us that God says, 'When I love My servant, I become the eye with which he sees, the ear with which he hears, the foot with which he walks, and the hand with which he smites.'[16] The Koran seems to affirm the same sort of mystical *imitatio Dei*: 'You slew them not, but God slew them' (8:17). In this, Islam is hardly unique. Other traditions which have developed a model of sacred warriorhood offer very similar reflections about the saint who fights. In the *Bhagavad Gita*, Krishna says: 'By Me alone have they already been slain: be thou merely an instrumental cause.'[17] Something similar happened in some dimensions of Buddhism: for many in the Mahayana tradition, a Boddhisattva does not violate his *dharma* if he kills a robber who is about to commit murder.[18]

In its historical evolution, therefore, Islam has not had difficulty with the category of a warrior saint, provided that the warrior is indeed striving to be such. War is no different from any other potentially problematic area of human responsibility, such as sexuality or the ownership of property, in that it ensnares the egotist but can uplift the unselfish. To object to the saints who bear arms is, to the extent that they are what they claim to be, no more theologically coherent than to object to the existence of majesty as well as beauty in God's world.

Ethical Dilemmas in the Classical Sharīʿa Theory

The theology of war was, however, never going to be this simple in practice. The very juxtaposition of good and evil in a world which cries out for political action also renders it vulnerable to subversion. The saint, like the prophet, will therefore be instinctively averse to war. A hadith reports the Prophet as having said: 'Do not look forward to an encounter with the enemy; but when you encounter him, stand firm.'[19] His community is told: 'Fighting is prescribed for you, though you dislike it' (Koran 2:216). The aversion is a virtue, but it must not be manifested as cowardice. Its utility lies in a preference for non-violent solutions, the avoidance of vainglory, in recalling the preponderance of mercy, and also in the cultivation of prudence.

A key question for the tradition, which this leaves unresolved, was this: does the caliphal duty to make war on the enemies of God's peace require offensive war, or is it to be purely defensive and reactive?

---

[16] Bukhārī, Riqāq, 38.

[17] *Gita*, XI.33.

[18] D. Keown, *The Nature of Buddhist Ethics* (Basingstoke, 1992), p. 152.

[19] Muslim, Jihād, p. 19.

One reason for the ambiguity of the Muslim response lay in the plurality of possible readings of the Koran. Fred Donner, author of a major study of the early Islamic conquests, notes this as follows:

> The Qur'ānic text as a whole conveys an ambivalent attitude towards violence. On the one hand, oppression of the weak is roundly condemned, and some passages state clearly that the believers are to fight only in self-defence. But a number of passages seem to provide explicit justification for the use of war or fighting to subdue unbelievers, and deciding whether the Qur'ān actually condones offensive war for the faith, or only defensive war, is really left to the judgement of the exegetes.[20]

And here is Alfred Guillaume, historian of the Prophet's life

> The texts which urge the Muslims to fight in the way of God quite obviously refer to the soil of Arabia, and though Jews and Christians are mentioned it is not at all clear whether all are included.[21]

One Koranic text reads: 'If they then withdraw from you, and do not fight against you, but offer you peace, God has not opened for you a way against them' (4:90). Another, however, tells us to 'fight the idolators totally, as they fight you totally' (9:36). The Prophet certainly fought against the idol-worshipping Meccan elite and their clan allies, but whether he envisaged the wars which conquered the Near East after his death has not been easy for modern scholars to determine.[22] The *jihād* partly originated as a means of suppressing the pagan blood-feuds which had been rampant among the Arab tribes, and historians surmise that the later conquests may have been launched by the caliphs as a means of cementing the unity of the same tribes after their conversion.[23] It was only much later that attempts were

---

[20]   Fred Donner, 'Sources of Islamic Conceptions of War', in Kelsay, John, and Johnson, James Turner (eds), *Just War and Jihad: Historical and Theoretical Perspectives on War and Peace in Western and Islamic Traditions* (New York, Westport and London: Greenwood Press, 1991), p. 47.

[21]   Alfred Guillaume, *Islam* (London, *c.*1956), p. 72.

[22]   See Fred Donner, *The Early Islamic Conquests* (Princeton, 1981), p. 271: 'It is also possible to argue that the conquests of Syria and Iraq were merely side effects of the state's drive to consolidate its power over all Arab tribes, including those living in the Syrian desert and on the fringes of Iraq. This process generated the direct clashes with the Byzantine and Sasanian Empires that ultimately led to the Islamic conquest of Syria and Iraq, but that does not necessarily imply that the conquest of Syria and Iraq was a conscious objective of the ruling elite from the start.'

[23]   Peter Partner, *God of Battles: holy wars of Christianity and Islam* (London, 1997), pp. 37, 41.

made to turn it into a formal legal doctrine.[24] Yet despite the undoubted element of *realpolitik* informing the conquerors' decisions, it is clear that they justified their actions religiously. If *jihād* was to be, not quite for the sake of Islam, but for the oppressed (*mustaḍ'afūn*),[25] then it was hard to see why non-Arabs should be excluded from its liberative scope.

Classical Sunni law, when it came to be formulated three or more centuries after the Prophet's death, typically decided the issue on the basis of its theology of Islam's caliphal and Ishmaelite responsibilities to all mankind. It read the Koran as justification for offensive war outside the Arabian peninsula, with the objective not of converting unbelievers by force (an act which Islamic law generally forbade)[26] but of broadening the Abrahamic tent in which members of non-idolatrous religions could worship, under the aegis of God's latest law.[27] This is the policy referred to by the modern Indian thinker Muhammad Hamidullah (1908–2002) as 'idealist' war (perhaps 'utopian' would be a better adjective).[28] Hamidullah surveyed and generally commended the views of his medieval predecessors for whom the world naturally divided into *Dār al-Islām*, the House of Islam, implicitly the lands whose rulers obeyed God and where peace prevailed, and the *Dār al-Ḥarb*, the House of War, meaning the places which, in a state of nature, were at war with themselves and against Islam. A third category, *Dār al-Ṣulḥ*, or the House of Treaty, came to be added by some jurists, reflecting the Prophet's practice of concluding truces with non-Muslim powers.

Jihād Theory in the Modern Period

All these categories were formulated in medieval times. In the nineteenth century, Hamidullah's 'idealist' paradigm came under increasing pressure from Europeanising reformers, who were no longer persuaded by the classical view that the lands outside Islam were places of mere pandemonium. In 1856, the Ottomans signed the Treaty of Paris, thereby joining the Concert of Europe and

---

[24]   Roxanne L. Euben, 'Killing (For) Politics: Jihad, Martyrdom and Political Action', *Political Theory* 30 (2002), 4–35; see p. 13, where *jihād* in Koran and Hadith 'appears less a fixed doctrine about warfare than a recurrent and flexible motif with multiple interpretive possibilities.'

[25]   Cf. Koran 4:75. For the arguments and a new insight see Rumee Ahmed, 'Rescuing the Wretched: Between Universal and Particular Readings of Q. 4:75, in the *Journal of Scriptural Reasoning* 8 (2009); etext.virginia.edu/journals/ssr/issues/volume8/number1/ssr08_01_e02.html

[26]   For the rule and the exceptions see Yohanan Friedmann, *Tolerance and Coercion in Islam: Interfaith Relations in the Muslim Tradition* (Cambridge, 2003), pp. 87–120.

[27]   On the basis of commentaries upon Koran 22:40.

[28]   Muhammad Hamidullah, *Muslim Conduct of State* (3rd edition, Lahore, 1953), pp. 167–9.

implicitly validating the nation-state model. In few areas of traditional consensus did Sharī'a laws change so drastically as in this domain; the only other case that might parallel it being the abolition of classical Muslim laws on slavery. Today, all Muslim countries belong to the Organisation of the Islamic Conference (OIC), which affirms the UN Charter and international law as the basis for the external relations of member states. Article 2(4) of the UN Charter prohibits armed aggression, and despite objections from religious radicals, every Muslim state, whether or not it claims to impose versions of Sharī'a domestically, has committed itself to this principle. Moves have been made at the OIC for the establishment of an international Sharī'a court that would mediate in international disputes, but such an institution would, on the current proposals, have no authority to override international laws save by mutual consent, which would seldom be forthcoming in the case of relations between a Muslim country and a non-Muslim neighbour.[29] Overall, the Muslim nation-states have insisted on full participation in the Western-authored 'international community'. As Naveed Shaikh observes:

> The very Charter of the Islamic Conference certainly makes no pretensions to challenge the operative expressions of the secular world order […] in fact, beyond the mere recognition, as fait accompli, of the constitutive rules of the (Westphalian) order of territorial states, Islamic states have willingly internalised the regulatory rules of étatism.[30]

Part of the background to this remarkable accession of Muslim jurisdictions to a global legal framework of purely European provenance is the retreat by most late twentieth century Muslim legal theorists from the so-called 'idealist' interpretation of the Koran's intentions. As Richard Martin summarises the position, 'the majority of contemporary Muslim jurists […] restrict jihad as it applies to modern Muslim nation-states to defense against outside attack and/or internal subversion.'[31] For instance, one of the leading figures of Islamic legal thought in the twentieth century, Shaykh Ṣubḥī Mahmassānī, was able to write as follows:

> Islamic law […] is essentially a law of peace, built on human equality, religious tolerance, and universal brotherhood. War, in theory, is just and permissible only as a defensive measure, on grounds of extreme necessity, namely to protect

---

[29]   Naveed Shaikh, *The New Politics of Islam: Pan-Islamic foreign policy in a world of states* (London, 2003).

[30]   Ibid., 130. Cf. also Hasan Moinuddin, *The Charter of the Islamic Conference and the Legal Framework of Economic Co-operation among its Member States* (Oxford, 1987).

[31]   Richard Martin, 'The Religious Foundations of War, Peace and Statecraft in Islam', in Kelsay and Johnson, p. 108.

freedom of religion, to repel aggression, to prevent injustice, and to protect social order.[32]

Does such a position envisage a role for the old 'idealist' Sharī'a view which tolerates pre-emptive action? More pointedly, can one invade a foreign, even a distant, country in order to protect oppressed Muslim communities? In 1994, the Organisation of the Islamic Conference passed resolutions authorising member states to disregard the UN arms embargo on Bosnia, citing the need to intervene to rescue the Muslims of the region from genocide. In the event, Western pressure forced the OIC countries back into the international camp. The OIC, purportedly the flag-bearer of Muslim unity and values, had shown the ineffectual nature of its modern *jihād* discourse in the face of Western policies and power.

Despite the willingness of mainstream jurists to redefine their reading of the Koran to reduce or abolish the scope for offensive war, the concept of *jihād* remains firmly part of Muslim discourse. Ann Mayer notes that the clearest example has been the reaction to the occupation of Palestine, which has called forth a range of official religious pronouncements, such as the 1973 *fatwā* (verdict) by the Shaykh al-Azhar, for many the highest religious authority in the Sunni world, to the effect that fighting for the liberation of Palestine was a religious duty, not just for Palestinians, but for all Muslims. The *fatwā* was reiterated at the Third Islamic Conference in Ṭā'if, in 1981. The regimes, due to religious apathy and Western pressure, seem to have paid no attention; but the preponderant juristic view remains that the Israeli occupation should be resisted by force.

This is not the first time that Palestine has been the proving-ground for *jihād* theories. For Muslims, the loss of Palestine, classified as a holy land by the Koran and the hadith literature, has entailed a deep offense to Islamic optimism about the discernability of God's purposes. For medieval historians such as Ibn al-Athīr, the Crusader intrusion had placed the City, and the Aqṣā Mosque, into the hands of followers of a radical misunderstanding of the will of Heaven. The community of the Messiah was supposed to be a Jewish community, and its Gentile extension, represented by the Crusader monarchies, was a *ghuluww*, an extremism, represented as much by its violence as by its excessive claims for Jesus. The seventh-century delivery of the Temple site into Ishmaelite hands, and the fulfilment of biblical expectations that it would be made a house of prayer for all nations, had now been brutally reversed. Famously, the first Palestinian refugees who reached Baghdad violated the Ramadan fast publicly in the mosque, to signal the profound breach of the religious order of the world that the sack of Jerusalem seemed to entail.[33]

If the Crusader intrusion resembled an attempt to defy God's purpose to open the Temple to all in the uniquely universal Ishmaelite *oecumene*, a regression to an order abrogated centuries before, the Zionist movement presented a still

---

[32] Ann Mayer, 'War and Peace in the Islamic Tradition and International Law', in Kelsay and Johnson, p. 203.

[33] Michael Foss, *People of the First Crusade* (London, 1997), pp. 186–7.

more shocking challenge to Muslim assurances. The Third Temple was now in the hands of a people who seemed to have no confidence in the two most recent, and climacteric, figures in the city's prophetic story. A series of attempts to destroy the Dome of the Rock, the first championed by Shlomo Goren, the chief rabbi of the IDF, but blocked by the politicians,[34] seemed more disturbing even than the increasing unlikelihood of a substantial return of refugees.

Today, one hears Catholic priests in Palestine call the Israeli prime minister the 'New Herod'. Perhaps, then, Hamas are the *sicarii*, the assassins willing to lose their own lives to bring death to the Romans.[35] The very word *ḥamās* means 'zealotry'. Ḥamās identifies Western support for the rejection of the 2006 election results as a delegitimisation of Maḥmūd 'Abbās; his faction, rebelling at the West's insistence against the elected government of Ismā'īl Hanīya, is therefore a 'Khārijite' formation: it is just to fight for democracy and faith against a Western-backed usurpation lacking popular mandate. Gaza is an embryonic House of Islam, and its *jihād* will ensure that oppression and alien occupation will be no more. Christian Westerners who support the occupation of any part of historic Palestine are co-conspirators with Israel in prolonging Palestinian misery; in some contexts, they too can form a target.

According to Ann Mayer, the creation of Israel has been the principal dynamo of Islamic radicalism. Although, as she points out, 'the connections between Islamic institutions and doctrines and any distinctively Islamic form of terrorism are very weak,'[36] a situation which remains the case with regards movements with no direct involvement in Palestinian liberation,[37] one notes a growing, and worrying, reluctance to apply to Ḥamās's actions against the occupation the same condemnation that was heard in the aftermath of the attacks on the United States.[38]

It may be, as a number of academics have speculated, that a major long-term consequence of the creation of the state of Israel will be the reversal of the once-strong trend towards the moderation of Islam's old *Dār al-Islām* versus *Dār al-Ḥarb* dichotomy. Ḥamās against Israel is seen as a kind of microcosm, or accentuated version, of Islamic fighters in their Manichean struggle against the whole West. And Ḥamās's struggle against the Western-backed Palestinian

---

[34]   Bernard Wasserstein, *Divided Jerusalem: The Struggle for the Holy City* (Yale and London, 2001), p. 328.

[35]   For the roots of the suicide bombing phenomenon, see Abdal Hakim Murad, *Bombing without Moonlight: the origins of suicidal terrorism* (Bristol, 2008).

[36]   Mayer, in Kelsay, p. 218.

[37]   Al-Qaʿida appears to have been uniformly condemned by the religion's leadership: for some representative voices see www.uga.edu/islam/nineeleven.html.

[38]   Note, however, the view of one secular philosopher, that 9/11 and similar atrocities were immoral, but that Palestinian resistance could be classified as 'just terrorism': Ted Honderich, *Humanity, Terrorism, Terrorist War: Palestine, 9/11, 7/7 ...* (London and New York, 2006), p. 184. Given such views, not uncommon on the secular Left, it is unlikely that Muslims themselves can be persuaded not to sympathise with Palestinian militant violence.

Authority is emblematic of the larger self-understanding of Islamic movements, which campaign against Westernised elites for the return of indigenous values to the public square. Returning the compliment, right-wing elements in the Washington administration speak of crusades, while the mainstream public discourse in the US becomes, often with the help of pro-Israel activists, generically anti-Muslim, so that the whole Muslim world is treated as a kind of House of War, in need of direct American garrisoning. The longer-term implications are disturbing. Will the zealots who react against this be defeated by the new Rome and its Herodian allies, this time around, given the possibilities of technological terrorism? A stalemate seems more likely. Gaza turned out not to be Masada, because the resistance seems unbroken, and even hard-hearted Westerners are increasingly anxious about Palestinian suffering.

Non-State Violence: *Baghy* and *Ḥirāba*

These medieval Sharī'a theories of *jihād*, amended and in some respects revived in modern times, paralleled in important respects medieval Christian thinking on just war, and several scholars have documented this convergence.[39] But as with the Christian theories, Islamic law was obliged to note the difficulty of dealing with an actual world in which clear dichotomies were far less common than situations of deep ambiguity. In particular, the Sharī'a thinkers struggled with the more difficult, non-territorial issue, of extremist rebels, or Khārijites, who were not external crusading armies, but internal Muslim formations which for a range of reasons, some clear and some indecipherable, took up arms against the authorities. This was a particularly sensitive topic for Muslims, since although pragmatism and the most evident sense of scripture indicated the propriety of a quietist obedience to Muslim rulers, even when unjust, it was not possible to ignore the fact that revered figures in early Islam, including the Prophet's widow 'Ā'isha, had unmistakeably 'come out' and offered battle to the established caliphal authorities.

The debate in medieval Islamic law here focussed on two categories rooted loosely in Koranic terminology: *baghy* and *ḥirāba*.[40] The former was generally understood as a religiously-based rebellion against lawful authority. The punishment was not fixed, but commonly those engaged in such rebellions were exempted from punishment if their penitence was evident, particularly if they abandoned their views before actually resorting to violence. *Ḥirāba*, by contrast, was defined

---

[39]   This is the perspective of several authors in Kelsay and Johnson, op. cit., see also Hilmi M. Zawati, *Is Jihad a Just War? War, Peace, and Human Rights under Islamic and Public International Law* (Lewiston and Lampeter, 2001).

[40]   A third category, *fasād fi'l-arḍ* ('corruption upon the earth'), also rooted in Koranic language, is recognised by jurists of the Mālikī school as a variety of *ḥirāba*, which can include acts of espionage or sabotage ('Abd Allāh ibn al-Sayyid al-Maḥfūẓ bin Bayyah, *al-Irhāb, al-tashkhīṣ wa'l-ḥulūl* (n.p, n.d., 29).

as a more severe form of insurrection that involved not only a military challenge to the ruler's army, but brigandage, rape, the wanton destruction of property, and the murder of civilians. In the definition of the chief judge of Muslim Lisbon, Ibn 'Abd al-Barr (d.1071): 'Anyone who disturbs free passage in the streets and renders them unsafe to travel, striving to spread corruption in the land by taking money, killing people or violating what God has made it unlawful to violate, is guilty of *ḥirāba*, be he a Muslim or non-Muslim, free or slave, and whether he actually realises his goal of taking money and killing or not.'[41] *Ḥirāba* was distinguished from more familiar crimes of murder and theft by the distinguishing intention to cause fear and helplessness.[42] The Arabic root underlying *ḥirāba*, *ḥ.r.b.*, has resonances of rage and fury, the qualities of untrammelled egotism which the Koran attributes to the Arab pagans (48:26), and which are the opposite of the detached, cold anger of the prophet or saint directed against those who damage God's peace. Today, this has allowed modern thinkers to identify it as the Sharī'a category into which acts of terrorism naturally fall:

> In effect, these extremists rely on and worship themselves. They are exhibiting the most serious crime condemned in the Qur'an, which is the root of almost all the other crimes, namely, arrogance. They are committing the crime of *hirabah*, which is the attack on the very roots of civilisation, and justifying it in the name of Islam. There can be no greater evil and no greater sin.[43]

The crime of *ḥirāba* is specified in the Koran, sura 5, verse 33, which also permits the judge to choose between a range of punishments, ranging from crucifixion, or the amputation of limbs, to exile. It is the most severely punished crime in Islamic law.

State suppression of *ḥirāba*-type movements continued to be sanctioned by Muslim jurists in an approximately classical way until well into the nineteenth century. The most serious case in the caliphate's declining years was the rebellion by members of the Wahhābī sect of Central Arabia, which was put down by an Ottoman army in 1818. The Wahhābīs had carried out large-scale atrocities against ordinary Muslims, demolished shrines deemed incompatible with Wahhābī tenets, and killed orthodox Muslim scholars who fell into their hands. Ottoman jurists such as Ibn 'Ābidīn (d.1837) issued formal rulings condemning them and validating their suppression by the caliphal armies.[44]

Modern Muslim writers, inhabiting a world without a caliph, and hence without a central institution for the identification and suppression of *ḥirāba*, find in the

---

[41]   Sherman Jackson, 'Domestic Terrorism in the Islamic Legal Tradition', *The Muslim World*, 91, (2001).

[42]   Khaled Abou El Fadl, *Rebellion and Violence in Islamic Law* (Cambridge, 2001), pp. 234–94.

[43]   Robert Crane, 'Hirabah versus Jihad', www.irfi.org/articles/articles_301_350/hirabah_versus_jihad.htm

[44]   Abou El Fadl, p. 333.

principle a useful parallel to Western understandings of terrorism (while noting that the parallel cannot be exact, in the absence of an agreed definition of the latter).[45] Although the American Muslim scholar Sherman Jackson, in a detailed study of Islamic legal definitions of terrorism, draws our attention to certain distinctions between *hirāba* and terrorism as legally defined in the US since it began as a legal category there in the 1960s, he is able to conclude that 'this law corresponds in its most salient features to domestic terrorism in the American legal system.'[46] In particular, he notes that *hirāba*, as a category that exists as a potential resource to be invoked when conventional penalties are insufficient, makes terrorism (if this is the translation to be used) an offence even more broadly and inclusively defined in Islamic law than in the US. He concludes: 'In this capacity, *hirābah* appears, again, to parallel the function of terrorism as an American legal category. Its function is not so much to define specific crimes but to provide a mechanism for heightening the scrutiny and/or level of pursuit and prosecution in certain cases of actual or potential public violence.'

Jackson's conclusion, however, should be tempered by the awareness that his comparison is with domestic terrorism. Whether *hirāba* is an offense analogous to international terrorism is a more ambiguous issue in Islamic law, since the classical Sharī'a manuals were composed long before the emergence of the modern nation-state model, and modern jurisdictions in the post-caliphal Islamic world either entirely ignore the categories of *baghy* and *hirāba*, or manipulate them opportunistically to signify any militant opposition to the state. Moreover, the current phrase 'war on terror' (*harb 'ala'l-irhāb* in the Arab media) is generally rejected by Muslim jurists, since *jihād* is defined as a war against particular human beings or their agencies, not against a principle as such, least of all one which seems to have assumed almost metaphysical status as a denoter of a cosmic, perhaps eschatological enemy.[47]

In this context of radical renegotiation and the absence of any properly-constituted Sharī'a judiciary, new definitions have emerged. In the discourse of radical groups, the term *hirāba* is now often reinterpreted to refer not to their own actions, but to the oppression of the regimes currently in place across the Muslim world. Ruling by torture and terror, these pro-Western tyrannies are guilty of this most serious crime, and to oppose them is not *hirāba*, but its opposite: a righteous struggle for the oppressed which must lead either to martyrdom or freedom. Sayyid Qutb (d.1966) is the best-known exponent of this radical inversion of traditional Sharī'a understandings of the *hirāba* principle.[48] His view is extreme, but reflects nonetheless the sense among many Muslims that classical legal assumptions about the inviolability of rulers are intolerable in an age when rulers openly flout religion, collaborate with foreign economic interests, and violate the rights of their populations.

---

[45]   Bin Bayyah, pp. 18–19, 127.

[46]   Jackson, 'Domestic Terrorism in the Islamic Legal Tradition,' pp. 293–310.

[47]   Cf. Bin Bayyah, pp. 127–31.

[48]   Abou El Fadl, pp. 338–9.

Possible Futures

The classical tolerance of offensive *jihād* has, as recorded above, been downplayed or reversed in line with the perceived requirements of living in a comity of modern nation states. Likewise, laws of *baghy* and *ḥirāba* have drastically mutated. However religious thinkers cannot escape their duty to quarry the old resources to find a religiously-unarguable rebuttal of the new radicals. In the case of Western invasions of Iraq and Afghanistan, most notably, the inactivity or tacit complicity of most Muslim regimes has substantially increased the appeal of hardline interpretations of the *jihād* principle, and the determination of these activists, even when subject to torture by Western governments or their perceived proxies,[49] indicates the persuasiveness of the new argument that *ḥirāba* is in reality the practice of the regimes, and that the insurrectionists, through a utilitarian calculus, are using ugly but ultimately less savage methods in order to bring about a just order where presently there is only hubris and corruption. To revert to the ancient metaphor, Al-Qaʿida sees the Muslim garden as invaded by rapacious neighbours, and its own gardeners as fifth-columnists for that invasion, resulting in nothing less than the destruction of the Abode of Islam and the imposition of alien values. The loss of Palestine supplies the key icon of this David and Goliath asymmetry; but every other Muslim country is seen as the stage for a similar, though usually less visible, drama. This polemic gained still more traction when during the Bush administration, as is examined in Chapter 4, the use of strong religious language by some Western leaders intensified this belief that Muslim values were at risk from inveterate Christian enemies, who wished to see only one set of values prevail throughout the world.[50]

Despite the current polarity, with Al-Qaʿida and the American 'theocons' determined to counter each other's violence through a preemptive violence of their own, most Muslims clearly abhor the escalation of global hatreds caused by the terror and the war-on-terror rhetoric and practice which have been deployed by zealots on both sides.[51] The scholarly mainstream has consistently and strongly condemned terrorism.[52] One reason is that most casualties, both of Islamist terrorism and of Western 'shock and awe', are Muslims. Muslims, whose countries are being progressively despoiled by this cycle of violence, should lead

[49] I agree that 'enhanced interrogation techniques' such as waterboarding should legally and morally be classified as torture; see the argument in the 'Open Letter to Attorney-General Albert Gonzales', issued by Human Rights Watch, dated 5 April 2006.

[50] See Abdal Hakim Murad, 'America as a Jihad State: Middle Eastern perceptions of modern American theopolitics' (www.masud.co.uk/ISLAM/ahm/America-as-a-jihad-state.htm).

[51] For a good global survey of Muslim attitudes, see John S. Esposito and Dalia Mogahed, *Who Speaks for Islam: What a Billion Muslims Really Think* (New York, 2008).

[52] E.g. the list at www.unc.edu/~kurzman/terror.htm ('Islamic Statements against Terrorism')

the way in encouraging the zealots on both sides to seek more constructive forms of engagement.

Only here, it seems, might a long-term solution be found. Nine years after 9/11, the West seems unsure of the success of its current strategies. When conventional methods fail, the United States is increasingly willing to use more controversial measures (Predator drone strikes in Afghanistan, no longer designated as 'assassinations', increased threefold in the first nine months of the Obama administration).[53] The military jargon of 'mowing the lawn', denoting the killing of insurgent suspects in the awareness that they will be replaced by others, suggests a widening mood of fatigue and scepticism. The Muslim world needs to seize this opportunity by embarking on several public diplomatic initiatives, all of which will require the inertia of the regimes, and the anger of the populations, to be bypassed. Such initiatives would include the following insights.

1. Muslims should not wait for the Western 'Quartet' to unlock the Palestine/ Israel impasse. It should be accepted that the Christian world, whether led by Bush or Obama, lacks the will to impose a truly just settlement. The Islamic world must find solutions to its global issues even if there is no solution for Palestine.

2. Muslims should make the case to Western belligerents that further wars against Muslim 'rogue states' would run counter to Western interests. It is likely that Al-Qa'ida's purpose in attacking America was to draw it into a ground war in Afghanistan which it could not win. The Iraq invasion, which toppled the Arab world's last major secular opponent of Western interests in the region, was, for Al-Qa'ida, an added and unlooked-for bonus. Invasions or large-scale bombardments of Iran and Syria would impose the risk of further strategic defeats for the West, including the disruption of energy sources and a consequent instability in the global economy.

3. Muslims need to adopt a strategy of what Heba Raouf calls 'preemptive civility'.[54] By showing the Muslim world as composed of reasonable human beings who desire peace and justice, and do not wish to invade and expropriate Western countries, such a presentation will make it more difficult for Western leaders to persuade their electorates or the UN Security Council of the desirability of further punitive wars. The 'Common Word' initiative of 2007, which attracted much media attention and comment from political as well as religious leaders, stands as a model of such preemptive action.[55]

---

[53]   Jane Mayer, 'The Predator War', *The New Yorker*, (October 26, 2009), pp. 36–45.

[54]   Heba Raouf Ezzat and Mary Kaldor, 'Not Even a Tree: delegitimising violence and the prospects for preemptive civility' in Helmut Anheier, Mary Kaldor, and Marlies Glasius (eds), *Global Civil Society 2006/7* (2006).

[55]   www.acommonword.com See also Aref Nayed's suggestion that America's 'security architecture' for control of the Middle East should be replaced by a 'Compassion

4. Muslim scholars should work to reinforce traditional universities and madrasas to increase the number of trained scholars able to defend classical distinctions between *jihād* and *ḥirāba*. The degrading of Islamic education under most regimes in the post-independence period has played a major role in the growth of Quṭbian radicalism.[56]

5. The Koranic insistence that Abraham's sons Isaac and Ishmael are not Cain and Abel, and are not emblems of an eternal mortal combat, but are both prophets of God who each launched a blessed story, must be at the theological heart of Muslim engagement with the West.

6. *Jihād*, as suggested above, takes its underlying motivation from the duty to empathise with the suffering of the oppressed. At its highest, this must include the oppressed Other. Examples of individuals with the courage to challenge their own religious parochialism are not abundant, but they do exist. Here, for example, is an Israeli journalist, making his own lonely but moral decision. He is stopped by US immigration officials, who think he may be an Arab, and he is asked: 'Do you read the Koran a lot?' The following exchange then ensues:

> It occurred to me that I should say plainly, 'I am not a Muslim.' But this did not seem fair. In occupied Denmark in 1940, Germans ordered the Jews to wear the yellow Star of David. The Danish King then wore such a star as a sign of his solidarity with his Jewish subjects. Would I fail this test of common humanity, and proclaim my non-Muslim origin? It would feel like sacrificing a Muslim in my stead. I tried to compromise: 'I do *not* read the Koran a lot,' I said. The officer, Gomez, a big, dark man, did not relent. 'But you read the Koran?' 'Occasionally,' I tried again. This pusillanimous response was the beginning of my undoing. I was searched and verbally abused, every piece of my luggage was checked and double-checked.[57]

No amount of just war theory can bring peace, if there is no heroic empathy with the Other.

Architecture'; cited in David Ford, *A Muscat Manifesto: Seeking Inter-faith Wisdom* (Cambridge and Dubai, 2009), p. 26.

[56] For the key role played by traditional scholars (as opposed to Salafī fundamentalists) in Sharīʻa reform, see Indira Gesink, *Islamic Reform and Conservatism: Al-Azhar and the Evolution of Modern Sunni Islam* (London, 2009). For the radical attack on the traditional colleges see Charles Kurzman, 'Bin Laden and other thoroughly modern Muslims', *Contexts: Understanding People in their Social Worlds*, 2 (Fall-Winter 2002).

[57] Israel Shamir, 'Maidens and Warriors', at www.israelshamir.net/English/maidens.htm.

Chapter 3
Challenging Al-Qaʿida's Justification of Terror

Ahmad Achtar

Overview

Al-Qaʿida and its associates manipulate the Divine Islamic sources and Islamic tradition to justify their views and violent actions. This chapter argues that Al-Qaʿida is a fringe group within the Islamic scene and does not speak in the name of mainstream Sunni Islam. Furthermore, the violence perpetuated by Al-Qaʿida is not religiously inspired. Rather, it purports to be religiously justified by manipulating Islamic law and its Divine sources.

This study is divided into three parts. Part one situates Al-Qaʿida as a fringe group within the spectrum of Islamism/Salafism and highlights the main differences between it and other movements and trends. The second part argues that the acts of violence committed by Al-Qaʿida are not religiously inspired. Religious justification is rather sought for them – including the frequently cited justifications for killing non-combatants – only *after* committing these acts. The third part challenges the justifications offered by Al-Qaʿida for killing non-combatants by drawing on mainstream Sunni legal thought and, in particular, the document produced by the one-time mentor of the Al-Qaʿida deputy leader, Ayman al-Zawahiri: Dr. Faḍl (Sayyid Imām) who renounced the ideology of Al-Qaʿida and its practices.

Typology of Contemporary Muslim Trends

Al-Qaʿida is a fringe group whose advocacy and practice of violence are alien to mainstream Islamic thinking. Such a group should not be confused with the other trends in the Islamic scene, especially Islamism and Salafism.

In the literature on modern trends among Muslims, there are various typologies that aim to differentiate between various orientations. Esposito distinguishes four of these: secularist, conservative, neo-traditionalist (or neo-fundamentalist) and reformist (neo-modernist).[1] The secularists call for the confinement of religion to the private sphere and the separation between religion and state. According

---

[1]   J.L. Esposito, *Islam: The Straight Path* (Oxford, 2005), p. 228.

to Esposito, the others 'advocate a return to Islam; however, their meanings and methods vary.'[2] In a similar approach, Shephard, in his analysis of ideological dimensions of Muslim thinking in the twentieth century, identifies three major orientations, with further subdivisions: secularist orientations, Islamism (Islamic Modernism and Radical Islamism), Traditionalism (neo-Traditionalism).[3] Abdullah Saeed offers a broader typology in which he identifies eight trends: legalist traditionalism, theological puritanism, militant extremism, political Islamism, secular liberalism, cultural nominalism, classical modernism, and progressive Ijtihadis.[4] He includes a classical modernist trend which is no longer present in the Islamic scene. His classification does not distinguish between national and transnational manifestations of 'militant extremism' and political Islamism, although these distinctions are important for our discussion.

These classifications are not sufficient for deep critical analysis. Until we have a better typology I will focus on two important trends, namely Salafism (theological puritanism) and Islamism. These two trends do not represent mainstream Sunni Islam but the reason for focusing on them is that Al-Qaʿida's ideology is developed out of these two currents.

Salafism (in Arabic Salafiyya) refers originally to the reform movement of Jamāl al-Dīn al-Afghānī (d. 1897) and Muḥammad ʿAbduh (d. 1905). Reformist Salafism tried to revitalize Islamic thought from its stagnation by advocating a return to the original source of Islam (Qurʾān and Sunna) as it was understood by the pious ancestors (*al-salaf al-Ṣāliḥ*).[5] Modern Salafi groups that emerged in the 1970s shared with reformist Salafism their refusal to imitate the classical jurists. But they differed in their approach to the Qurʾān. While the reformist Salafism engaged in a creative interpretation of the foundational texts, the modern Salafis tended either to interpret them literally or to move from texts to implementation without passing through the process of interpretation, especially the interpretative methods

---

[2]   Esposito, ibid.

[3]   W. Shepard, *The Diversity of Islamic Thought: Towards a Typology, in Islamic Thought in the Twentieth Century*, (eds.) Suha Taji-Farouki and Basheer M. Nafi (London, Tauris, 2004), pp. 61–103.

[4]   A. Saeed, 'Trends in Contemporary Islam: A Preliminary Attempt at a Classification', *The Muslim World*, vol. 97, July 2007, 395-404.

[5]   Shahin, Emad el-Din, 'Salafīyah' In *The Oxford Encyclopedia of the Islamic World. Oxford Islamic Studies Online*, http://www.oxfordislamicstudies.com/article/opr/t236/e0700 (accessed 13-Jun-2009).

of classical jurists. Salafism also needs to be distinguished from Wahhabism[6] since Wahhabism is a form of Salafism but not vice versa.[7]

Three major trends can be distinguished within contemporary Salafism.[8] Traditionalist Salafis oppose all forms of political activity, including violence because this might lead to civil strife; activist Salafis engage in non-violent political activism; and armed Salafis, such as those who joined the *mujahidin* in Afghanistan in the 1980s, abandon political activism and engage in armed operations.[9]

Islamism: various definitions have been proposed for Islamism. For Roy it refers to conceiving Islam as a political ideology.[10] Denoeux defines it as 'a form of instrumentalization of Islam by individuals, groups and organizations that pursue political objectives'. It 'provides political responses to today's societal challenges by imagining a future, the foundations for which rest on re-appropriated or reinvented concepts borrowed from the Islamic tradition.'[11] On the other hand, the authors of the International Crisis Group's report *Islamism* define it as synonymous with 'Islamic activism' in the sense of 'the active assertion and promotion of beliefs, prescriptions, laws, or policies that are held to be Islamic in character.'[12] This definition is too broad and considers Salafism as a sub-category of Islamism which is not helpful for critical analysis. On the other hand, the report warns against representing Islamism as a monolithic phenomenon and the branding of Islamists as radicals by Western analysts. It argues that Islamism 'has a number of very different streams' and that the West needs 'a discriminating strategy that takes account of the diversity of outlooks.'[13]

---

[6]   'It is distinguished from other Sunni Muslim religious discourses by its own specific interpretations and interpreters. *Wahhābiyya* is simply a religious worldview that can promote both consent and contestation, depending on the context in which its teachings and texts are interpreted. Politically,*Wahhābiyya* can be both quietist and revolutionary', M. Al-Rasheed, *Contesting the Saudi State: Islamic Voices from a New Generation* (Cambridge, 2007), p. 2.

[7]   Khaled Abou El fadl, *And God Knows the Soldiers: The Authoritative and Authoritarian in Islamic Discourses* (University Press of America, 2001), p. 170.

[8]   Bernard Haykel, 'Salafī Groups', in *The Oxford Encyclopedia of the Islamic World. Oxford Islamic Studies Online*, http://www.oxfordislamicstudies.com/article/opr/t236/e1244 (accessed 13-Jun-2009).

[9]   *Understanding Islamism*, Crises Group Middle East/North Africa Report No 37, (2 March 2005), p. 4.

[10]   Olivier Roy, *The Failure of Political Islam*, (London, 1994), p. ix.

[11]   Guilain Denoeux, 'The Forgotten Swamp: Navigating Political Islam', *Middle East Policy*, vol. 9 (June 2002), p. 61, quoted by Mohammed Ayoob in 'Political Islam: Image and Reality', *World Policy Journal*, (Fall 20040, p. 1.

[12]   *Understanding Islamism*, Crisis Group Middle East/North Africa Report No 37, 2 March, 2005, p. i.

[13]   *Understanding Islamism*, Crisis Group Middle East/North Africa Report No 37, 2 March, 2005, Executive Summary.

Two Major Trends can be Identified within Islamism:

1. *Political Islamism*: the actors here try to achieve their goals by political means. These movements adopt modern models of political organization and try to gain political power within the boundaries of respective nations by political means, thus accepting the legitimacy of the nation-state as a framework of their activities. Examples are the Muslim Brothers in Egypt, *Jamaat-i Islami* in Pakistan and the Justice and Development Party in Turkey.

2. *Armed Islamism*: The actors here engage in armed activities to achieve their aims. Three sub-categories can be distinguished within this trend:

   (a) Armed activities against occupying powers. The actors in this category blend Islamism 'with nationalism, particularly in the context of resistance against non-Muslim foreign domination and/or occupation. Islam thus becomes an instrument of the mobilization of Muslim populations against control or domination by predominantly non-Muslim political authorities or foreign occupiers, thus giving the resistance its religious colour.'[14] The actors here use 'the concept of jihad to justify resistance against foreign domination, thereby popularizing the modern interpretation of jihad as primarily defensive war against foreign occupation, aimed at driving out the occupier.'[15] This type of armed activity is sometimes contested by local and international players, as in Afghanistan (between the *mujahidin* and the Arab fighters in the 1980s), and subsequently in Bosnia and Iraq.

   (b) Armed activities against what the actors consider as nominal Muslim regimes: 'the nearer enemy.' The targets of the armed activities are Muslim regimes which are considered to be infidels because of their failure to implement Islamic law in all spheres of life. Consequently these regimes are legitimate targets for militant activities. For the actors here, jihad is considered as an individual obligation (*wājib*) incumbent on every Muslim and this view of jihad will be adopted by Al-Qaʻida, as we will see later. These views are clearly manifest in the writings of the ideologue of *tanẓīm al-Jihād* (al-Jihad organization) in Egypt, 'Abd–al-Salām Faraj who in his book entitled *al-farīda al-ghā'iba* (the neglected duty) considers al-jihad as the sixth pillar of Islam. (The group later assassinated the Egyptian president Anwar al-Sadat in 1981 whom they considered as the nearer enemy).[16] Generally speaking, the main characteristic of

---

[14]   Mohammed Ayoob, ed, *The Many Faces of Political Islam: Religion and Politics in the Muslim World* (University of Michigan Press, 2008), p. 112.

[15]   Ayoob, ibid., p. 113.

[16]   'Abd al-Salām Faraj. Al-farīda al-ghā'iba, translated by Johannes J. G Jansen as *The Neglected Duty: The Creed of Sadat's Assassins and Islamic Resurgence in the Middle East* (Macmillan, 1986), p. 192.

these forms of armed activities is that both are confined to a specific operational context within the domain of a nation-state, unlike Al-Qaʻida.

(c) Al-Qaʻida came into existence as a result of the merging of two groups who fought with the mujahidin in Afghanistan: the armed Salafi groups, and elements from the al-Jihād organization headed by Ayman al-Zawahiri. The most important feature of this new transnational formation is the change in the direction of their militant activities from the nearer enemy to the further enemy, especially the United States and its allies. The ideology and practices of Al-Qaʻida stand in marked contrast to the mainstream of Sunni thought.

Al-Qaʻida's Justification for Killing Non-Combatants

Al-Qaʻida and its associates called for Muslims to participate in what it claims to be jihad against 'the further enemy' without distinguishing between combatants and non-combatants, declaring all of them to be legitimate targets. All of this is reflected in a fatwa issued by bin Laden and others in 1998:[17]

> The ruling to kill the Americans and their allies – civilians and military – is an individual duty for every Muslim who can do it in any country in which it is possible to do it, in order to liberate the al-Aqṣā Mosque and the holy mosque [Mecca] from their grip, and in order for their armies to move out of all the lands of Islam, defeated and unable to threaten any Muslim. This is in accordance with the words of Almighty Allah, 'and fight the pagans all together as they fight you all together,' and 'fight them until there is no more tumult or oppression, and there prevail justice and faith in Allah.'

It was only six months after 9/11, on 24 April 2002, that Al-Qaʻida produced a detailed religious justification, with supporting Islamic texts, for its acts of terror. This was on the *al-nedaa* website, which is run by people associated with Al-Qaʻida.[18] The justification is found in a document entitled 'A statement from *Qāʻidat al-Jihād* regarding the mandates of the heroes and the legality of the operations in New York and Washington.'[19] It is reported that the Saudi Al-Qaʻida member, Yūsuf al-ʻUyayrī, who died in June 2003, was in charge of this website.[20]

---

[17] The Federation of American Scientists (FAS), http://www.fas.org/irp/world/para/docs/980223-fatwa.htm (accessed 20 October 2009).

[18] The website was shut down in 2002 see: http://www.time.com/time/world/article/0,8599,332914,00.html (accessed 1 Nov. 2009).

[19] The English version can be accessed from http://www.mepc.org/journal_vol10/alqaeda.htmland the Arabic from http://www.mepc.org/journal_vol10/alneda.pdf (both accessed 1November 2009).

[20] http://www.freerepublic.com/focus/f-news/924769/posts (accessed 1 Nov. 2009).

It is very likely that it was he who wrote this statement, because towards the end of the document it is indicated that, 'These comments about the permissibility of the martyrdom operations in the attack of New York and Washington are taken from the book, *The Truth about the New Crusader* War.'[21] This book was written by Yūsf al-'Uyayrī.[22] In the introduction to the second edition, al-'Uyayrī states that he wrote the book in 9 days and he wanted to correct the first edition.[23] The date of the first edition became clear in a tribute[24] to al-'Uyayrī written by another Saudi Al-Qa'ida member, 'Isāb. Sa'd al-awshan.[25] He states that al-'Uyayrī started writing his book after the events of 9/11 in order to justify 'martyrdom operations and refute all the doubts that were raised about them.' When this book reached bin Laden he said 'it seems that this book was authored before the operation because it is not possible for it to be written in such a short time.'[26] Then al-Awshan adds, 'I testify before God that al-Shaykh Yūsuf wrote this book only after the event.'[27] From all of the above, it is clear that there was no detailed justification based on Islamic sources before 9/11. It was only six months later – on 24 April 2002 – that Al-Qa'ida used the justification of al-'Uyayrī, after mounting criticism of its actions. I argue, therefore, that in no way can Al-Qa'ida's actions be described as religiously inspired violence. Rather Al-Qa'ida committed the acts of terror first and only after that tried to justify them religiously by using Islamic sources and legal tradition. Furthermore, the mere fact of Al-Qa'ida's attempt to manufacture a justification for its actions indicates that these actions are not supported by any textual evidence in the Qur'ān and prophetic tradition. Nor are they considered legal by mainstream Sunni juristic thought. These actions had to be legally justified somehow so that Al-Qa'ida could give credibility to itself in the eyes of Muslims.

---

[21] http://www.mepc.org/journal_vol10/0306_wiktorowiczkaltner.asp (accessed 1 November 2009)

[22] The book can be downloaded from this link: http://www.4shared.com/get/101457408/a29d6ad6/___.html (accessed 2 Novmber 2009).

[23] The second edition of this book is dated Rajab 1422 AH (1st of Rajab is 19 September 2001).There is no indication about the precise date but it must fall between 20 September and 18 October 2001 which indicates that he wrote the book and revised it in a very short time.

[24] See http://www.majahden.com/vb/showthread.php?p=119098 (accessed 1 Nov. 2009) and the section on al-Ayiri in the following document www.almedad.com/temp/seyar.doc *(accessed 2 Nov. 2009).*

[25] Died July 2004 http://www.alyaum.com/issue/article.php?IN=11360&I=192263 (accessed 1 November 2009).

[26] http://www.majahden.com/vb/showthread.php?p=119098 (accessed 2 November 2009).

[27] http://www.majahden.com/vb/showthread.php?p=119098 (accessed 2 November 2009).

The statement of Al-Qa'ida mentioned above gives two sets of justifications: one for killing non-Muslims and the other for killing Muslims. Regarding non-Muslim persons, the statement indicates that 'the prohibition against the blood of women, children, and the elderly is not an absolute prohibition. Rather, there are special conditions in which it is permissible to kill them if they are among the people of war, and these conditions exist in specific circumstances.'[28] The statement confesses that among the victims were some people belonging to the above category (non-Muslim women, children etc) but claims that it is permitted to kill them for seven reasons and that only one reason is sufficient for the act to be legal.[29] Regarding the justification for killing Muslim persons, the statement gives six reasons.

The most often cited justifications by Al-Qa'ida for killing non-combatants are two:

First: it is allowed for Muslims to kill protected ones among unbelievers as an act of reciprocity.[30] If the unbelievers have targeted Muslim women, children, and elderly, it is permissible for Muslims to respond in kind and kill those similar to those whom the unbelievers killed. As Allah almighty says, 'So if anyone commits aggression against you, attack him as he attacked you.' Q (2:194)

Second: it is allowed for Muslims to kill protected ones among unbelievers when the enemy is shielded by their women or children.[31] Moreover, when Muslims are killed by these acts, they are considered to be shields used by the enemy as well and their killing is justified by invoking the legal maxim of necessity.

The other five reasons for killing non-Muslim non-combatants given by the document are: the difficulty of distinguishing between combatants from non-combatants in case of raids; the assistance of non-combatants to the war efforts by act, word, opinion or any other form; unavoidable killing of non-combatants due to the need to weaken the enemy in order to conquer a place; unavoidable killing of non-combatants due to the use of heavy weaponry when the army is attempting to conquer a place; and finally violation of treaty with Muslims.[32] Generally speaking, all of these reasons for killing non-combatants are manipulations of what is found in Islamic legal tradition regarding unintentional killing of non-combatants or when non-combatants actively engage in the act of war and therefore lose their immunity. In no way does the Shari'a or Islamic legal tradition give permission for the deliberate killing of non-combatants. Furthermore, the exceptional reasons that justify non-intentional killing of non-combatants are discussed in Islamic legal tradition in the context of offensive war which requires a legitimate leader or Caliph

---

[28] 'A statement from *Qā'idat al-Jihād* regarding the mandates of the heroes and the legality of the operations in New York and Washington' in http://www.mepc.org/journal_vol10/0306_alqaeda.asp (accessed 2 November 2009).

[29] http://www.mepc.org/journal_vol10/0306_alqaeda.asp

[30] http://www.mepc.org/journal_vol10/0306_alqaeda.asp

[31] http://www.mepc.org/journal_vol10/0306_alqaeda.asp

[32] http://www.mepc.org/journal_vol10/0306_alqaeda.asp

to initiate. Al-Qaʿida declares its jihad to be of a defensive type. Its manipulation and appeal to these reasons is, therefore, misleading and illegitimate because its leaders have neither religious nor political authority over the Muslims. Even if we assume for the argument's sake that non-combatants might be unintentionally killed in the case of defensive jihad in addition to offensive jihad, Islamic law, as we will see later, is very clear in its prohibition of deliberate killings of non-combatants in all contexts.

I will now deal with the first two reasons because they are the most often cited ones to legitimize deliberate targeting of non-combatants by Al-Qaʿida and its associates.

Challenging Al-Qaʿida's Justifications

Within mainstream Sunni legal writings on the conduct of war, it is forbidden intentionally to kill certain individuals classified under the category of non-combatants. This is attested in the legal writings on Jihad from the second AH/ninth CE up till now. In the book of al-Shaybānī (d. 804) on the law of nations we find 'The Apostle said: Fight in the name of God and in the "path of God" [i.e., truth]. Combat [only] those who disbelieve in God. Do not cheat or commit treachery, nor should you mutilate anyone or kill children.'[33] The prophet also 'prohibited the killing of women.'[34] Other categories of persons that are not to be killed intentionally are slaves, old people, the lame, the blind and the helpless insane.[35] Nevertheless, Islamic law accepts the reality that Muslims, while fighting a legitimate war, might indirectly harm non-combatants, including Muslims and non-Muslims alike. John Kelsay comments on this issue:

> The reasoning [behind this view] is quite reminiscent of Western Just-war tradition and its approach to collateral damage. One would be quite wrong, in the case of just war or of Shariʿa reasoning, to read such a passage as negating respect for the immunity of noncombatants. The point is that the attacks are not directly and intentionally aimed at noncombatants. Without this overarching categorization, the military acts described would be unjust, and those engaging in them would need to make restitution.[36]

The general consensus on not deliberately targeting non-combatants is attested in the writings of later Muslim theologians such as al-Māwardī (1058). He states that, 'It is not permissible to kill women and children whether in a war or otherwise so

---

[33]   Al-Shybānī. The Islamic law of Nations, translated by Majid Khadduri (The John Hopkins Press, 1966), p. 76.

[34]   Ibid., p. 87.

[35]   Ibid., pp. 101–102.

[36]   John Kelsay, *Arguing the Just War in Islam* (Harvard, 2007), p. 109.

long as they don't fight because the messenger of God forbids their killing.'[37] A few centuries later, Ibn Taymiyya (1328), whose legal verdicts on Jihad[38] have been often taken out of context by militant groups including Al-Qa'ida, contends that noncombatants who do not participate in the war efforts either by deeds or by words, such as 'women, children, the monk, old man, the blind and the chronically ill should not be killed according to the majority of the scholars.'[39]

Al-Qa'ida and its associated groups departed from the consensus of Muslims with regard to the unlawfulness of deliberately killing non-combatants. This departure is a tragic consequence of the Salafis' claim that 'every believer should interpret the scriptures according to his own lights'[40] and their 'radical rejection of all Muslim scholarship.'[41] Al-Qa'ida could not argue against the Divine sources and the consensus of the jurists regarding the sanctity of life and the prohibition of intentional targeting of non-combatants. They had, therefore, to make up their own justification for their unprecedented views about the legitimacy of targeting non-combatants. Furthermore, Al-Qa'ida's justifications of its actions in attacking non-combatant Muslims and non-Muslims are based on manipulating Islamic sources and juristic verdicts by taking them out of context and stretching them to support their terror.

In what follows I will present a refutation of the most often cited justifications by Al-Qa'ida for killing non-combatant Muslims and non-Muslims alike, by drawing mainly on the writing of the founder of the Egyptian Jihad organization and mentor of the deputy leader of Al-Qa'ida : Dr. Faḍl (Sayyid Imām). Dr. Faḍl released a document entitled[42] *Tarshīd al-'amal al-jihādī fī miṣr wa al-'ālam* ("Rationalizing the jihadi action in Egypt and the world") which was published by the Kuwaiti newspaper al-Jarīda between November-December 2007.[43] In this document, Dr. Faḍl reassessed the militant ideology he had himself propagated in earlier writings and challenged the practices of Al-Qa'ida. The document is a big

---

[37]   Al-Māwardī, *Al-Ahkām al-Sulṭaniyya* edited by Ahmad Mubarak al-Baghdadi (Kuwait, 1989), p. 57.

[38]   Ibn Taymiyya, *Muslims under Non-Muslim rule*, translated by Yahya Michot (Oxford, 2006).

[39]   *Ibn Taymiyya, al-Sīyāsa al-Shari'yya fī islāh al-ra'ī wa al-ra'iyya*, edited by Ali b. Muhammad al-Imaran (Saudi Arabia, 2008), p. 158.

[40]   Abdul Hakim Murad, *Bin Laden's violence is a heresy against Islam* in http://groups.colgate.edu/aarislam/abdulhak.htm (accessed 2 Nov. 2009).

[41]   Ibid.

[42]   'Imprisoned Leader of Egypt's Islamic Jihad Challenges al-Qaeda' in *The Jamestown Foundation* http://www.jamestown.org/single/?no_cache=1&tx_ttnews% 5Bswords%5D=8fd5893941d69d0be3f378576261ae3e&tx_ttnews%5Bany_of_the_ words%5D=Abdulaziz%20al-Sharif&tx_ttnews%5Btt_news%5D=4597&tx_ttnews%5Bb ackPid%5D=7&cHash=50522ce7d7 (accessed 2 Nov. 2009).

[43]   http://www.aljarida.com/book/00_Book.pdf

blow to Al-Qaʿida's ideology to the extent that al-Zawahiri circulated a book of 188 pages refuting the document.[44]

The Legality and Limits of Reciprocity

Reciprocity is the most often cited principle by Al-Qaʿida to justify the killing of non-combatants. Al-Qaʿida did not, however, quote the whole verse Q (2:194) in their justification of the principle of reciprocity. The verse in full reads, 'A sacred month for a sacred month: violation of sanctity [calls for] fair retribution. So if anyone commits aggression against you, attack him as he attacked you, *but be mindful of God, and know that He is with those who are mindful of Him.*'

As is clear from the verse, even when retaliating, Muslims have to be mindful of God by observing his other commands throughout the Qurʾān such as Q (6:164), 'Say, "Should I seek a Lord other than God, when He is the Lord of all things?" Each soul is responsible for its own actions; no soul will bear the burden of another. You will all return to your Lord in the end, and He will tell you the truth about your differences.' It can be also observed that 'each of the Qurʾānic verses permitting reciprocity are followed by admonitions for restraint and even forgiveness as the better moral choice.'[45] But all these admonitions have been ignored by Al-Qaʿida because they would refute their argument.

In his criticism of Al-Qaʿida's employment of the principle of reciprocity, Dr. Faḍl contends that, even though some countries transgress against some Muslim countries and kill Muslims without discrimination, this does not give Muslims a license to reciprocate:[46]

> because God the most high forbid us committing transgression in all our affairs including the state of jihad and fighting. God says in the Qurʾān (9:10), 'Fight in God's cause against those who fight you, but do not overstep the limits: God does not love those who overstep the limits.

Furthermore, 'The Prophet (May peace be upon him) said 'convey the trust to the one who entrusted you with it and do not betray the one who betrayed you'. Transgression and betrayal are not, therefore, to be reciprocated because of the above mentioned evidence. Among the forbidden acts of transgression committed by Al-Qaʿida are: killing those who should not be targeted (non-combatants), treachery, violation of pacts, and unnecessary destruction of urban areas. Dr. Faḍl summarized his argument saying that 'Muslims should refrain from committing

---

[44]   http://www.jamestown.org/single/?no_cache=1&tx_ttnews[tt_news]=4891

[45]   Sohail H. Hashmi, 'Saving and Taking Life in War: Three Modern Muslim Views', *The Muslim World*, vol. 89, no. 2, April, 1999, p. 178.

[46]   http://www.aljarida.com/book/00_Book.pdf, Episode 7 (accessed 2 Nov. 2009)

unethical acts even when these acts are committed by the enemy because of God's commands'.[47]

The Legality and Limits of the Shielding Argument: the Principle of Necessity

The idea of necessity is a well-established legal principle in Islamic law. The Qur'ān legitimizes certain injunctions on the ground of necessity and on this basis a legal maxim has been formulated. This states, 'necessity makes lawful the forbidden.' Three offences are forbidden regardless of the situation. They are 'murder, the amputation of a limb, or serious wounding likely to cause death'.[48] Other offences, such as stealing in case of hunger or eating forbidden food, are all legitimate. Al-Ghazālī (d. 1111) used the example of shielding in war to explain the limits of applying this principle. When Muslims, fighting an enemy who threatens to take the land of Islam and kill all Muslims, use Muslims as shields, it is lawful for a Muslim army to kill these Muslims that are used as shields for the sake of the public interest. According to Islamic law, killing such Muslims is forbidden. But in this case their killing 'does not incur moral culpability because (1) it is a matter of vital necessity (*ḍarūra*); (2) it is a case of clear-cut certainty (*qaṭʻiyya*); (3) its importance is universal (*kulliya*).'[49] Al-Ghazālī here restricts the application of the principle of necessity to a very narrow situation affecting the whole Muslim community.

On the use of shielding as a justification for killing Muslims, Dr. Faḍl argues that killing Muslims who are mixed with non-Muslims by using the argument of shielding is not allowed because there is no clear text that supports this act.[50] The argument of shielding is based on personal legal reasoning and it is only allowed in the case of necessity. There is no necessity in the case of these operations in non-Muslim lands because they are unnecessary offensive operations. Dr. Faḍl thus argues against Al-Qaʻida who considers these operations as a form of defensive jihad. The jurists allowed killing Muslims used as shields only in the case of defensive jihad and only in the case of emergency when Muslims fear that by not attacking the shield their enemy will kill all of them. Only in this situation is it authorized to kill the Muslims who are used as shields. But this is not the case with the operations that have been carried out by Al-Qaʻida in non-Muslim lands. When the jurists allowed killing the shield this was in the context of a non-Muslim army putting Muslim hostages in the front as human shields to deter the Muslim army from attacking them. At present, those Muslims living in non-Muslim lands are not hostages. They are rather citizens of these countries or residing there and not part of an army in war. The argument

---

[47]   http://www.aljarida.com/book/00_Book.pdf, Episode 7 (accessed 2 Nov. 2009)

[48]   Linant de Bellefonds, Y. "Ḍarūra." *Encyclopaedia of Islam, Second Edition*, Volume II, page 163.

[49]   Hashmi, *Saving and Taking Life in War*, p. 177.

[50]   http://www.aljarida.com/book/00_Book.pdf, Episode 7 (accessed 2 Nov. 2009)

of necessity does not, therefore, work in this case because the conditions for using the principle of necessity articulated by al-Ghazālī are not satisfied.

As for killing non-combatant civilians in non-Muslim lands, Dr. Faḍl argues that only in a state of war in case of military necessity may non-combatants be killed if they are used as human shields by their army. In a state of war, intentional killing of civilians in planes, trains and buildings is, therefore, not allowed because they are not military buildings and there is no military necessity.

Furthermore, he argues that for Muslims to enter non-Muslim countries with a visa is like signing a contract granting safe passage. Any Muslim who enters non-Muslim countries with a visa should, therefore, fulfill the terms of his contract and not betray these countries by committing terrorist acts because Q (5:1) clearly states, 'You who believe, fulfil your obligations.' Killing the people of these countries – whether military personnel or civilians – and destroying their buildings, bombing their planes and trains are all acts of betrayal and treachery which are forbidden by the Qur'ān and the tradition of the Prophet.[51]

Conclusion

Al-Qa'ida – in both its ideology and practices – is a new, unique and fringe phenomenon within the Islamic scene. The tendency of some Western analysts and writers on the subject to lump together all forms of armed activities by Muslims as a form of 'terrorism' is, at best, misleading and, at worst, dangerous. It criminalizes all forms of legitimate and just struggle and risks alienating large segments of the Muslim world who might perceive this attitude as a 'war on Islam,' with a negative impact on their cooperation. This hinders efforts to prevent any future terrorist acts which affect Muslims and non-Muslims alike.

The acts of terror committed by Al-Qa'ida are not religiously inspired but 'religiously' justified by Al-Qa'ida only after carrying out these acts in order to legitimize itself in the eyes of Muslims. Its justification for killing non-combatants is characterized by disregard and erosion of all the constraints that are recognized by mainstream Sunni legal thought. Whereas there is a consensus among the jurists that non-combatants should not be targeted intentionally in war, Al-Qa'ida removed their immunity and considered them legitimate targets. Al-Qa'ida manipulated Islamic Divine sources and used classical legal verdicts out of context in order to justify its terrorist acts. The religious rhetoric Al-Qa'ida employs to justify itself and its actions has been challenged and shown to be baseless within the mainstream Sunni discourse.

---

[51]   http://www.aljarida.com/book/00_Book.pdf, Episode 7 (accessed 2 Nov. 2009)

Chapter 4

Challenging the Political Theology of America's 'War on Terror'

Richard Lock-Pullan

The events of 11 September 2001 and the response of the US to them have confronted many Christians with the question what is an appropriate Christian response to the challenges of living in an age of terror. In this context one can ask what insights Christian doctrine, as opposed to Christian ethics, has to contribute to understanding the present era and how these can then shape the nature of Christian engagement with the current issues as explored in later chapters on Just War thinking.

This chapter will argue that one can generate a Christian perspective and subsequent ethics on the basis of seeing theology as an essentially interpretative task that mediates between Christian doctrine and political events. Using this approach President Bush's use of 'evil' is examined and shown to be a source of absolutist and self-righteous thinking, leading to a disastrous and unjust foreign policy. As an alternative, Reinhold Niebuhr's reinterpretation of the doctrine of sin will be shown to be an effective doctrinal lens to avoid these pitfalls, whilst itself generating a practice of Christian Realism that takes seriously the context of international affairs and Christian vision. The revisions of Niebuhr's theology are then used to develop a more liberal approach which gives the church a transformative role in addressing the 'war on terror', and concludes by examining how Obama's post-Niebuhrian liberal religious views shape current policy.

Political Theology

Relating Christian doctrine to Christian practice in a particular context requires holding all three aspects in tension. As Stephen Pattison argues, it is possible to have a three way critical conversation that takes place between the Christian tradition, one's own faith presuppositions and a particular situation.[1] The way to hold the tension between the three aspects is to focus on the specific situations under

---

[1]   Stephen Pattison, 'Some Straw for the Bricks: A Basic Introduction to Theological Reflection', in James Woodward and Stephen Pattison (eds.), *The Blackwell Reader in Pastoral and Practical Theology* (Oxford, 2000), p. 136.

consideration, as Alastair Campbell outlines.[2] Political theology is understood here as an act of imagination creatively integrating doctrine and practice in a concrete context making it hermeneutical, an 'interpretative discipline.'[3] This process is understood as 'reading in communion', whereby a Christian learns in and through their community how to be a wise reader capable of embodying the Christian narrative in their life and generate the 'skills to negotiate the dangers in our environment in a manner appropriate to our nature'[4]

This methodology is used to examine current US foreign policy by looking at the doctrines of 'evil' and 'sin.' First, President Bush's use of the term 'evil' will be examined and the consequences of its application for US foreign policy and international relations analysed. Second, the alternative of using Reinhold Niebuhr's doctrine of sin and its consequent practice of Christian Realism will be examined. Both sections focus on the political mainstream and aim to elucidate what political theology can say to leaders in the current international climate. The final section will address some of the challenges Niebuhr has faced and how he can be adapted for Christians to understand and act in the current unstable international environment and in the light of the Obama administration.

President Bush and Evil

'What has failed in Iraq has been not just the strategy of the administration of George W. Bush, but the whole way of looking at the world.'[5] The way of looking, or the hermeneutic, which George Bush has, is based on an intuitive understanding of faith guidance which often rejects church advice and upon a questionable reading of Christian doctrine. Consequently, his practice is flawed.

How America uses military force is, like all countries, shaped by its strategic culture, namely those variations in history, geography, political culture and such like which shape national behaviour. As Michael Howard observes, 'different cultures have different attitudes to war, and these, far more than any rational calculations, will shape their strategy and explain their successes and failures.'[6] Christianity has infused US politics and foreign relations from its Puritan foundation onwards

---

[2]   Alastair Campbell, 'The Nature of Practical Theology' in James Woodward and Stephen Pattison (eds), *The Blackwell Reader in Pastoral and Practical Theology* (Oxford, 2000), p. 85.

[3]   Edward Farley, 'Interpreting Situations: An Inquiry into the Nature of Practical Theology', in Woodward and Pattison, *The Blackwell Reader*, pp. 118–127.

[4]   Stanley Hauerwas, 'A Story-Formed Community: Reflections on Watership Down', in his *A Community of Character,* (Notre Dame, ID, 1981), p. 15.

[5]   Anatol Lieven and John Hulsman, *Ethical Realism* (New York, 2006), p xi.

[6]   Michael Howard, 'Review of *The Making of Strategy: Rulers, States and War'* (eds.), Williamson Murray, Macgregor Knox, and Alvin Bernstein, *War in History* (vol. 4. no 1. 1997), pp. 105–10.

and so been a key feature of American strategic culture. One is able to discern two major lines of emphasis in Christianity in the US, both of which draw on the American Christian heritage of moral politics and the sense of national mission. James Monroe has termed them the 'puritans' and the 'social gospel' groups.[7] A clear illustration of the influence of these two groups can be seen during the Interwar period – when the Puritan trend of prohibition was concerned with enforcing a private virtue of no alcohol, whilst the social gospel 'New Deal' aimed to promote social virtues through community service and social reform. The 'social gospel' was the predominant trend in American society from the 1930s to the 1960s, and Niebuhr was one of its most prominent, if critical, voices, before the emphasis on 'puritan' individual vice and virtue would return with the rise of the Christian Right. The growth of the Christian Right was also the period of the birth of the neo-Conservative movement, which was similarly a reaction against the perceived liberality and social failings of the 1960s and a call to reintroduce religious and moral values into the political mainstream. They made common cause in their moral campaign, which culminated in the Bush administration.

As Gary Scott Smith's *Faith and the Presidency* shows, religion has been a fundamental part of the presidency since Washington's inaugural; it is a fundamental part of the civic tradition of the US.[8] But the Bush presidency was different. President Bush was 'the most aggressively religious president in American history.'[9] His first executive order was to set up the Office of Faith-Based and Community Initiatives in the White House. There are well-documented cases of how his religious viewpoint shaped policy, such as his opposition to abortion, stem cell research and the withholding of $34 million to the UN Population Fund on the grounds that it co-operates with abortions. Bush placed his faith at the forefront of American diplomacy, using it to build bonds with fellow Christians such as Tony Blair and alienating secularists such as Jacques Chirac and Gerhard Schroeder. By examining his use of the term 'evil' it is possible to elucidate the Christian hermeneutic at work and the consequences for American foreign policy and the world.

Rather than see the use of the term 'evil' as a rhetorical device, in the way 'war on terror' or 'war on drugs' are, it is necessary to see the religious thinking that lies behind it and what the consequences are for US foreign policy. One who has taken Bush's religious rhetoric seriously is the ethicist Peter Singer, who has analysed the President's morality.[10] As he says, Bush has a universalist view of morality that sees morality as timeless and true in all places. Singer notes that Bush spoke about evil in 319 separate speeches between taking office and June 16 2003, and used

---

[7]   James A Monroe, *Hellfire Nation* (New Haven, 2003).

[8]   Gary Scott Smith, *Faith and the Presidency* (Oxford, 2006).

[9]   Arthur M. Schlesinger, Jr, *War and the American Presidency* (New York, 2005), p. 143.

[10]   Peter Singer, *The President of Good and Evil,* (London, 2004).

evil as a noun far more than as an adjective (914 against 182).[11] For example, on 26 October 2001 Bush said, 'We are at the beginning of what I view as a very long struggle against evil. We're not fighting a nation; we're not fighting a religion; we're fighting evil.'[12] Five years later he still saw the enemy as evil.[13] Rhetorically there have been appeals to the dangers of evil before. Ronald Reagan famously referred to the Soviet Union as the 'evil empire' but Reagan was pragmatic and shifted his position as Gorbachev reformed the Soviet Union. His reference to 'evil' was a statement that there was no moral equivalency between the US and the USSR. However, 'Bush is not thinking about evil deeds, or even people, nearly as often as he is thinking about evil as a *thing*, or a force, something that has a real existence apart from the cruel, callous, brutal, and selfish acts of which human beings are capable.'[14] For critics, the President is actually advocating an apocalyptic Manichaeism, where his readiness to see America as pure and good, and its enemies as wholly evil, moves beyond a traditional Christian understanding of evil. There are three aspects which draw these failings out – the flawed ontology of how Bush understands evil, the absolutism it leads to and the self-righteousness it engenders.

Ontology

Christianity does not have a positively stated orthodox doctrine of evil, as it sees evil more as a verb rather than noun.[15] Evil is understood in a general way as that which destroys life or prevents it from flourishing, a perversion, whilst sin is viewed as deliberate and free behaviour, thoughts or desires which are against God and create alienation from Him. Christianity makes the distinction between physical evil, which is the product of an incomplete creation such as a tsunami killing thousands, and moral evil where suffering and violence is inflicted by people, and is the product of sinful human nature.

The early church focused on the need of all people for Christ's grace of forgiveness, not on the nature of evil.[16] The doctrine of original sin was developed to explain why life is marred by hatred, brutality and tragedy, even though creation is good and there is hope in divine redemption by Jesus. The doctrine weaves them into a unified framework. Original sin was thus developed to address an

---

[11]   Singer, *The President of Good and Evil*, p. 2.

[12]   George W. Bush, 'President Bush Calls for Action on the Economy and Energy', 26 October 2001, www.whitehouse.gov/news/releases/2001/10/print/20011026–9.html, accessed 10 April 2007.

[13]   George W. Bush, 'President's Address to the Nation', 11 September, 2006,www. whitehouse.gov/news/releases/2006/09/print/20060911–3.html, accessed 10 April 2007.

[14]   Singer, *The President of Good and Evil*, p. 2.

[15]   Robert R Williams 'Sin and Evil' in Peter Hodgson and Robert King (eds.), *Christian Theology* (London, 1983), p. 168.

[16]   Tatha Wiley, *Original Sin* (New York, 2002), pp. 3–4.

experience of reality and articulates what redemption transforms. The doctrine, as espoused by Augustine, was refined by arguing against the optimism of Pelagius and the pessimism of Manichean thinking.

Pelagius was concerned that if sin cannot be avoided because it is inherent in the fallen nature, there is no motive to be good. Pelagius thus argued that the capacity to do good was still possible due to the moral nature of humans, whereby humans imitated Adam's behaviour but they did not inherit it. At the other extreme was Manichaeism which espoused a cosmic dualism with a conflict between God (light and Spirit) and Satan (darkness and the material world). Evil is equated with finitude and has an ontological status.

Augustine's Christian formulation rejected the Manichean metaphysical dualism as incoherent and saw the Genesis story ruling out equating evil with finitude or the world. God created being and being was good and sin occurred freely and contingently.[17] Like Pelagius, Augustine saw that every human being is good, and that evil is the voluntary defection from this state through an act of will, meaning there is no ontological foundation for, or explanation of, evil. As Augustine says 'the evil will is itself not an effect of something, but a defect.'[18] However, Augustine had a more pessimistic view of human nature than Pelagius, as he argued that, due to Adam, humans were biased toward evil and in need of salvation. Augustine's doctrine was a *via media* between the two positions. For Augustine the story of the Fall and the hereditary principle explained the source and continuation of sin. This is a crucial point, because the whole purpose of the doctrinal development of original sin is as an explanation of why humans need Christ. Humankind needs to be reconciled to the totality of which it was originally a part, and God reconciled the world to Himself in Christ. Thus, as Paul Ricoeur shows, theologically the doctrine cannot be understood without including the doctrine of salvation, with original sin as an antitype.[19] It is the symbolism of a loss of the covenant bond with God. Original sin is consequently not a concept but a symbol of what Christians declare most profoundly in the confession of sins.

By using 'evil' as a noun Bush has been Manichean and not followed traditional doctrine. To stay within the bounds of Christianity he must use 'evil' as an adjective as evil motives and deeds can be separated. Hannah Arendt's work shows that the agent of evil deeds, such as Adolf Eichmann, does not need to have evil motives – they could be banal.[20] However, by using 'evil' as the key hermeneutical term to understand the age of terror he undermines the soteriological – the salvation – role of the doctrine, which in Bush's terms is not seen as coming, as in the doctrine, through Christ but through the President's actions. This leads to absolutism.

---

[17] Williams 'Sin and Evil,' pp. 172–5.

[18] Augustine, *City of God against the Pagans* (Cambridge, 1998), p. 507.

[19] Paul Ricoeur, ' "Original Sin": A Study in Meaning' in his *The Conflict of Interpretations* (London, 1989), p. 286.

[20] Hannah Arendt, *Eichmann in Jerusalem* (2nd Edition, New York, 1965).

Absolutism

By appealing to evil President Bush creates fixed absolutes, bringing about a clash of mentalities and the closing down of religion and politics. Bush's absolutism is a statement of certainty, which is 'a quest for security, an attempt to flee from contingency, uncertainty, and ambivalence of everyday life.'[21] Absolute faith overwhelms a need for analysis and lessens the need for engagement. The emphasis on 'evil' blocks serious deliberation and diplomacy; it hampers the creation of alternatives, it justifies military interventions, and rules out democratic discussions that respect dissenting views and the evaluation of views.[22] As Bush's former Secretary of the Treasury put it, if you know the answer to everything then it is not penetrable to the facts.[23] One can see the effects of this mindset most clearly with the policy towards Iran, which is placed in the 'Axis of Evil' and thus blocked from attempts at traditional diplomatic negotiations. Evil as a hermeneutical key to understanding current events has a hugely negative effect, seen very clearly in the practice of unilateralism by the administration and the doctrine of pre-emption – both of which led to the invasion of Iraq.

In the same way that normal politics is suspended once something is deemed a 'security' issue, by being made 'evil' people and countries are placed outside the accepted norms of international and national behaviour. They become the inhuman other, as with the illegal internments at Guantanamo. The Bush administration allowed torture, introduced the Patriot Act, had extraordinary renditions and reconceived 'justice' in its response to the events 11 September.[24] It is not a Christian response embodying values such as social justice, human dignity and peace. There is a need to mediate the absolutist position of the President to avoid the dangers of Christian militarism.[25]

Self-Righteous

The fears of Christian militarism growing because of seeing the 'war on terror' as fighting against 'evil' are entirely reasonable. They lead to self-righteousness. On the first anniversary of 9/11 at Ellis Island the President substituted the ideal of America for the Christian original found in John's gospel: 'America is the hope of all mankind. That hope drew millions to this harbour. That hope still lights our way. And the light shines in the darkness. And the darkness will not overcome

---

[21]   Richard J. Bernstein, *The Abuse of Evil* (Cambridge, 2005) p. 24.

[22]   Bernstein, *The Abuse of Evil*, p. 84.

[23]   Kaplan, Kaplan, Esther, *With God on Their Side* (New York, 2005) p. 12.

[24]   David Cole, *Justice at War* (New York, 2008).

[25]   Ronald H. Stone, *Prophetic Realism* (London, 2005).

it,' thereby associating God and the American anti-terror project.[26] It was self-righteousness of the highest order. The 'threat' from Islam is part of the broader fear of a 'clash of civilisations' which, for the security community, was expressed in the idea of fourth generation warfare where wars would be ideological and cultural.[27] The US would be fighting for God against evil.

There is no doubt that there has been great suffering and violence as the result of terrorist acts, but abrogating God's place is not the way forward. How to understand and act in the light of faith in the context of events that generate such suffering and violence is fundamentally a question of theodicy – the problem of suffering – and Reinhold Niebuhr's theology is an extended work of theodicy.[28] He addressed these issues by reinterpreting Augustine for his age and generating a different hermeneutical lens.

Reinhold Niebuhr

The American theologian Reinhold Niebuhr (1892-1971) articulated a theology of 'Christian Realism.' Niebuhr is relevant to the current debate because he explicitly addressed US foreign policy and its elite in an earlier generation where his theological and ethical concerns and methods were very influential, particularly in the early Cold War years. His approach was based on his understanding of sin, and generates a better Christian practice and perspective for the current context. Since 9/11 there has been a resurgence of interest in Niebuhr's writings. Niebuhr drew on the American tradition of pragmatism, and articulated a doctrine of sin that allowed him to address the 'evil' of communism in a far more measured manner than the Bush administration's tackling of 'evil.'

Niebuhr started as a liberal 'social gospeller' but his views changed due to his pastoral experience in Detroit where he saw that progress was not inevitable. As Hans Morgenthau noted, Niebuhr's major contribution to theology and politics was his rediscovery of 'political man,' where the lust for power and the social configurations which arise from it are seen as an intrinsic aspect of human nature.[29] This led to his emphasis on creating 'systems of justice which will save society and themselves from their own selfishness,' with justice as the route to a more loving world.[30] Niebuhr was deeply engaged with the issues of his time.

---

[26]   Kaplan, *With God on Their Side*, p. 18. George W. Bush, 'President's Remarks to the Nation', Ellis Island, September 11, 2002, http://www.whitehouse.gov/news/releases/2002/09/20020911–3.html, accessed 10th April 2007.

[27]   William S. Lind, et al., 'The Changing Face of War Into the Fourth Generation', *Military Review*, 69/9, (1989), pp. 2–11.

[28]   Mark F. W. Lovatt, *Confronting the Will to Power* (Carlisle, 2001).

[29]   Hans J. Morgenthau, 'The Influence of Reinhold Niebuhr in American Political Life and Thought', in Harold R. Landon (ed.) *Reinhold Niebuhr* (Greenwich, CT, 1962), p. 100.

[30]   D.B. Robertson (ed.), *Love and Justice* (New York: World Publishing, 1957), p. 28.

Niebuhr was traditional in his theology as he saw that Jesus was the revelation of the goodness of God and the goodness of man, and that it was in God's nature to 'swallow up evil in himself and destroy it.' The cross reveals that the defect in life is contingent not inherent, and that salvation comes from realising the defect of sin and repenting. Christians can be saved by hope and faith.[31] Niebuhr avoided synthesis or irreconcilable opposites by keeping the dialectical tension open and developed a methodology that was 'paradoxical' and contextual. His perspective was actually a complex of 'theological conviction, moral theory, and meditation on human nature' with the elements mutually reinforcing each other, rather than being developed systematically.[32] His theology thus changed over time, and was an engaged and fragmentary hermeneutic drawing on many sources, based on a re-conception of sin.

Sin

For Niebuhr the religious dimension of sin is 'man's rebellion against God' and the moral and social dimension of sin is 'injustice.'[33] The key contemporary theological position he addressed was the predominant liberalism of his day – enlightenment rationalism and liberal Protestantism – which saw progress as inevitable and believed in the fundamental goodness of humanity. Liberalism saw conflict in international life as caused by a poorly managed international system, not sinful greed, competitiveness and egoism. Niebuhr abandoned this liberal position because of the war, his experience of the unjust exploitation of workers at Henry Ford's Detroit works and the Depression in America. They exposed the forces at work in society and what creating a just society needed to address.

Niebuhr criticised the idea of inevitable progress, as he saw it as Christianity without the doctrine of sin – a secularised Christianity – the removal of which leads to a simple optimism 'which fails to do justice either to the unique freedom of man or to the daemonic misuse he may make of that freedom.'[34] Niebuhr was thus Augustinian in his view of human nature, which greatly influenced his 'realism.' Niebuhr saw that Augustine articulated an interpretation of human selfhood which 'enables him to view the heights of human creativity and the depths of human destructiveness, which avoids the errors of moral sentimentality and cynicism.'[35] As Niebuhr famously pointed out, these two aspects need to be held in tension and shape the nature of politics, as 'man's capacity for justice makes democracy

---

[31] Larry Rasmussen (ed.), *Reinhold Niebuhr – Selected Writings* (London, 1989), p. 94.

[32] Robin W. Lovin, *Reinhold Niebuhr and Christian Realism* (Cambridge, 1995), p. 3.

[33] Reinhold Niebuhr, *The Nature and Destiny of Man,* vol.1 (London, 1941), p. 179.

[34] Niebuhr, *Nature and Destiny of Man*, vol.1, p. 24.

[35] Reinhold Neibuhr, *Christian Realism and Political Problems* (London, 1954), p. 12.

possible; man's inclination to injustice makes democracy necessary.'[36] His emphasis on sin was a corrective to the optimism of inevitable progress and of inherent human goodness.

Sin was conceived of in terms of the tension created by the limited human self meeting the unlimited potential of freedom, and the anxiety this causes. Freedom generates an existential crisis, anxiety, which was part of the human condition. The anxiety was not itself sinful, but the turning to the self to cope with the anxiety and insecurity was. As he says, 'Man is insecure and involved in natural contingency; he seeks to overcome his insecurity by a will-to-power which overreaches the limits of human creatureliness.'[37] Sin placed the self in central prominence, as 'self-love' (excessive love of self) is the source of evil as it makes itself its own end.[38]

In recognising that all are sinful and all have equality before God, Niebuhr suggested a less clear distinction between the righteous and the wicked than Bush's self-righteous rhetoric. 'If only we could only fully understand that the evils against which we contend are frequently the fruit of illusions which are similar to our own, we might be better prepared to save a vast uncommitted world …'[39] This hope, as expressed in 1952, was sadly unfulfilled in the Bush administration.

Christian Realism

Niebuhr's emphasis on realism and the tragic aspect of human nature are the defining features of his viewpoint. The open and contingent method of political theology Niebuhr developed was 'Christian Realism', and 'realism' was understood as having a full and accurate picture of what is going on, taking in 'all factors in a social and political situation which offer resistance to established norms into account, particularly the factors of self-interest and power.'[40] His sense of tragedy gave a critical humility to the sense of vision which underpinned his writings but, unlike some other realists, there was a duty towards justice that came with power. For Niebuhr it was about achieving a relative justice in the world.

The practice of Christianity in the context of international affairs was particularly important for him as he saw history as deeply contingent, with a leading role for responsible agency. The aim was to make relations between states work better, rather than follow one's own interest in ignorance of others' legitimate requirements and interests, or in search of an ideological solution. Thus for Niebuhr it is legitimate and natural for states to further their interests but that does not mean there should be a simple anarchic competition between states. Niebuhr advocated

---

[36]   Reinhold Niebuhr, *The Children of Light and the Children of Darkness* (New York, 1944), pp. 6–7.

[37]   Niebuhr, *Nature and Destiny of Man*, vol.1, p. 178.

[38]   Neibuhr *Christian Realism and Political Problems*, p. 117.

[39]   Reinhold Niebuhr, *The Irony of American History* (London, 1952), p. 14.

[40]   Reinhold Niebuhr, 'Augustine's Political Realism' in his *Christian Realism and Political Problems* (London, 1954), p. 114.

the idea of national restraint and the development of international organisations, unlike the Bush administration's policies.

Niebuhr's approach challenges the exclusive absolutism of the Bush administration as he was concerned with showing that all lived under God, so no state or person could be seen as absolute.[41] He understood the forces at work in the world as fluid and in this sense he is very modern. He has an ontology of radical change, relativity, contingency and autonomy running throughout his work, tempered by the Augustinian sense of sin and coming grace, which stopped him embracing an unapologetic understanding of liberal progressivism.[42] His method was very much a middle way between those who aimed to achieve too much, and those who wished to avoid involvement. The opening to his famous 'Serenity Prayer' summed this up neatly: 'God grant me the serenity/ to accept the things I cannot change;/ the courage to change the things I can;/ and the wisdom to know the difference...'

The United States

Niebuhr was very clear that there were peculiarities to how the US saw and acted in the world as it was founded on utopian hopes.[43] The US has a messianic vision exemplifying the virtues of democracy and looking to extend the principles of self-government throughout the world. However, as Stone explains, Niebuhr aimed:

> to persuade an empire tempted by swings toward isolationism, imperialism, moralism, Manichaeism, and materialism to conduct its affairs diplomatically and persistently in a manner of broadly conceived national interest and national restraint.[44]

The critique of Bush's unilateralism and Manichaeism is clear. For Niebuhr peace is understood as an armistice, rather than being a 'natural' state of affairs and the major powers had responsibilities to make a peace for all – not just the US. The use of coercive powers may be necessary, but Niebuhr's understanding challenges the simplicity of belief and action underpinning the thinking regarding Iraq. He warned of the dangers of the pride of power, pride of the intellect and the pride of self righteousness[45] – all of which the administration fell into, and it cost them dearly.

---

[41]   Roger L. Shinn, 'Christian Realists in a Pluralistic Society: Interactions between Niebuhr and Morgenthau, Kennan, and Schlesinger', in Patterson, *The Christian Realists*, p. 192.

[42]   Langdon Gilkey, *On Niebuhr: A Theological Study*, (Chicago, 2001) pp. 248–9.

[43]   Reinhold Niebuhr and Alan Heimert, *A Nation So Conceived* (London, 1963).

[44]   Stone, *Prophetic Realism*, p. 62.

[45]   Eric Patterson, 'Niebuhr and His Critics: Realistic Optimism in World Politics' in his *The Christian Realists* (Lanham, MD, 2003), pp. 25–51.

Politics does not work in absolutes because it is about the ability to work in concert seeking reciprocal agreements.[46] Niebuhr's political theology, which has at its core prudence, responsibility, study, humility and a 'decent respect' of the views and interests of other nations, is a way of addressing the self-deceiving, morally arrogant approach and messianic tendencies to which US foreign policy can be prone.[47] It allows the realisation of the God-given value of others, their concerns and interests. In addition, Niebuhr's method of biblically formed engagement using the philosophy of Pragmatism avoids absolutes and embraces contingency and a wider audience.

Obama and a Post-Niebuhrian Approach

Niebuhr has not been without his critics. Martin Luther King, for example, thought him too pessimistic of human nature, whilst feminists have critiqued his focus on aggressive personality types, and others see his focus on policy makers as a problem. However, his strength is that he 'can explain to people how it is that one can subscribe to a faith in Christ and yet opt for a public life.'[48] At root what Niebuhr was trying to do was promote the long-term goals of peace, order and justice, whilst being aware of the theological and political aspects which resisted those goals. However, the critics are pointing out that, whilst Niebuhr makes sin intelligible, he underestimates the transformative nature of the sinful self through the graceful formation provided by the church.[49] This is a key criticism and by critiquing his analysis of power and the church, a post-Niebuhrian hermeneutic for political theology becomes possible.

There are two major problems with Niebuhr's understanding of power. First, he saw it as always negative and corrupting, and second, he had a pre-modern understanding of it.[50] First, Christianity has traditionally not seen power as inherently corrupt because it is possible to exercise power to further mission – as a dangerous expression of service and love. This view is essentially affirmative of power but not without reservations and the need for humility and an alertness to failings.[51] For example, Augustine's *City of God* talks of the art of governing in the imperfect city.[52] Second, a pre-modern understanding sees power as a quality or substance. A more modern understanding, in the works of Michel Foucault for instance, sees it as a more contested concept, viewing power in relational terms involving consent

---

[46]   Charles Davis, *Religion and the Making of Society* (Cambridge, 1994), p. 128.

[47]   Lieven and Hulsman, *Ethical Realism*, pp. 53–86.

[48]   Robert B. Westbrook, *Democratic Hope* (Ithaca, 2005), p. 211.

[49]   Stanley Hauerwas, *With The Grain of the Universe: The Church's Witness and Natural Theology* (London, 2002), pp. 138–40.

[50]   Lovatt, *Confronting the Will to Power*, p. 180.

[51]   Stephen Sykes, *Power and Christian Theology* (London, 2006), pp. 27–53, 152.

[52]   Augustine, *City of God*, Bk. 5, Ch. 24.

and resistance. It involves direct and indirect disciplinary practices.[53] Niebuhr, by understanding power as the will of the individual – something internalised in human personality – misses the social and relational nature of it.

Niebuhr's lack of ecclesiology follows the same limitation, as he focuses on the individual. One can apply a more social re-reading of this shortcoming too, by understanding the church and its hermeneutic as involved in character formation, where Christians learn the Christian narrative and learn, by 'reading in communion', to embody it in life. This makes it possible to maintain the understanding of humanity as the source of sin, but to see that the church is part of the transformation of that sin, both individually and collectively.

From this position it is possible to advocate that the church can use and generate power in society by imagining a different future to the one bound by simple political concerns or by fears of terror. William Cavanaugh has shown how this was possible in Chile under Pinochet and how the individualisation the dictatorship tried to impose was countered by the communitarian aspects of the church, founded on the experience of the Kingdom rooted in the Eucharist.[54] It brought together doctrine, context and practice in the community. With this hermeneutic the church's practice became a witness to an alternative reality and developed political challenges to the state, such as its human rights work. This is what a political theology based on a 'reading in communion' hermeneutic can achieve. It fits Niebuhr's non-utopian liberalism but is post-liberal and gives grace, power and the church greater roles in the analysis of the context and practice of faith. Faith, not self righteousness, is the true source of security because it provides a different understanding of security, to one based on fearful will-to-power.

President Obama

President Obama has already begun to pick up the threads of the Niebuhrian approach. On the campaign trail he explained the influence of Niebuhr on his thinking. He saw him as 'one of my favourite philosophers' who had outlined that there was 'the compelling idea that there's serious evil in the world, and hardship and pain. And we should be humble and modest in our belief we can eliminate those things... I take away ... the sense we have to make these efforts knowing they are hard, and not swinging from naïve idealism to bitter realism.'[55]

Obama embodies the shift from the Puritan-individualistic trend in American Christianity back to the social gospel model, though one that relates far more to Niebuhr's earlier liberalism, pragmatism and pluralism. Obama comes from a totally different religious background to Bush. Where for Bush Christianity saved

---

[53]   Michel Foucault, 'Truth and Power' in *Power* (London, 2001), pp. 111–133.

[54]   William T. Cavanaugh, *Torture and Eucharist* (Oxford, 1998).

[55]   Jim Winters, 'Obama Cites Influence of Niebuhr' http://public.elmhurst.edu/news/7207811.html, accessed 10 May 2007.

him from alcoholism, for Obama it gave him a community and identity as a mixed-race young man and he embodies the progressive, social justice liberal agenda.[56] So, though he was raised outside churches, he attended the politically active liberationist church of Reverend Jeremiah Wright and this provided much of his character formation. The radical nature of Wright's theology and anti-American statements were to become a political liability on the campaign trail, but the influence has been formative. Furthermore, Obama had worked as a community organiser in Chicago, so has a far more communitarian background than Bush's individualistic faith.

Obama's approach is in stark contrast to Bush's as there is a clear humility towards his own views and the position of the US. Following Niebhur he has a clear sense of the role of sin rather than evil in life. He points out that he is 'human, limited in my understandings of God's purpose and therefore prone to sin,' whilst the US has on occasion contradicted its founding principles.[57] Following Niebuhr, he balances the demands of political compromise whilst maintaining an emphasis on the ultimate ethical basis of his policies. As he said in his inaugural speech: 'security emanates from the justness of our cause; the force of our example; the tempering qualities of humility and restraint.'[58] Furthermore the role of his faith as the driver of his politics is tempered by his understanding of American democracy and pluralism: 'What our deliberative, pluralistic democracy does demand is that the religiously motivated translate their concerns into universal, rather than religion-specific, values. It requires that their proposals must be subject to argument and amenable to reason.'[59] This makes him much closer to the Niebuhrian and post-Niebuhrian model of political theology addressing the pragmatic, contingent and pluralistic nature of life. This approach renounces the attractions of absolutism or total relativism by seeing inquiry as a self-correcting mechanism. It is an approach or practice which is reliant on openness and a willingness to test ideas in public and situate human beings as agents, not as spectators to their destinies, in a fluid conception of life. It is the model of the self-critical or reflexive Christian hermeneutical method. For him the source of American confidence is still faith based as it comes from 'the knowledge that God calls on us to shape an uncertain destiny.'[60]

Shaping that uncertain destiny has certainly been a challenge since Obama's assumption of power with the fragility of the world economy. This crisis has led to a high degree of inter-governmental co-operation to address the problems, and the economic consequences alone will force a degree of 'realism' on his international and domestic policies that will leave the many electrified by his election rhetoric

---

[56] Stephen Mansfield, *The Faith of Barack Obama* (Nashville, 2008).

[57] Barack Obama, *The Audacity of Hope* (Edinburgh, 2007), pp. 223, 281.

[58] Barack Obama, Inaugural Address in his *Change We Can Believe In* (Edinburgh, 2009), p. 295.

[59] Obama, *The Audacity of Hope*, p. 219.

[60] Obama, 'Inaugural Address', p. 298.

disappointed. However, it is possible to see already that his approach has been a clear reorientation of rhetoric and priorities underpinned by pragmatism. He held on to Robert Gates as Defense Secretary, for example. His naturally consensual approach can be seen in his domestic policies over healthcare and his chairing of the UN Security Council – the first US President to do so. He chaired talks on UN peacekeepers in September 2009.[61] Multilateral institutions and allies are back in favour in Washington. The rhetoric is of engagement and admission of failings, matched by far less confrontation. There is no longer unlimited support for Israel. He has shown himself willing to commit the prestige of his office, if somewhat prematurely, in the Israel/Palestine issue as this is seen as a key factor in developing peace in the Middle East, a view not held by his predecessor. More markedly, he has been willing to have open negotiations with the Iranians, though the time limit on that is now reaching termination and the disputed Iranian elections have raised issues about the principles of human rights for the presidency, as well as the concerns about uranium enrichment. His openness is matched by a strong stance on sanctions to halt the enrichment programme. Rather boldly his security agenda now includes not building the missile defence system in Eastern Europe, thereby ameliorating the poor relations with Russia and enabling them to work together over the issue of Iran. The legitimacy of other countries' concerns are now being engaged with, and the principles that are supposed to underpin US foreign policy are brought to the fore as he aims to close Guantanamo and to bring terror suspects to trial in civil rather than military courts.

Obama's ability to realise these aims and bring them to a successful conclusion are for the future. But the place and orientation of his theological liberalism gives him a different approach to his predecessor and one that uses Niebuhr's principles, though in a more liberal way. Obama's religious views and experiences give him a unique perspective as a president of the United States as they enter a new era. His major speech in Cairo in June 2009 shows an understanding and appreciation of Islam and its contribution to civilisation and the arts that no other previous president could have managed, brought up as he was for a period in the Indonesia. As he said he seeks,

> a new beginning between the United States and Muslims around the world, one based on mutual interest and mutual respect, and one based upon the truth that America and Islam are not exclusive ... they overlap, and share common principles – principles of justice and progress; tolerance and the dignity of all human beings.[62]

---

[61]   Barack Obama http://www.whitehouse.gov/blog/09/09/24/President-Obama-Meets-the-Peacekeepers/, accessed 24/9/09.

[62]   Barack Obama http://www.whitehouse.gov/the_press_office/Remarks-by-the-President-at-Cairo-University-6–04–09/, accessed 24/9/09.

Religion is thus not to be a dividing factor for him in the 'War on Terror' but an engine of reconciliation, as befits a man who sees the uncompromising principles of religion as a 'dangerous' basis for policy.[63] It is a far humbler security policy that is aware of the need to work with others, to recognise America's strengths and weaknesses, but also to keep the aim of justice clearly in view. He stands clearly in the mainstream of American strategic culture defending US interests but articulating them in terms of the 'social gospel' rather than 'puritan' trend of his predecessor. How far he is able to realise these aspirations cannot be judged so early in his term. But the American 'war on terror' and its self-understanding are on the move to a wiser and broader understanding of security based on a doctrine of sin, not a flawed view of evil.

Conclusion

This chapter has analysed the suitability of using the doctrines of evil and sin for analysing the context of the US response to the events of 11 September 2001 and the war on terror. The limitations of President Bush's use of the term 'evil' have been examined and shown to be the source of the absolutism and self-righteous foreign policy that has been so disastrous, illegal and unjust. Reinhold Niebuhr's reinterpretation of the doctrine of sin has been shown to be an effective doctrinal lens to avoid these pitfalls and able to generate a practice of Christian Realism that takes seriously the nature of self-interest and power in international affairs. Obama embodies a liberal version of this. Underpinning this analysis is the model of political theology as a task that aims to relate doctrine, context and practice by generating a performative hermeneutic undertaken in the broader context of the church community. This process is understood as 'reading in communion', a process of life-long learning aiming to embodying that reading in life. This methodology is used to refine the shortcomings of Niebuhr's over-emphasis on the individual and the limitations of his analysis of power and the church. The church is given a key transformative role in the public debate.

From this position it is possible to see the limits of using evil as the key hermeneutic of international affairs. 'Evil' can be used adjectively as long as it starts with the sense of sin, but the dangers of absolutism and self-righteousness are enormous. The 'war on terror' is not between good and evil, but is much more a part of the broader human predicament. This, as Niebuhr showed, does not mean a descent into chaos, but a sense of the mutual failings or sinfulness of those involved, which one cannot legislate away. It also requires embracing a far more pragmatic approach that avoids absolutism, where the state can become in danger of being treated as a god, or at least as godly. The messianic drive that comes from this destabilises politics and shuts down debate. The emphasis on 'sin'

---

[63]   Obama, *The Audacity of Hope*, p. 220.

allows Christians to understand why the US has acted in the way it has, and how Christians can judge and critique it. The doctrine provides insight.

Advocating the use of 'sin' as a crucial doctrine for generating Christian practice in the international context is not to argue for a deeply negative view of human nature, but to generate an open, contingent, self-critical and contextual method of looking and acting as a Christian in the world. It is a way of looking in an imaginative fashion, fighting for justice in a tragic setting and doing so via the performative and transformative church. Niebuhr shows how a tragic sense of history can still maintain an optimistic viewpoint; how to be a non-utopian liberal. This is important because, when Niebuhr was writing, he was calling out to a complacent country. Now there is a need to have a call of hope, but one that recognises the tragic, the realistic aspects of life[64] – the non-utopian liberalism he advocated, which mediates between the extremes of absolutism or utter relativism – the 'audacity of hope' Obama refers to.

Political theology recognises that the practice shapes the understanding of doctrine. By seeing 'sinful' Christians acting in 'tragic' history it is possible to see the redemptive acts of God rooted in history, and to see how partial our understanding and perception of God are. We are flawed but we are responsible. The paradoxical dialectic at the heart of God and ourselves is lived and learnt through learning to read and live in the transformative church which draws on scripture, tradition, reason and experience. In that practice and from that position one is able to condemn Bush's rhetoric and policies and work to realise an alternative approach to the 'war on terror.' As the strategist Basil Liddell Hart said, 'The object in war is a better state of peace – even if only from your own point of view. Hence it is essential to conduct war with a constant regard to the peace you desire.'[65] The contingent peace that Niebuhr advocates, has greater strength than the absolutist approach of the Bush administration, and is one Obama is working towards.

Finally, it is an understanding of religion that sees it promoting justice and peace, rather than the more usual view of religion as a source of violence. Bush's view plays into the myth of religion as having to be absolutist, anti-rational and divisive.[66] For disproving that alone Niebuhr's theology and Obama's efforts should be welcomed.

---

[64]   Shinn, 'Christian Realists in a Pluralistic Society', p. 194.

[65]   Liddell Hart, Basil, *Strategy* (2nd Revised Edition, London, 1954/67), pp. 338, 353.

[66]   Cavanaugh, William T., *The Myth of Religious Violence* (New York, 2009).

PART TWO
Responding to the Terrorist Threat

Chapter 5

Philip Bobbitt's *Terror and Consent*: a Brief Critique

Michael Howard

The phrase 'War on Terror' was coined by the American government in the aftermath of the terrorist attacks on New York and Washington on 11 September 2001. It was an immediate reaction in a moment of enormous stress, so no one should expect those responsible to be too pedantic about their definitions. An appalling 'act of war' had clearly been committed against the people of the United States although the identity of the perpetrators was still obscure, so 'War on Terror' seemed good enough to be going on with. But the shortcomings of the term were rapidly revealed. 'War' may be a reasonable metaphor to describe action against such specific anti-social activities as crime or drug-trafficking, but against an abstract concept such as 'Terror' it makes very little sense. Moreover, the use of the term 'war' creates a dangerous state of mind that tempts both governments and peoples into extreme actions more likely to damage than to help their cause. The Bush Administration used it as a justification not only for instituting draconic constraints on the civil liberties of its own citizens by the so-called 'Patriot Act', but for jettisoning most of the laws governing relations between sovereign powers that the United States had done so much to create. Elsewhere the term never caught on, and even the American government has now officially abandoned it in favour of one less contentious if even less precise 'The Long War'. But when a scholar of Professor Bobbitt's eminence not only continues to take the term seriously but publishes a six-hundred page volume justifying it, it is clear that the term cannot be totally ignored.[1]

Bobbitt's starting point seems to me fundamentally sound. The world is no longer divided, as Grotius and his successors saw it, into discrete and sovereign states, each responsible for the maintenance of its own internal order and external security (the first the realm, as Bobbitt sees it, of Law, the second of Strategy: two dimensions that can never be entirely separated). Nor can relations between states any longer be effectively regulated by an 'international' law that assumes the inviolable sovereignty of its members. 'Globalisation' has now produced a degree of interdependence so complete that not only the economic but the political well-being, if not indeed the actual survival, even of the most powerful state is

---

[1]   Philip Bobbitt, *Terror and Consent: the Wars of the Twenty-First Century* (London & New York, 2008).

now affected by that of all the others. To maintain this global order it may thus be necessary for 'law-abiding' states to intervene, if necessary by force, in the internal affairs of others. But Bobbitt insists that if this intervention is carried out on behalf of the international community as a whole, it must be, and be seen to be, 'legal'. Its rationale, conduct and aftermath must all be contained within a universally accepted framework of law. 'Strategy', as Bobbitt puts it, must continue to respect 'Law'. But 'Law' may have to be adjusted to accommodate the ineluctable demands of 'Strategy'. That is where the problems begin.

There is nothing new about this problem: *Terror and Consent* should be seen in the context of a debate about 'intervention' that dates back at least to the sixteenth century. In fact the 'Grotian' world in which states enjoyed absolute sovereignty was very short lived, if it ever lived at all. It existed after a fashion in Europe for some forty years; between the mid-eighteenth century, when wars of dynastic intervention at last came to an end, and the French Revolution when 'democratic' states first asserted the right to intervene on behalf of neighbouring peoples 'struggling to be free'. The debate about the legality of intervention (or what the British Prime Minister Lord Palmerston who disapproved of it, called 'interference') continued throughout the next two centuries, eliciting major contributions from thinkers of the stature of John Stuart Mill and Michael Walzer.

Today, as Bobbitt properly points out, this perennial topic has been given new urgency by two contemporary developments. The first is a trans-national revolutionary movement, rooted in Islamic fundamentalism, whose leaders aim not simply at regime-change within individual states, but at a global transformation of power and ideology that threatens the stability of the entire international community. The second, and by far the more serious, is the capacity of terrorists, by using 'weapons of mass-destruction', to wreak damage on a scale so catastrophic as to pose an existential threat not only to regimes but to entire peoples; terrorists, moreover, inspired by an ideology that legitimises such destruction, not simply as a means to a political end but, by destroying an intrinsically evil culture, as a moral end in itself. The events of 11 September 2001 give only a mild foretaste of what such destruction might achieve. This combination of unlimited means with unlimited ends, Bobbitt argues, makes it necessary to abandon the traditional concept of terrorism as a disagreeable but not unusual weapon in the hands of 'non-state actors'. The transformation, he claims, is so profound that it is now appropriate to reify such activity as 'Terror' and regard it as an appropriate object of 'War'.

Bobbitt brings to his subject the authority not only of an academic with an unusual mastery of the fields of law, international relations and strategic studies, but that of a former government official with extensive experience in planning for the protection of 'critical infrastructure'. Further, he presents his case with an attractive lucidity, and a wealth of illustrative examples, that makes it highly persuasive and likely to be widely influential. Finally, kindly but embarrassingly, he dedicates the work to me. For this I am flattered and grateful. None the less, I believe that he has gone badly wrong.

First, Bobbitt generalises from an extreme situation. There are indeed extremist fanatics who preach the use of terror to overthrow existing world governance and create a universal Muslim *umma* where obedience would if necessary be enforced by 'terror', but – as Ahmad Achtar explains in Chapter 3 – few experts on the subject regard such thinkers as in any way typical. Such chiliastic fanatics always appear in times of stress. They were familiar figures in Europe during the era of the Protestant Reformation, but their influence was local and temporary, and they were far from typical of the reform movement as a whole. Today we certainly face a widespread resentment within the Muslim world against a Western political and cultural hegemony that has been growing in intensity over the past two hundred years; a resentment that can now find expression not only in local rebellion as it did throughout the nineteenth and twentieth centuries, but in acts of violence with global implications. In recent years this sentiment has been intensified, partly by the policies pursued in the Middle East by, in particular, the United States – especially her role in the conflict over Palestine – but more generally by racial tensions within the West wherever Muslim immigrants have failed to integrate with the indigenous populations.

But that resentment, however much it may be fuelled by extremist rhetoric, normally arises from specific grievances – political, social, or economic – which bulk far larger in the minds of rebel activists than does any serious aspiration to destroy Western civilisation and create a new 'terror-dominated' world. To be sure, the longer such grievances are left to fester, and the more remote any hope of remedying them becomes, the more likely are those who hold them to turn to desperate measures and fanatical leaders, whether they share the apocalyptic beliefs of those leaders or not. But to see in these protest movements, however linked they may be by a common rhetoric, an undifferentiated entity to be labelled as 'Terror' against which we must 'wage war', is to fall into the exactly the same error as did a slightly earlier generation of American publicists, who saw in every left-wing movement and government throughout the world a manifestation of an undifferentiated entity called 'Communism', against which they summoned 'the Free World' to wage an equally global struggle.

Further, Bobbitt sees in 'Terror' not merely a means, but an end. He sees the object of those who use such methods as being not only to overthrow existing regimes, but to create what he terms 'states of terror', Orwellian dystopias whose members are terrified into perpetual subjection. These he distinguishes from those he defines as 'states of consent', which he summons to wage 'a historic struggle to preclude a world in which terror rather than consent establishes the State's legitimacy'.[2]

Now to draw the world in such black-and-white terms is a true *reductio ad absurdum*. That such 'states of terror' have existed and continue to exist is unfortunately all too true, although Bobbitt does not help his case by citing such bizarre examples as those established by mutinous soldiers in the sixteenth century and Caribbean pirates in the eighteenth – small local regimes that established

---

[2]   *Terror and Consent*, p. 12.

themselves where legitimate authority was ineffective or non-existent. These were not 'states', in any recognised sense of the word, but criminal groups concerned, like the Mafia, to exploit the weakness of legitimate order rather than to overthrow it. Nevertheless Western history certainly provides many examples of true 'states of terror'. The Normans imposed one on England in the eleventh century, as did Henry VIII in the last years of his reign. Robespierre's France was an avowed, if mercifully short-lived, 'state of terror'. The Soviet Union could certainly be defined as such until the death of Stalin, as could the Peoples' Republic of China until the death of Mao Zedong; while today the survival of Robert Mugabe disastrously prolongs one in Zimbabwe. On the other hand, there are also, happily, 'states of consent' such as those in the United States and Western Europe, where, as Bobbitt puts it, 'all persons can exercise the rights of conscience and in which the individual conscience plays the decisive role by means of a constitutional, consensual system of laws'.[3]

But these are extremes in a very broad spectrum. Most political communities throughout history have been, and many still are, states neither of 'terror' nor of 'consent', but of *acquiescence*. Without giving positive and explicit 'consent' to their governments, their members accept them as 'the powers that be'. Their obedience is not so much explicit and cerebral as innate and tribal: they have been born into the community and accept its norms, however oppressive these may be. I am, I hope, a loyal citizen of my country, but that is not because I can 'exercise [my] rights of conscience' and vote to elect a government once every five years. It is because this is a community rooted in the soil where I feel at home; one created over many centuries by its history, its culture, its language, and its traditions, and to whose method of governance I have become accustomed. The constitutional mechanism of 'consent' has very little to do with it. When my countrymen fought two world wars it was to defend, not 'democracy', but their 'country'; a huge jumble of memories and aspirations, prejudices and affections that they would have been hard put to it to explain or justify to an unsympathetic outsider but which they all understood perfectly well. Patriotism has more to do with emotions than with constitutions.

All this was expounded and argued two centuries ago in their different ways by Edmund Burke in Britain and Johann Gottlieb Fichte in Germany, to explain why their countrymen found the rationalist dogmatism of the French Enlightenment so unacceptable. Those explanations and arguments are equally valid for those who find Western-style democracy so alien today, and who fight against it with the same stubborn conviction that led the British to defend an aristocracy, the Prussians to defend a monarchy and the Spaniards to defend a clerical absolutism against the attempt of the French to dragoon them all into sharing the benefits of enlightenment democracy.

Further, even in the most democratic and best-ordered states, there will always be those who accept authority only from fear of the consequences if they do not.

---

[3]   *Terror and Consent*, p. 523.

No state can exist without some element of coercion, which may seem often to border on 'terror' by those anti-social elements against whom it is directed. The borderline between terror and coercion, coercion and acquiescence, acquiescence and consent, is often very blurred, and most historic communities have mutated from one to another over the centuries. There are times indeed when states may paradoxically be ones both of 'consent' and of 'terror'; a condition that prevailed in the Third Reich in the final stages of, and the Soviet Union throughout, the Second World War. States of unadulterated 'terror' have seldom persisted for more than a few decades before softening into 'states of acquiescence'.

To divide the world as does Professor Bobbitt, Manichean-fashion, into 'states of terror' and 'states of consent' is in fact to perpetuate a tendency that runs through much American thinking: the imposition, on a highly diverse world, of a procrustean framework comprising 'freedom' or 'democracy' on the one hand, and 'tyranny' or 'despotism' on the other; the two being locked in an ineluctable conflict in which if the forces of freedom do not prevail they will be irretrievably lost. This is perhaps an extrapolation to the rest of the world of their own tragic experience: a terrible civil war fought in the belief that their Union could not survive 'half slave and half free' and that freedom was therefore indivisible; a belief they believe to be as valid globally as it once seemed nationally. What is surprising is that a scholar with the subtlety and learning of Professor Bobbitt should share a parochial misconception that has misled so many of his countrymen.

Professor Bobbitt justifies his reasoning by arguing that the transition from the 'nation state' to the 'market state' that he analysed so brilliantly in his previous work *The Shield of Achilles* has resulted in a change in the nature of war.[4] This leads him to suggest that Al-Qaʻida should now be regarded as a 'state', on grounds that would apply equally to any multi-national corporation or, come to that, the Roman Catholic Church. He would be on firmer ground if he argued that what has changed is the nature, not of war, but of *peace*; the conditions needed for the preservation of order in a globally interdependent world. The use of force by legitimate authority to maintain a 'just' order may involve the conduct of campaigns against specific adversaries such as that being conducted at present in Afghanistan, but these are quite distinct from the total commitment against a global enemy implied in the term 'war against terror'. Indeed the whole concept of legitimacy depends on the maintenance, and acceptance, of that distinction.

Oddly enough, this is recognised by Bobbitt himself when he goes on to explore the boundaries of legitimacy, both for states when they intervene in the internal affairs of others, and for the officials of those states in handling individual 'combatants'. The care and precision with which he does so is exemplary, whether or not we accept his definitions and recommendations; though it must be admitted that when he is dealing with the question of 'preclusive war', in the first category, and torture, in the second, he ventures on to very uncertain ground, as David Fisher and Brian Wicker

---

[4]   Philip Bobbitt, *The Shield of Achilles: War, Peace and the Course of History* (London & New York, 2002).

make clear in their chapters. But his very concern for ensuring the legality of both state and individual actions show that he is dealing with the maintenance of peace, not the waging of war.

Why, therefore, does Bobbitt talk about 'waging war' at all? I suspect that there are two reasons. The first is a quite proper concern to emphasise the urgency of the problem that we face and the radical nature of the measures that may be needed to deal with it. The second is his understanding, even if he does not share it, of the cultural disposition of his countrymen referred to above, to see the world in Manichean terms, a disposition that leads them to take action in international affairs only when roused by the belief that they are confronting apocalyptic forces of 'evil' which threaten to destroy them. In 1917 Woodrow Wilson justified his declaration of war on Germany, not because that country was threatening the political and commercial interests of the United States, but in order, as he put it, to ensure 'the ultimate peace of the world and the liberation of its peoples [so that]…the world …[can] be made safe for democracy.'[5] Again, in 1941, when the Japanese attacked the American fleet in Pearl Harbor in a pre-emptive strike to prevent the United States from interfering with their expansion into China, President Roosevelt declared that America was 'fighting for its existence and its future life [and] for a world in which this nation, and all that this nation represents, will be safe for our children'.[6] And in March 1947, in order to persuade Congress to fund a Greek government fighting against a largely Communist (but not Soviet-supported) insurgency, President Truman enunciated the 'Truman Doctrine', declaring:

> At the present moment in world history nearly every nation must decide between alternative ways of life …. One way of life is based upon the will of the majority, and is distinguished by free institutions, representative government … and freedom from political oppression. The second way of life is based upon the will of a minority forcibly imposed upon the majority. It relies upon terror and oppression … I believe that we must assist free peoples to work out their own destinies in their own way.[7]

Whether Truman was correct in his appreciation of the 'Communist threat' in 1947 is still a matter of dispute among historians; but it is in almost the identical terms as those in which Truman summoned the American people to take arms against the Communist threat that Professor Bobbitt now urges them to conduct a 'War against Terror'. 'Waging war against terror', he declares, 'is a historic struggle to preclude a world in which terror rather than consent establishes the

---

[5]   Patrick Devlin, *Too Proud to Fight: Woodrow Wilson's Neutrality* (Oxford, 1974), p. 670.

[6]   Henry Steele Commager (ed.), *Documents of American History* (New York: Prentice Hall, 1946), p. 639.

[7]   David McCullough, *Truman* (London & New York, 1992), p. 547.

state's legitimacy.' [8] These are battle-cries to which the American public can be relied upon to respond. To define the challenge in terms of keeping the peace, rather than of waging war, is far less likely to be effective. To put it in the crudest political terms, the American electorate is traditionally happier to provide funds for the Department of Defense than it is for the Department of State, while the Pentagon is temperamentally more at ease in the role of fighting wars than in of maintaining peace. In order to persuade the American people to take action necessary to preserve peace, it may be necessary to tell them that they are fighting a war.

Now, 'war-fighting' may often be an essential tool in 'peace-keeping', but it should be regarded as an instrument of last resort; much as 'armed response' may be a necessary instrument in domestic peace-keeping, or lethal poisons a necessary element in the pharmacopaeia of medical practitioners: exceptional measures to be employed only in emergencies and then under stringent control. They have to be regarded as exceptional, if only for the corrosive effect they are likely to have on the minds of their users. As I have written elsewhere: 'The leaders of nations at war have always considered themselves entitled, if all else fails, to use any means to defeat their adversaries and avoid defeat themselves, whether it be the torture of individuals or the destruction of entire cities, and they will usually enjoy massive popular support when they do so.'[9] Warriors may strive to observe the restraints dictated by their peculiar cultures, whether they be those of religion, feudal chivalry or liberal humanism; but these rapidly erode under the stress of conflict, or when the price of adhering to them appears to be not only personal annihilation but the destruction of one's own society. 'The bottom line' in war-fighting is that victory must be achieved 'whatever it takes'.

That is not the ethic of policing. By definition, the police can only act within the law, and when they break it they are themselves subject to its penalties. Nor, fundamentally, is it the ethic of Professor Bobbitt. Indeed, he makes his own position clear when he replies to the question 'What in the "War against Terror" constitutes "Victory"?' 'Winning', he tells us simply 'consists in not losing.'[10] Victory is achieved when policing action is effective, justice takes its course, and the legitimacy of the responsible authorities is maintained: in short, when peace is preserved. But this depends, as Bobbitt repeatedly stresses, on the legitimacy of the enforcing authority being evident, both from the source of its mandate and the manner in which that mandate is enforced. Once that legitimacy is forfeited, the enforcer becomes simply another belligerent, on the same ethical level as those it is fighting. Law may have to take account of the changing demands of Strategy; but Strategy, if it is to be effective, must never exceed the limits prescribed by Law. That indeed is the lesson that runs throughout this large and learned book.

---

[8]   *Terror and Consent*, p. 12.

[9]   *Survival* (IISS, 2008), vol. 50, pt 4, p. 254.

[10]   *Terror and Consent*, p. 183.

Terror and Consent is in fact a major and authoritative study on how peace should be kept and order upheld in an increasingly dangerous world. But it will only be effective if it is seen as such, not as a primer for the conduct of a particular kind of war.

Chapter 6
Just War and State Sovereignty

Brian Wicker

Overview

In the last chapter Michael Howard examined Philip Bobbitt's views on 'the war on terror.' This chapter considers his observations on the disintegration of the global order of separate sovereign nation-states, and the implications of this disintegration for the defence of people against terrorism. For, as Audrey Kurth Cronin has said, in her important recent work *How Terrorism Ends*, 'the twenty-first century state is evolving beyond the classic nation-state anyway.'[1] With the rise of global terrorist gangs like Al-Qaʻida the very notion of a just war waged by sovereign states against terrorists seems inappropriate if not impossible. This is because globalisation in its multifarious forms is undermining the very legitimacy of the sovereign state system. It marks a shift in the political tectonics of the twenty-first century world. To tackle an organisation like Al-Qaʻida requires an equivalent shift in our approach to ending it for, as Cronin observes, 'we have tested the effectiveness of military force and come up short'.[2]

As with plate tectonics, the process is mostly very slow, and it will probably take a long time to evolve. Nevertheless, sudden and unexpected movements sometimes occur. An obvious example is the 2008 collapse of the global banking system. But more important are two potentially lethal threats to the very existence of the current nation-state system, both of which are being confronted as this book is being assembled. The first is global warming and climate change. The full effects of this were discussed internationally in Copenhagen in December 2009, although no agreement was reached on the way forward. Secondly, failure at the forthcoming Review Conference of the Nuclear Non-Proliferation Treaty (to be held in May 2010) could spell a suicidal spread of nuclear weapons around the most dangerous parts of the globe, including to terrorist gangs. Failure at either or both of these meetings could mean catastrophe for all the states conducting them.

As we have said in the Introduction, this book is concerned with the ethics of fighting terrorist gangs. Now for the purposes of a just war against such gangs in modern conditions, a key criterion is right authority. As just war theorists have always insisted, without this it cannot be just to go to war. Where could we find this right authority to go to war against (for example) Al-Qaʻida? Well, up to fairly

[1] Audrey Kurth Cronin, *How Terrorism Ends* (Princeton and Oxford, 2009), p. 193.
[2] Ibid., p. 194.

recent times the emphasis on right authority has concentrated on the *sovereignty* of the just belligerent. Going to war 'had to be a matter for decision by the lawful sovereign – whether an individual monarch or a collective supreme council – since overarching responsibility for the well-being of the people rested on the sovereign's shoulders.'[3] Today, of course, the tradition of right authority has to take account of a number of international legal institutions: the United Nations, the International Court of Justice, the European Union, and so on. It is commonly accepted that without their permission or authorisation, going to war today can hardly be just, since these institutions have a part to play in the well-being of the people of any belligerent state.[4] Nevertheless, the argument for a just war is still widely accepted, on the grounds that the sovereign state still has the primary responsibility for its people's well-being, and that the various institutions mentioned are founded upon the system of sovereign nation-states which we have inherited from the treaties of Augsburg (1555) and Westphalia (1648).

Of course, it was always a weakness of the notion of a just war (some would say a fatal weakness[5]) that the belligerent who goes to war will inevitably claim that he alone has right authority on his side. But today things are much more awkward than this. For the fact is that in the contemporary world the very notion of nation-state sovereignty is disintegrating.[6] Economic globalisation, the development of supranational institutions such as the European Union, the internet, global warming and climate change, the threat of nuclear proliferation, global resource depletion, mass tourism, the near-global meltdown of the banks: all of these contemporary developments are having a profound impact on the hitherto sacrosanct principle of the 'sovereignty' of the nation-state. A resort to protectionism in the context of recession in many states is widely recognised today as a serious threat to the stability and prosperity of the global economy. As is widely said by heads of governments the world over, the financial and economic crisis of late 2008 cannot be solved unless states co-operate, regardless of their sovereignty claims, for 'the era of globalisation has eroded national sovereignty.'[7]

Sovereign States as False Gods

Of course, the division of humankind into distinct political communities has evolved over time into very different forms. Although each form of community tends to be regarded by those within it as immortal, the fact is that all such realities

---

[3]   Guthrie and Quinlan, *Just Wa*, (London, 2007), pp. 26–7.

[4]   Cf. Lord Bingham (former Senior Law Lord), *The Guardian*, 18 November 2008), p. 1.

[5]   Stanley Windass, *Christianity Versus Violence* (London, 1964) p. 77.

[6]   On this see Joseph A. Camilleri and Jim Falk, *The End of Sovereignty* (Aldershot, 1992), passim.

[7]   Cf. *The Observer*, 16 November 2008.

develop and evolve with time. In the course of history humankind has almost inevitably developed 'independent political communities each of which possesses a government and asserts sovereignty in relation to a particular portion of the earth's surface' and in itself there was nothing wrong with that.[8] But Aristotle's city-state, or the princedoms of mediaeval Europe, were very different from the sovereign nation-states created by the Treaties of Augsburg and Westphalia. These have now become our 'gods', as perhaps Hobbes foresaw they would.[9] Today, when states act like personalities writ large, their will is law and cannot be gainsaid, even though (like the gods of ancient Athens) their voices are mutually contradictory. The deepest source of the trouble is that these sovereign national powers trump the common good of *all*. (The common good of *all* is a constant theme of papal pronouncements in international affairs, as witness the recent statement of Benedict VI to the newly-appointed US ambassador to the Holy See, 29 February 2008, and his speech to the United Nations, 18 April 2008). Thus, every time a political leader of a state affirms his determination to ensure, above all else, the safety and security of his own citizens, if necessary at the expense of the citizens of other powers, or even at the price of undermining the rule of law, he reveals himself a willing victim of the false god of state sovereignty. Every time a state, contrary to international law, tries to justify attacking or even invading another state, say for purposes of extirpating terrorists (as with American air-attacks on Pakistan, or Turkey's invasion of Kurdistan) it is exemplifying (however unavoidably) its commitment to the same false god. The same goes for attempts by any one of the powers to claim a right to torture its alleged enemies, as with American water-boarding or other illicit practices at places like Guantanamo Bay. Even the United Nations, with its international laws, is built upon the same false gods, despite valiant efforts to tame their worst effects.

Yet the supposedly sovereign power of states is still regarded by most politicians as an axiom of our modern existence. We can't seem to get away from it, notwithstanding that these sovereign states are only characters in a myth, written and revised over the centuries, the current version of which we in the twenty-first century constantly re-tell to ourselves as if it were the only possible story. But perhaps the false gods do not need to be placated for ever.

Sovereignty and the Market State

Philip Bobbitt has been hinting as much for some time. In his books, *The Shield of Achilles* (2002) and *Terror and Consent* (2008), he maintains that the sovereign nation-state is already being superseded by what he calls 'market states'.[10] His

---

[8] Hedley Bull, *The Anarchical Society* (New York 1977), p. 131.

[9] Thomas Hobbes, *Leviathan* (London: J.M. Dent, 1962), Part 1, Chapter 17.

[10] Philip Bobbitt, *The Shield of Achilles* (London and New York, 2002) and *Terror and Consent* (London and New York, 2008).

thesis is that boundaries behind which a state could do pretty much what it liked for and to its own people, as long as it did not directly attack others, are crumbling fast. National security no longer just means freedom from invasion. The alleged vital interests of (say) the USA or China now extend as far away as the oil fields of Iraq and the Sudan or the mineral deposits of Zaire and the Congo. Pressure is steadily increasing at the UN and elsewhere to use national military forces for policing and peace-keeping roles in troubled areas of the world, sometimes in the name of a global 'Responsibility to Protect' regardless of state frontiers.[11] At the same time, global terrorism by groups that have no allegiance to a particular state, and no respect for international law, is undermining the concept of national sovereignty from within, by simple but deadly forms of subversion, such as suicide bombing.

What then of what he calls 'transparent' national sovereignty? This holds that 'because a regime's sovereignty arises from its compact with its people ... sovereignty can be penetrated when a state commits widespread acts of violence against its own people, or acquires weapons of mass destruction in violation of its international agreements, or supports global terrorists who threaten the civilians of other states.' Thus the immunity of the state from attack from outside ought (Bobbitt argues) to be forfeit if and when its government does any of these things against the best interests of its people. In such a case armed intervention is legitimate despite the UN Charter article 2(4). This means a revision of the law much more drastic than the mere Responsibility to Protect suggests. If Bobbitt is right, the law should make room for the anticipatory *preclusive* use of force which will be needed if the world is to defeat the critical threat of global terrorism. – of which Al-Qaʿida is only an early example. The *ad bellum* criterion of right authority has to be completely rethought.[12]

If the division of human kind into separate sovereign nation-states is obsolescent, what is to take its place? On what principles should the future be organised? This is the key question Bobbitt asks. His reply is that the world will be run as a global market. If the primary objective of the nation state was 'maintaining, nurturing and improving the material conditions of its citizens', the over-riding objective of the market state will be to open up opportunities to every citizen who is able to benefit.[13] Of course, the global market is a very long-term goal, which may well take as long to achieve as the sovereign state did. Nevertheless, ultimately all kinds of organisations, from farming co-operatives and IVF clinics to multinational corporations and tribal groupings, will eventually run things for one overriding purpose: to increase their market share by offering ever-increasing opportunities to people the world over, regardless of nation or race or territory, to buy into the world's goods. These will include not just the material necessities or luxuries of life. As Karl Marx recognised, almost everything may be bought and sold as a

---

[11]   *Responsibility to Protect: Report of the International Commission on Intervention and State Sovereignty* (Ottawa, 2001).

[12]   *Terror and Consent*, pp. 469–70.

[13]   *Terror and Consent*, p. 86.

commodity, even other human beings. (It is already possible for women to buy embryos from donors anywhere in the world).[14] But not only shall we be able to obtain our food and our household needs and even our children, off globally sourced shelves in real or virtual supermarkets; we shall be invited to choose our thoughts, our artistic tastes, our ethical values, even our religious beliefs, from the same shelves. The market will encourage us to buy, from whatever source we like, the beliefs we prefer to entertain in order to justify what we do. The truth or falsity of these beliefs and the justice or otherwise of the values, will be irrelevant. As long as they are available the market will promote them, for as Bobbitt says, the market is not interested in such things as justice, or even culture.[15] It will be up to us as individuals to use them as we see fit.

Many global corporations are already richer, greedier, and more powerful than some nation-states. So they will tend to worm their way into the global woodwork. But as the market expands, so too will its vulnerability to attack. If Walmart is already a virtual state so too is Al-Qaʻida. In the end, the logic seems to suggest, states as we know them will wither away and people will simply become customers and producers of global goods made and sold anywhere, often via the internet. Ultimately we shall find ourselves competing for resources and riches anywhere on the planet. And the enemies of this global market will be the underdogs who for any reason are excluded from its benefits, and will therefore have reason to disrupt it, out of sheer hatred and despair at what the rest of us enjoy.

But it is not wholly clear what a market state is, given that multinational corporations and even Al-Qaʻida are already virtual market states. The assumption appears to be that market states will emerge out of the familiar nation-state Western democracies, because these are transparent 'states of consent' which govern 'on the basis of authority freely derived from the unfettered consent of the governed'.[16] Bobbitt divides the modern world into 'states of consent' and 'states of terror', but does not tell us which states fit into this framework. He makes clear that the USA, the UK and the EU are clearly states of consent; but nothing is said about the status of (say) Brazil or China. The danger is that by emphasising the 'Western' democracies as the states of consent he is under-estimating the power of the new economic giants, or the way they are able and willing to undermine the schemes of 'the West' in pursuit of their own national interests, for example by refusing to 'play ball' in the failed DOHA round of trade talks. Bobbitt does not take into account the obvious fact that this opposition to the West does not automatically make them into 'states of terror'.

But even market states will need to defend themselves from terrorism. Indeed, the more successful a market state becomes, in enlarging its market share by privatising, outsourcing and delegating its activities, the more vulnerable it will become, because the fragile protection of state frontiers and state-run monopolies

---

[14]   *The Guardian*, 30 July 2008, G,2 pp. 6–11.

[15]   *The Shield of Achilles*, p. 230.

[16]   *Terror and Consent*, p. 182.

will tend to fragment and even disappear. Unscrupulous groups who think it worthwhile to attack and undermine market states for their own ends, can easily dream up a convenient ideology to justify their depredations. Bobbitt concludes that there will inevitably be – indeed there already is – a war to be waged by states of consent (i.e. roughly: the liberal democracies most plausibly describable as proto-market states) against terrorism in the shape of Al-Qaʿida and its associates. And this war, or wars, will require the West to revise its laws and ethics to accommodate many highly undesirable, perhaps even wicked defensive strategies, often under seldom-defined claims about the rule of law.

Preclusive War

Bobbitt insists that war on terror must be *preclusive*. He uses this term to replace the old distinction between preemptive war (licit as long as the threat is imminent and certain) and preventive war, which is illicit because the threat is distant and uncertain. *Preclusive* war is conflict of a new kind, because to overcome global terror it must ensure that terrorist attacks cannot happen. Preclusive war is designed to make terrorism impossible. Yet 'armed forces will increasingly have to learn how to conduct high intensity combat, counterinsurgency, peace support and reconstruction simultaneously' all within the rule of law.[17] For this purpose many different kinds of organisations and activities need to work together: the military, the police, the media, the legal system and the courts, intelligence services, civil and social engineers, and so on, all dedicated to the reconstruction of a fragmented terrorised world. But if the twenty-first century faces quite new problems and dangers it is surely unhelpful to employ the old language of warfare to describe it. As Bobbitt insists, it is necessary to combine *strategy* with *law* (that is victory and maintaining the rule of law) and to bring them into a new joint enterprise to cope with the new world of terror and consent. Yet, as Michael Howard has suggested in the last chapter, whereas an American scholar may find it politically necessary to go on talking about war, the fact is that we need to get ourselves out of thinking in this old-fashioned way.

If *The Shield of Achilles* suggests a relatively benign world of market states, despite the competition between them to maximise market-share, *Terror and Consent* describes a much more sinister aspect of that world. For now (since 9/11) Bobbitt recognises that those who are not beneficiaries of this market-competition are likely to mount violent campaigns against the market-state world. These campaigns are as global as their targets, and (if Bobbitt is right) require the states of consent to stoop to activities which are close to torture of suspects (perhaps by re-defining torture itself), and a deterrent willingness for continental annihilation of innocent and guilty alike if necessary in order to maintain themselves in

---

[17]   *Terror and Consent*, p. 147.

existence.[18] That such activity is manifestly contrary to any coherent theory of just war is beside the point. Bobbitt thinks the just war criteria must be re-defined to allow for them. The world of market states in this respect is no ethical improvement on the world of sovereign nation-states which is being left behind.

One of the ways in which Bobbitt tries to justify the unjustifiable is by advocating a consequentialist ethic to be followed by government officials. He borrows the term consequentialism from Elizabeth Anscombe's essay 'Modern Moral Philosophy' (1958)[19], but without noticing that she shows that it is incoherent. For this reason he fails to provide the necessary foundation for his key arguments that (a) law and strategy on the part of the states of consent (the key opponents of the states of terror) must be brought together, and (b) that the rule of law must be brought up to date, and indeed revised, to make this possible. The issue of nuclear weapons dramatises his failure.

In Bobbitt's market-state world, nuclear weapons remain pretty well as they are, in the hands of the current nuclear powers, as deterrents to other states who might think of harbouring terrorists. In other words, nuclear deterrence is both strategically and legally OK, even necessary, in the War on Terror, for its purpose is to protect civilians from harm – the essential aim of any such war. Some reduction of nuclear arsenals, as proposed by Gordon Brown at the 2009 UN General Assembly, is all very well as a move in the right direction because it may lead towards nuclear disarmament. But it is not nearly enough. The trouble is that, as we have seen, nuclear deterrence cannot avoid harbouring an ultimate willingness to 'obliterate' our foes – including many innocents.[20] But intentionally killing them is always murder.[21] So the colossal corruption of the national will implicit in nuclear deterrence, whether by nation-states or by market-states, undermines the claim to legitimacy (or indeed credibility) in the conduct of a just war on terror.

The reason for insisting upon the ethical category of the innocent is that without it there is no fundamental limit to what may be done by either law or strategy. In speaking of the need to revise international law Bobbitt fails to indicate where these boundaries are to be found. He needs some criteria by which to distinguish genuine future developments in international law from aberrations which simply undermine the virtue of justice, which is what the law ideally exists to maintain.

---

[18]   *Terror and Consent*, p. 134.

[19]   *The Collected Philosophical Papers of G.E.M. Anscombe* (Oxford, 1981), vol. 3, pp. 26–42.

[20]   Michael Portillo, defending nuclear deterrence while Secretary of State for Defence, *Sunday Times*, 19 June 2005. Philip Bobbitt uses the term 'continental annihilation' (*Terror and Consent*, p. 134).

[21]   On this see my 'Double Effect' in *New Blackfriars*, vol. 90, no. 1028, July 2009, pp. 448–457.

Perhaps these criteria need to be parallel to those which Newman used to distinguish genuine from aberrant developments in the history of Christian doctrine.[22]

A Patchwork of Territories

Bobbitt also suggests that future market-states may be more like multinational corporations than territorial nation-states. Global terrorist organisations like Al-Qaʿida are simply the sinister underbelly of such a non-territorial system. But is this plausible? Surely the history of humanity, not to mention the geological pre-history of the planet, has bequeathed to us a patchwork of territories on which people have to live, thrive and build cultural identities. This bewildering variety of inherited (and created) landscapes has bequeathed to humanity diverse ways of living and prospering (or not), as well as cultural, religious and sociological habits and customs. While these legacies have made immense human diversity inevitable, their products are also constantly shifting. And today forces like humanly-determined climate changes are reshaping the planet even as we try to tame and enjoy it. If there is to be a future at all, it can only be through some kind of territorial patchwork corresponding roughly to the physical conditions we have been given by the planet, or are creating on its surface.

However, it is also widely accepted now that simply drawing lines on the ground cannot create the right sort of boundaries. While there are sometimes major physical features which largely determine the limits of a politico-cultural community, as in Tibet or Iceland, so that such communities can survive unscathed for a long time, under modern conditions even mountains or oceans cannot provide adequate boundaries for communities. In other places, as in India/Pakistan, Israel/Palestine or Ireland boundaries drawn on the map create more problems than they solve. But more importantly, for the future what will these boundaries be for? Not, I have argued (following Bobbitt) for the defence of the territory of sovereign states. Furthermore, even between settled states on the current pattern, boundaries are becoming ever more permeable, for a host of financial, climatic, economic, cultural and electronic-technological (not to mention tourist) reasons. In a world of market-states such boundaries will almost disappear, or be constantly redrawn according to the influences of climate, culture, technology and patterns of communication. Hence Philip Bobbitt's difficulty in saying where such states appear on the map. What then would a world of market-states and virtual market-states look like?

There are various ways in which the patchwork of political communities may be able to sustain itself. One is the model of the European Union, in which a multiplicity of states pool some of their sovereignty and resources for the good

---

[22]   On this see my *Law and Justice*, No. 154, (Hilary/Easter 2005) pp. 35–55 and *The Development of International Law* at http://www.ccadd.org.uk under publications/ discussion papers.

of a larger whole, while trying to retain their national identities. How far this promising model will develop is anybody's guess. As a federation? Or some other kind of political compromise? Or will it simply disintegrate for lack of the moral and theological virtues necessary to sustain it? Another model may be suggested by Tibet, which wishes to retain its culture, and to value its history and religion, but as a semi-autonomous part of China. This model might provide a useful one for other parts of the world. That there will be conflicts between the communities, within a patchwork of landholdings that lacks stable or clear boundaries, is I think, unavoidable. The question is how such conflicts will be conducted. On any large scale, dealing with them by threatening the use of weapons of mass-destruction seems likely to be suicidal. But in any case, the whole tradition of just war as understood in the modern world of nation states is under strain from collapsing sovereignties. This is because that tradition is built upon a notion of self-defence. In its literal meaning self-defence simply denoted one individual's use of force against another. Any extension of this idea to a whole community under attack needs careful scrutiny. St Augustine regarded killing a single enemy attacker in self-defence to be intrinsically sinful, since it rested upon an illegitimate lust to preserve an unworthy good, namely one's own life.[23] But Aquinas disagreed, on 'double effect' grounds.[24] He rejected St Augustine's basis for refusing to kill in self-defence, on the ground that all living things have a natural inclination, implanted in them by God, to preserve themselves. This is why he had to resort to 'double effect'. It is worth noting, however, that Aquinas employs the double effect argument only in the case of the individual's defence of himself – and even then quite unconvincingly, in so far as he tries to justify lethal self-defence *only* as long as it is motivated solely by the intention to defend one's own life, and *not* deliberately to kill the attacker. For surely in most cases of lethal self-defence the individual *intends* to kill the attacker precisely as the means of saving himself.[25] But in so far as all modern formulations of the tradition (including that of the UN Charter Article 51) presuppose self-defence of the entire sovereign state as the only basis for just war, the blurring of territorial boundaries, and their replacement by the intrinsically vague notion of the market state, with its unstable and constantly redefined territory and indifference to culture and justice (or any of the other virtues), renders the very concept of the self that is to be defended today increasingly obscure. Extending the concept of the self further still, to encompass a state's vital interests far beyond its territory, only makes the metaphor of self-defence even more problematic. This is a more fundamental problem for the theory of just war even than the development of weapons of mass-destruction which turn major war into mass-murder.

---

[23]   *De Libero Arbitrio, PL32*, pp. 1227–8.

[24]   *Summa Theologiae*, II ii Q. 64 Art. 6.

[25]   Windass, *Christianity Versus Violence*, pp. 85–9.

The Church as Catholic in a Globalised World

For the future, then, diplomacy, compromise, and the readiness to share resources for the good of *all* seems the only possible solution to any conflicts that will inevitably arise. This of course is precisely what the church teaches: namely that communities, like individuals, must cope with their mutual differences by the practice of the virtues, especially justice and peace, for the good of all. The relationships between the culturally diverse dioceses of the church could serve as models, or sacramental signs, of such practice for political communities.

Although we cannot predict how this practice is to be maintained, we can I think rule some solutions out. For example, global Islamisation under a single universal Caliphate is surely unacceptable if, like a global Christianity rooted in a dominant *caesaro-Papism*, it tended to eliminate the diversity of cultures, traditions and ways of life that human history and human freedom inevitably throws up. While the *umma* should function sacramentally as a virtual political community[26] (as the church *qua* sacrament does) this is not what Al-Qaʻida or those who think like them have in mind. In this respect Al-Qaʻida's version of Islam would be quite alien to those who envisage the church as sacrament of human diversity, rooted in justice, peace and charity. It would be comparable with the failure of the centralised Roman church to understand the point of the seventeenth-century Jesuit attempts to incorporate elements of Chinese culture into Christianity, and of Nobili's failed attempt to become a Brahmin in India. These failures have been called 'great blunders of history'.[27] Another set of blunders occurred when the genuine teaching of the Renaissance theologians and missionaries such as Victoria and Las Casas, about the rights of the American Indians to their own land and way of life, was sidelined by the imperialist states abetted by churches who saw their mission in their own states' terms. A single globalised Islam might well make the same mistake.

Is there an alternative way of organising humankind? It is at this point that I want to suggest the church has something to say to, because it is already embedded within, this predicament. For the church is the sacrament of a different world; an embodiment of how a different future could offer itself to us in the present.

As I have said, even in the globalised world of the market, humankind will continue to live in various delimited spaces in order to cultivate its variegated national virtues, its sense of communal identities, its cultures. The creation by God in Christ of a universal church in no way contradicts this ordinary human necessity for local variety. On the contrary it cherishes the differences, as development within the early church of separate competing identities and later of dioceses each

---

[26]   On the *umma* as a 'virtual' or 'sacramental' political community see David Burrell, *Freedom and Creation in Three Traditions* (Notre Dame 1993), pp.162ff. I am indebted to Nicholas Lash for drawing my attention to this important book and its understanding of Islam.

[27]   See J.M. Cameron, *On the Idea of a University* (Toronto, 1978), p. 22.

with its bishop, or overseer shows. While the precise meanings of these terms, and the practices they represented, remained contentious for some time, the teaching of the churches developed steadily until it became clear that various local groups, with their differentiated cultures, were here to stay in the form of episcopal jurisdictions.[28] Yet, while dioceses varied enormously, they nevertheless belonged to the one global or catholic body of Christ.

These local churches, or dioceses, were and are more than mere components of the catholic church. For each diocese is the whole church for that place. The relation of local church to global church is more like that of an individual animal to its species than it is to (say) a cog in a machine. If I am baptised into the diocese of (say) Southwark I am, nevertheless, baptised into the whole church, because that diocese embodies all that is necessary for me to understand what being the church amounts to. This is why the church is sacramentally a challenge to the political organisation of humanity into competing sovereign states.

But what does this mean? Well, if I observe the diocese in which I live, or the congregation of my parish, I can say various things about it. For example, it is a) a body of people, members of the species *home sapiens*, gathered in this place. But it is also b) a body of *inhabitants of the British Isles* in this place. Furthermore, it is also c) a body of *citizens of the UK* in this place. And it is d) the *Body of Christ* in this place. All of these statements are true. But they mean different things, at different levels. The first is a biological, the second a sociological, the third a legal, the fourth a theological interpretation of the same reality.

To speak of the church as the Body of Christ is to speak of this body of people in words that operate at a higher, or deeper, level of meaning than is operative at the biological, sociological, or legal levels. Indeed, the theological meaning is the deepest level of all. So talking of this body of people as the Body of Christ in this place is not an alternative to talking of them, for example, as members of the state, as though these truths were on the same level of meaning. The various depths of meaning are not competing with each other in the same logical space.

Nevertheless, the deepest theological level of meaning constitutes a permanent challenge to any merely political or legal grouping, since this body of people is now gathered together not only by human laws but by the overarching power of love; that is by the gift of God in Christ, who is the image of the invisible God. (Colossians 1: 15ff) Of course, the sin of the world being what it is, such gathering in love is bound to be a miserable failure. But then that is part of the point. For the founding of this loving community in the crucifixion of Jesus was itself a mark of failure. The 'man born to be king' had to be killed like a slave and criminal. Christianity was based on human failure in order to reveal the triumph of God's gift of supernatural love in the resurrection. This love is a constant reminder to the state of its own inadequacies as a gathering together of people in this place.

The diocese is founded on the love of the Father for the Son who is incarnate in the risen body of Jesus Christ in this place. That is how these people constitute

---

[28]   Hans Kung, *The Church* (London, 1967) pp. 410ff.

his Body which is the church. For the love of God which binds the church together cannot be identified with the necessarily imperfect relations of people as citizens of a state, or even as members of a fallen species. It is a love which can only be consummated in the future Kingdom – when of course people will no longer need the church or its sacraments. The sacramental order belongs to the interim time before God's will is finally done. So although this Body of Christ exists here and now on earth, in this place, its whole existence points to that future. The church is not merely open to all in the here and now. It also points to what is to come. It is the sacrament of the future.

The Church and the Sovereign State

This excursion into theology is necessary in order to indicate the meaning of the existence of separate sovereign states. As I see it, their rise was an inevitable, and in its time a positive, answer to the centuries of conflict among the princedoms of late mediaeval Europe. Post-Westphalian society seemed a logical and practical answer to the chaos of earlier times. Unfortunately and tragically the church allowed itself to be dragged into this new structure of potentially warring states, especially after the movements of legitimate protest and reform begun by Luther and others ultimately rejected the sacramental basis of Catholic theology and associated themselves with, or even (as in England) became departments of, the new sovereign-state structure. The result was the division of Europe, and later of the European-inspired empires, into Catholic and Protestant sovereignties.

But nothing lasts for ever. While the state of affairs just described has lasted, more or less, for roughly three hundred years, it has become increasingly shaky in recent times. In effect the 'Long War' of 1914–1989 made obsolete the post-Westphalian regime of sovereignties in Europe, although it will take a very long time for that structure to transform itself completely into something else. The globalisation which has followed the long war requires a new world order (which will itself doubtless be superseded by something yet more remote). Of course there are those who are sceptical of all such developments, and want to turn the clock back into the Westphalian past. But in my opinion, unless a new political order, of which the church (itself duly purged of its post-Westphalian residue) is the model or sacrament, can be brought into being, the chances are that the mass-destruction weapons still wielded by sovereign states, or eventually obtained by terrorist gangs, will eventually bring about the collective global suicide of civilisation, even if climate change does not do the job first.

Unfortunately, the post-Westphalian churches have sometimes behaved like states, or seen themselves as just the 'spiritual' aspect of the state they are associated with. But this has always been an aberration. The church does not just offer to the state a religious dimension which that state would otherwise not have. On the contrary, it embodies a model by which human beings can organise their affairs that is subversive of the state's false god as commonly understood today. For the church is a challenge to all political arrangements and all religions. Thus a diocese is first of all the body of the risen Christ in this place. And what this means is that those who are leaders of the diocese – the bishop, but also all the others who have been given other charisms, exist to serve their fellows. 'Let the greatest among you become as the youngest, and the leader as one who serves. For which is the greater, one who sits at table, or one who serves? Is it not the one who sits at table? But I am among you as one who serves'. (Luke 22.26f) This picture of *diakonia* is the principle of the church's practical or political organisation. Of course, the arrangements that the church community needs in order to function have to be appropriate to its constitution. They need to develop 'in order to ascertain where, as a whole and at individual points, the original intention and the real meaning can be found...in order to see how the *ius conditum* always points to a better *ius condendum*.'[29] And the whole of this activity has to be founded on love, for the reign of God even in the church here and now is 'a kingdom of truth and life, a kingdom of justice, love and peace.' (John 13:35) This requires that the members of the church 'by their competence in secular disciplines ... (should) vigorously contribute their effort so that created goods may be perfected by human labour, technical skill and civil culture for the benefit of all ... (and be) more equitably distributed among all men, and may in their own way be conducive to universal progress in human and Christian freedom'.[30] This also entails that the world's leaders 'extend their thoughts and their spirit beyond the confines of their own nation, that they put aside national selfishness and ambition to dominate other nations, and that they nourish a profound reverence for the whole of humanity.'[31]

In short, the local church is to serve the whole of humanity, not just its own members. It shares this objective in common with all Abrahamic faiths, and is at the opposite pole from the sovereign nation-state. For the primary responsibility of the sovereign state lies with furthering the interests of its own citizens. Now it is perhaps just possible to suppose that a world of market-states, devoted to giving individuals maximum opportunities and choices, could be a way of furthering this concern for the common good of *all*. But only as long as it also exists as a community of justice, love and peace. And as we have seen, these are not particular concerns of the market. Worse still, as long as the world of market states is unavoidably enmeshed in warfare against terrorism (as Bobbitt argues) its life is irreconcilable with the church's vision of peace and good will towards all. 'The world is constantly beset by strife and violence between men, even when no war is being waged ... since these same evils are present in the relations between various nations as well, in order to overcome or forestall them and to keep violence once unleashed within limits, it is absolutely necessary for countries to cooperate to better advantage, to work together more closely, and

---

[29]   Hans Kung, *The Church*, p. 429.

[30]   *Gaudium et Spes (Constitution of the Church)* Second Vatican Council 36.

[31]   *Gaudium et Spes*, p. 82.

jointly to organise international bodies and to work tirelessly for the creation of organisations which will foster peace'.[32]

Although this was written in 1965, well before the advent of the post-Cold War, market-driven world, the Second Vatican Council accepted 'the increasingly close ties of mutual dependence today between all inhabitants and peoples of the earth' and went on to affirm that 'the fitting pursuit and effective realisation of the universal common good now require of the community of nations that it organise itself in a manner suited to its present responsibilities, especially towards the many parts of the world which are still suffering from unbearable want.'[33] This emphasis on the church's responsibility for the common good, including the material good, of all humanity as the first requirement of global justice and peace, is the key point of the Council's reflections on the world scene.[34] It is a far cry from the drive to increase market share, in order to maximise choices for those able to take advantage of them (but not for others) which lies at the root of Bobbitt's market state world.

Translating this ethic of the common good of all into practical politics is, of course, extremely difficult, as the recent global collapse of the banking system has shown. But it is just what is needed all the same. As an example one may cite the recently failed DOHA round of trade liberalisation talks among rich and poor regions of the world in 2008. This process was an expression of a new fact in the global economy, namely that the West, which hitherto has been able to dominate the world's trade, is now confronted by burgeoning new economic powers, notably Brazil, India and China, who have to be placated and are not prepared to be dictated to. For it was they who scuppered the bargain which the United States and the EU had hoped to steer through the negotiating procedure. How soon and under what terms these new superpowers will eventually become market states is anybody's guess. As things are at present, the transition looks like being long and tortuous, if it comes to anything at all. Meanwhile, the stalemate among the nation-states of the world looks like continuing to the detriment of almost everybody, but especially of the poorest.

This crisis has to be resolved if there is to be a genuinely just distribution of agricultural and manufactured goods for the common benefit of everybody. States have to overcome their own prejudices if they are to benefit not just those in other states, but their own citizens too. Protectionism by separate sovereign nation-states is, in the long run, no protection at all, however tempting such protectionism may be in a period of global recession. Even market states will have to come to terms with this fact, however difficult it is to see how an elected government, which seems to be systematically disadvantaging its own voters for the sake of those in other states, can long survive.

---

[32] *Gaudium et Spes*, p. 83.

[33] *Gaudium et Spes*, p. 4.

[34] On this point, see Clifford Longley in *The Tablet*, 23 August 2008, pp. 10–11.

Furthermore, the maximisation of choices which is the market's *raison d'etre* has nothing to do with the intrinsic worth of these choices. Yet some options are surely better than others. A few ought to be prohibited under any circumstances (such as for example the choice by some states of a strategy which entails being willing, in certain critical circumstances, intentionally to kill the innocent as a means of keeping the peace). But in themselves, mere choices, indiscriminately provided, are no formula for human flourishing. At the same time, the indifference of the market to justice and peace is no accident: it is intrinsic to the very existence of the market itself as a system for maximising profit. For this reason alone a global market is grossly inadequate as a picture of how mankind should organise its affairs for the future. There has to be another way. The church's example is a sign, indeed a sacrament of how this may be done. In Australia Pope Benedict XVI has recently said as much:

> Life is not just a succession of events or experiences, helpful though many of them are. It is a search for the true, the good and the beautiful. It is to this end that we make our choices, it is for this that we exercise our freedom, it is in this – in truth, in goodness, in beauty – that we find happiness and joy. Do not be fooled by those who see you as just another consumer in a market of undifferentiated possibilities, where choice itself becomes the good, novelty usurps beauty, and subjective experience displaces truth.[35]

The Church as Sacrament of the Future

As sacrament of the future the church is the sign of what must come to be. Of course it is embedded in human history, as a gathering of people within this world. But this gathering exists precisely as a sign of what this world needs to be if it is to be properly human. If and when, as has regularly happened when it has allowed itself to be practically incorporated into the political system of states, the church becomes simply one more component of this world, it ceases to function as the sign of what the world needs to become. It then turns into just another religion among the rest. But because a word has meaning only because it is part of a language, that is a system of signs that communicate meanings, the church is a sign that has meaning only as part of a system of meanings, a new language that goes beyond the merely this-worldly.[36] In other words, the church as sacrament is not a sign which points to something else beyond itself, as (for example) a sign-post indicates a place beyond itself. On the contrary, it is a sign that in itself communicates its meaning by being what it is, a sign within but not confined to, the language of ordinary political community-relations. Exactly how this new

---

[35] *The Tablet*, 26 July 2008, p. 11.

[36] Herbert McCabe OP, 'Sacramental Language' in *God Matters* (London, 1987) pp. 165–179.

meaning will be embodied in the future history of human politics it is impossible to predict. For example, how the church would express its sacramental meaning in a world of market-states is hard to say, because it is hard to say just what a world of market-states would look like. But one thing is clear: the church as sacrament of the future will remain – as it always has, even when deeply compromised by the things of this world – as a sign pointing to something beyond the world of such states. And the way the church exists as a gathering of distinct communities, or dioceses, each with its own culture and history, but united in love for the common good of all, will be the sign of how things must become.

As sacrament of the future, the church suggests that *warfare* with terrorist gangs like Al-Qaʿida, which are emerging from globalisation, is unthinkable. For *Gaudium et Spes* insists it is possible, and therefore necessary, for the globalised world so to organise itself as to foster justice and peace, and reject violence. Just as war between dioceses of the church – for all their radical differences of culture and national identity – is surely unthinkable, so too the political order which the church teaches is achievable, and of which it is itself the sacrament, can and must be refashioned in like manner. If there is any justification for the use of violence in such a political context, it can only come from a Responsibility to Protect those who are vulnerable to harm from groups which are liable to spawn terrorist activities. Indeed, in so far as the market state, the more successful it is, unavoidably makes itself increasingly vulnerable to such attack, the likelier it is that the Responsibility to Protect will need to be invoked, and forceful means to put it into practice deployed. But exercising this responsibility is a response to globalised *crime*.[37] What this means is that we need global laws and means to enforce them. Inter-national law is only a first step towards this. What a system of global law, for the whole planet, with global courts and a global police force, would look like it is, at present, impossible to say, perhaps even impossible to imagine. This is doubtless why some people want to go backwards, into a Westphalian past. But St. Augustine would have found it equally impossible to envisage the Islamisation of North Africa, or Aquinas the European colonisation of America. Yet these things happened. A globalised world requires a globalised system of law. And if and when it exists, it will become obvious that terrorism is just organised crime, which needs global policing. I have no idea how it will come into existence; I merely note that sometimes things change by volcanic eruptions rather than through centuries of evolution. And a guide as to what it might be like is the church as sacrament of the future.

---

[37]   See Baroness Shirley Williams, *God and Caesar* (London, 2003) Chapter 6 on 'War and Peace'.

Chapter 7

Terror and Pre-Emption – Can Military Pre-Emption ever be Just?

David Fisher

In the aftermath of the devastating terrorist attack on New York and Washington on September 11 2001, the US Government developed a new security strategy. This was published a year after the attack on 17 September 2002, at a time when a spectacular terrorist assault was widely expected to mark the first anniversary. At the core of the strategy is the declaration that, 'We will not hesitate to act alone, if necessary, to exercise our right of self-defence by acting pre-emptively against such terrorists, to prevent them from doing harm against our people and our country.'[1] So emerged the new strategic doctrine of pre-emption.

The doctrine was the brain child of the Bush Administration. Some of its features, particularly its unabashed unilateralism, provoked criticism from Democrat opponents. President Obama is committed to pursuing a consensual and multilateralist approach in international relations. The Obama administration has not, however, formally repudiated the doctrine of pre-emption and, indeed, explicitly retained the option to use military pre-emption to prevent Iran from acquiring a nuclear capability.[2] Moreover, the need for a new strategic approach to counter the new terrorist threat attracted widespread support in the US, including from such a distinguished academic and former senior adviser to Democrat administrations as Philip Bobbitt in his penetrating analysis of the threat published in 2008, *Terror and Consent*.[3] Great powers are reluctant to forswear the option of pre-emption. So is there any legal or moral basis for the new doctrine of pre-emption? Do states have a right to take pre-emptive military action? Can military pre-emption ever be just?

In international law, the short answer is that states have no such right except in very narrowly defined circumstances. In 1837 British marines boarded a private schooner, the *Caroline*, which was engaged in gun running from the US to Canadian

---

[1]   *The National Security Strategy of the United States of America,* President George W. Bush, The White House, (17 September 2002), p. 6, viewed at www.whitehouse.gov/nsc/nss.pdf.

[2]   Hillary Clinton, confirmation hearing as Secretary of State, Senate Foreign Relations Committee, (13 January 2009).

[3]   Philip Bobbitt, *Terror and Consent – The Wars for the Twenty-first Century* (London and New York, 2008).

rebels. The marines set the ship on fire and cast her adrift to be carried across the Niagara Falls by the current, although, in the event, the ship ran aground before reaching the Falls. The action was justified by the British ambassador as an act of pre-emptive self-defence. In the acrimonious debate that ensued, the generally accepted test set for pre-emptive self-defence was that proposed by Daniel Webster, the US Secretary of State, in his response to the British Ambassador, 'the necessity of that self-defence is instant, overwhelming, and leaving no choice of means, and no moment for deliberation.'[4]

Even those carefully circumscribed grounds were not recognised by the authors of the UN Charter. Article 2(4) prohibits states from 'the threat or use of force against the territorial integrity or political independence of any state.' The only concession granted to states is in Article 51: 'Nothing in the present chapter shall impair the inherent right of individual or collective self-defence if an armed attack occurs against a Member of the United Nations until the Security Council has taken measures necessary to maintain international peace and security.' The language clearly suggests that the armed attack is taking or has taken place, not that it is merely anticipated. The UN Charter was an agreement struck between sovereign states at the end of a long war where their sovereignty had been threatened by the aggressive ambitions of the fascist states. In such circumstances the inviolability of state borders was, not surprisingly, accorded high importance. Moreover, a strict constraint on the exercise of any right of pre-emption fitted well with the strategic doctrine of deterrence forged in the immediate post-war years following the atomic detonations at Hiroshima and Nagasaki. For it was feared that the stability of the system of mutual nuclear deterrence would be put at risk if pre-emptive action were countenanced by either side. In a nuclear world pre-emption was deemed both unwise and dangerous.

So in the post-war years pre-emption remained generally in disfavour. There were exceptions but they were few and far between. The Israeli Air Force launched pre-emptive air strikes on 5 June 1967 against the Egyptian and Syrian forces that were massing on her borders. This action evoked a broad measure of sympathy outside the Arab world since there was compelling evidence that Egypt and Syria were not only uttering bellicose threats but also taking active military preparations against Israel. But such exceptions were rare and so tended to underline the general presumption against pre-emptive military action.

The Impact of 9/11 on Strategic Thinking

But then, as a literal bolt from the blue, came the terrorist attacks of 9/11. Al-Qa'ida operatives crashed airliners into the Twin Towers in New York and the Pentagon in Washington, killing nearly three thousand innocent civilians. There

---

[4]   John Bassett Moore (ed.), *A Digest Of International Law*, (Washington, DC, 1906), vol. 2, p. 409.

were subsequent bombings in Bali on 12 October 2002, Madrid on 11 March 2004 and London on 7 July 2005.

Terrorism is hardly a new phenomenon. The scale of such a direct attack on the US was, however, without precedent since Pearl Harbor. There were also a number of other worrying novel features about the attacks.

The attacks demonstrated the global reach of Al-Qaʿida. The organisation was based in Afghanistan and, after its expulsion from there, in the Pakistan borderlands. But it was able to mount attacks in the US, Europe and elsewhere in the world. It did so through the novel approach of outsourcing its operations to local groups and individuals. The attacks were undertaken by suicide bombers, acting without regard to their own safety and with little apparent concern about alienating the public or their own supporters. Previous terrorists might have worried that too much collateral damage could lose them support. Not so with Al-Qaʿida whose 'Holy War' was aimed at civilians. 'The ruling to kill the Americans and their allies – civilians and military – is an individual duty for every Muslim who can do it,' so thundered the 1998 Al-Qaʿida fatwa.[5] The subsequent attack on 9/11 was designed to maximise civilian casualties. The attack had been undertaken with conventional weapons and had killed nearly three thousand civilians. There was considerable concern about how much greater would be the devastation if the terrorists were to acquire weapons of mass destruction.

Nor was this an idle fear. Osama bin Laden had openly proclaimed in an interview with *Time* magazine in early 1999 that the acquisition of such weapons 'for the defense of Muslims is a religious duty.'[6] Following the collapse of the Taliban Government in Afghanistan in November 2001, US and coalition forces uncovered documents and computer disks detailing the Al-Qaʿida biological programme, as well as contacts between Al-Qaʿida and rogue Pakistani nuclear scientists.[7] Moreover, just when academe was generally dismissive of the prospects of nuclear proliferation to rogue states and terrorists and the BBC was making a documentary, *The Power of Nightmares*, claiming the whole terrorist threat was politically manufactured, the British Secret Intelligence Service, working in conjunction with the CIA, was uncovering an extensive network of illegal nuclear proliferation activities.[8] This network had been controlled and run – for commercial

---

[5]   World Islamic Front statement issued 23 February 1998, see Appendix to Chapter 4 'Arguments Concerning Resistance in Contemporary Islam', by John Kelsay in Richard Sorabji and David Rodin (eds.), *The Ethics of War – Shared Problems in Different Traditions* (Aldershot, 2006), p. 90.

[6]   Osama bin Laden, 'Conversation with Terror', interview by Rahimilla Yusufzai, Time, 11 January 1999, p. 39.

[7]   Kamran Khan and Molly Moore, 'Nuclear Experts Briefed Bin Laden, Pakistanis Say', *Washington Post*, 12 (December 2001), p. 1.

[8]   *The Power of Nightmares*, BBC three-part series, broadcast January 2005.

profit – by the top Pakistani nuclear scientist, A.Q. Khan.[9] Khan had himself stolen nuclear technology from the European company, URENCO, for whom he had worked, to assist in the development of Pakistan's bomb. He had been involved in illegally exporting nuclear technology from 1976. His customers included North Korea, Iran, South Africa and Libya. The rogue Pakistani nuclear scientists, with whom Al-Qa'ida had been in contact, were linked with Khan's programme. Khan's activities finally came to an end on 4 October 2003 when agents boarded the *BBC China*, a ship flying a German flag, in the Italian port of Taranto and seized thousands of centrifuge components, in an operation coordinated by UK, US, Italian and German authorities. The illegal exporting of nuclear technologies was no longer a frightening possibility but a reality. There was thus a very real fear that terrorists might acquire weapons of mass destruction.

So how was the new terrorist threat to be countered? In the past, massing of armies and armour had been the signs of impending attack. But terrorists could now mount devastating attacks, anywhere in the world, swiftly, clandestinely and without visible preparations. Effective defence against the new scourge of terrorism could not be assured. Indeed, the spectacular success of the 9/11 attacks had demonstrated how difficult it was to mount an effective defence against the new terrorists.

But nor could deterrence be relied on to dissuade would-be terrorists from mounting attacks, at least not deterrence of the kind that had prevailed during the Cold War era. Deterrence – through the threat of massive reprisal – had helped maintain peace during the Cold War. Such deterrence had presupposed a substantial degree of rationality on the part of each side. The deterrent threat had been effective because each side was assumed to be capable of rational calculation and so dissuaded from reckless action by the threat of the dire damage that would be inflicted on them. This was not only theory but worked in practice, as demonstrated during the Cuban missile crisis. Russia blustered but backed off. Even the US made secret concessions over nuclear bases in Turkey, as subsequently became public knowledge. Despite all the pressures, both sides refrained from action that might lead to nuclear use.

It is, however, far from certain that a suicide bomber, armed with a nuclear device, would be amenable to such rational calculations. Indeed, as Michael Clarke has suggested:

> Terrorist groups would hardly be deterred by nuclear threats; indeed, the mentality of the suicide bomber would probably rejoice at the prospect of provoking an incoming nuclear strike against many innocent others.[10]

---

[9]   Khan's activities are described in *The Review of Intelligence on Weapons of Mass Destruction* (House of Commons 898 of 14 July 2004) – the Butler Committee Report – chapter two, paragraphs 64–75.

[10]   Michael Clarke, 'Does my bomb look big in this? Britain's nuclear choices after Trident', *International Affairs*, vol. 80, 2004, p. 59.

States lending support to terrorists may be susceptible to international pressures but the terrorists themselves may not be so amenable. Terrorists do not usually own or control territory, the role of the Taliban in Afghanistan being unusual in this respect. There may, therefore, be no targets that can be held at risk to underpin a deterrent threat. Indeed, a terrorist, armed with weapons of mass destruction, may have encroached upon our own territory, perhaps be hiding in a major city. A threat against the terrorists themselves could pose a direct threat to our own citizens or those of our allies and so its utterance would be self-deterring. The threat would lack credibility.

So neither defence nor deterrence through the threat of reprisal would necessarily work against the new terrorist threat. Was there then no choice but to wait until after an attack had taken place and only then take action against those who had perpetrated the attack? When the victims of the attack could be many thousands of innocent civilians, a policy of 'wait and see' was not an attractive option for a democratic government whose duty was to protect its citizens. In order to avoid this agonising dilemma the new doctrine of pre-emption was accordingly forged.

A New Strategic Doctrine

It was not acceptable to wait until an attack had taken place. For, as Philip Bobbitt, an advocate of 'preclusive' action against threats of sufficient gravity to imperil international security, even in advance of imminent aggression, explains, 'once a terrorist mass atrocity is actually executed in Manhattan, only tragedy and terror will follow.'[11] In an era 'of disguised attack using terrorist networks, the proliferation of WMD can make pre-emption an absolute necessity.'[12] 'Preclusion is the "new deterrence" i.e. it will be the central doctrine of warfare.'[13] Preclusion is also the new deterrence in that it is a form of deterrence through denial: denying the terrorist the means of mounting an attack through anticipatory action.

The shift in the US Government's strategic thinking was explained by the authors of *The New National Security Strategy of the United States of America*:

> For centuries, international law recognised that nations need not suffer an attack before they can lawfully take action to defend themselves against forces that present an imminent danger of attack. Legal scholars and international jurists often conditioned the legitimacy of pre-emption on the existence of an imminent threat – most often a visible mobilisation of armies, navies, and air forces preparing to attack.
>
> We must adapt the concept of imminent threat to the capabilities and objectives of today's adversaries. Rogue states and terrorists do not seek to attack using

---

[11]   Bobbitt, *Terror and Consent*, p. 529.

[12]   Bobbitt, *Terror and Consent*, p. 530.

[13]   Bobbitt, *Terror and Consent*, p. 138.

conventional means. They know such attacks would fail. Instead, they rely on acts of terror and, potentially, the use of weapons of mass destruction – weapons that can be easily concealed, delivered covertly, and used without warning.

The targets of these attacks are our military forces and our civilian population, in direct violation of one of the principal norms of the law of warfare. As was demonstrated by the losses on September 11, 2001, mass civilian casualties is the specific objective of terrorists and these losses would be exponentially more severe if terrorists acquired and used weapons of mass destruction.

The United States has long maintained the option of pre-emptive attacks to counter a sufficient threat to our national security. The greater the threat, the greater is the risk of inaction – and the more compelling the case for taking anticipatory action to defend ourselves, even if uncertainty remains as to the time and place of the enemy's attack. To forestall or prevent such hostile acts by our adversaries, the United States will, if necessary, act preemptively.[14]

The new strategy acknowledges that in the past pre-emption was only justified where an attack was imminent. It argues, however, that the changed nature of the threat post 9/11 – where devastating attacks can be mounted swiftly and secretly – means that this criterion is no longer appropriate. In future, it will be the gravity or sufficiency of the threat that justifies pre-emptive action 'even if uncertainty remains as to the time and place of the enemy's attack.' According to Bobbitt, what justifies a shift towards preclusive action is 'the potential threat to civilians posed by arming, with whatever weapons, groups and states openly dedicated to mass killing.'[15]

Evaluation of the New Doctrine

So is this shift in strategic thinking justified? The new strategic doctrine is not legal under current international law since it would permit action in a much wider range of circumstances than envisaged by the test formulated following the *Caroline* affair. But this objection would not dissuade advocates of pr-emption from advancing the merits of the new doctrine. For they would argue that it merely showed that international law is out of date and needs to be reformed to reflect what Bobbitt calls 'the new changing strategic context.'[16] We need, therefore, to consider whether the change, even if not currently legal, could still be morally justified according to just war thinking.

One objection that was immediately raised to the new doctrine of pre-emption is its unabashed unilateralism, a difficulty Philip Bobbitt wisely emphasises in the Afterword. The report's authors unabashedly proclaim, 'We will not hesitate to act

---

[14]   National Security Strategy of the United States of America, p. 15.

[15]   Bobbitt, *Terror and Consent*, p. 137.

[16]   Bobbitt, *Terror and Consent*, p. 531.

alone, if necessary.' 'The United States will, if necessary, act pre-emptively.' If the US, as a sovereign state, arrogates a right of pre-emption to itself, why should not other states do so similarly? Indeed, even North Korea could do so. But with such a proliferation of pre-emptive rights, international anarchy would appear to threaten.

It might be countered that the new terrorist threat was aimed – as Al-Qaʿida's leaders made clear – particularly at the US, as the leader of the Western world whose values Al-Qaʿida rejected. So, as the principal target for the new terrorism, it could be argued that the US should have particular rights to take defensive action. That is perhaps so. But it is still important that those rights should be specified in terms that would be equally applicable to any other nation similarly threatened. So, if the US had a right to act unilaterally in such circumstances, even against a threat that was not imminent, so would any other nation facing a similar threat. Our concern might then be whether other states, to whom such a right were conceded, would exercise it responsibly. This might lead us to insist that any such action by other states should require international consultation and approval. But if the action of other states should be subject to such consultation, it may be difficult – by parity of reasoning – to resist the conclusion that so should our own. The UN Security Council offers an appropriate and ready-made forum for such consultation.

It is unrealistic to insist that a state should secure the backing of the UN Security Council on every occasion before any kind of pre-emptive military action is taken. States, as we have already noted, can under international law act in self-defence against a threat that is imminent. The Security Council is made up of sovereign states that, notoriously, do not always act from the best of motives and are driven by their own motives of *real-politik*. Moreover, pre-emptive military action may take a variety of forms, ranging from the mere deployment (without use) of military force through a single missile attack up to a full scale military operation. We might be prepared to concede that actions at the lower end of the scale, where there is a need to act swiftly, decisively and on the basis of intelligence that could not be widely shared without compromising sources or losing surprise, could, exceptionally, be undertaken without such authorisation.

But even with such qualifications, the way the new doctrine of pre-emption was formulated still seems objectionable because of its apparent presumption in favour of unilateralism, even where military action is undertaken against a threat that is not imminent. In such circumstances the requirement for UN authorisation to confer the competent authority on which just war teaching insists would seem strong. This point was well made by the report of the UN High Level Panel on Threats, Challenges and Change. The Panel argued that where the threat, however serious, was not imminent the case for military action, 'should be put to the Security Council, which can authorise such action if it chooses to. Allowing one to act (unilaterally) is to allow all.'[17]

---

[17] *A more secure world: Our shared responsibility, Report of the Secretary-General's High Level Panel on Threats, Challenges and Change* (United Nations, 2004), paragraph 190, p. 55.

The Panel acknowledged, however, that, 'The Council may well need to be prepared to be more proactive on these issues, taking more decisive action earlier, than it has been in the past.'[18] The Panel clearly looked forward toward a reformed and more effective Security Council. But, in view of the current imperfections of the Council's operations, it might be argued that circumstances could still arise where unilateral action against a sufficiently dire, although non-imminent, threat might – exceptionally – be permitted. But, even if such a concession were made, the presumption should be in favour of a multilateral approach, with military action endorsed by the UN Security Council. The new doctrine's presumption in favour of unilateralism should be reversed.

But should pre-emptive military action as envisaged in the US National Security Strategy be permitted at all? Just war commentators sometimes rely on a distinction between pre-emption, aimed at grave threats that are imminent, and prevention aimed at threats that, while equally grave or graver, are as yet more distant. The former, it is suggested, may be morally permitted, while the latter remains forbidden. On such grounds it could be argued that the new doctrine of 'pre-emption' should be rejected. For, while it was labelled a doctrine of pre-emption (that could be justified), it was actually a doctrine of prevention aimed at countering threats that were not necessarily imminent. The label was misleading. The doctrine was accordingly unjustified.

This criticism proceeds, however, too quickly. It also relies on a distinction between 'pre-emption' and 'prevention' that is not borne out by our ordinary usage of these words.[19] In ordinary parlance 'prevention' is not somehow regarded as bad in a way pre-emption is not. Indeed, if anything the reverse is the case. We need, therefore, to probe deeper.

Just war thinkers certainly took the imminence or immediacy of a threat as an important guide whether pre-emptive action could be justified. Grotius, for example, says:

> War in defence of life is permissible only when the danger is immediate and certain, not when it is merely assumed.[20]

But Grotius also explains why immediacy is important as a test:

---

[18]   *A more secure world*, paragraph 194.

[19]   As noted by Nigel Biggar, 'Just war thinking in recent UK religious debate', in Charles Reed and David Ryall (eds.), *Price of Peace* (Cambridge, 2007), p. 70. Because of the popular confusion between pre-emption and prevention, Philip Bobbit prefers the term 'preclusion' for military action against grave but non-imminent threats, as he explains in the Afterword.

[20]   Hugo Grotius, *De Iure Belli ac Pacis*, Book II, Chapter I, section V, in Gregory M. Reichberg, Henrik Syse, Endre Begby (eds.), *The Ethics of War* (Oxford, 2006) p. 403.

Fear with respect to a neighbouring power is not sufficient cause. For in order that defence may be lawful it must be necessary and it is not necessary unless we are certain not only regarding the power of our neighbour but also regarding his intent, the degree of certainty being what is accepted in moral matters.[21]

Grotius' argument suggests that imminence or immediacy may provide a useful practical guide to what kind of threat would justify action but that neither is necessarily an end to be pursued in itself. It is rather, as Grotius says, 'the degree of certainty being what is accepted in moral matters.' The harm caused by war is both serious and certain. Just war teaching, accordingly, counsels that war can only be justified if it is designed to avert even more serious harm, as judged by both the gravity of what is threatened and the high probability that it will occur. For, otherwise, we risk causing more harm than good by military action and so breaching the just war principle of proportion. A dire event that is assessed to be of very low probability would not justify military action. A threat that is immediate or imminent is a threat about which we are likely to have good grounds for judging both its gravity and the high probability of its occurrence. If the threat is imminent, there may also be no time to take alternative action and so the just war requirement that force should only be used as a last resort can also be met.

It is, according to Grotius, the degree of certainty that counts in moral matters. There could, therefore, at least in theory, be a threat of an event that, while distant, was of such gravity and so certain to occur that it would be justifiable to take military action to counter it, if it could not be averted by non-military means. So, pre-emption could, in principle, be justified against a sufficiently serious threat, even if this was not imminent. But could all these conditions be met in practice?

One possible historical example where the conditions were met was the Israeli attack on the Iraq nuclear reactor at Osirak on 7 June 1981. The Israelis had learnt that the reactor was about to go live, after which it could not be attacked without risk of radiation fall-out. They had good reason to believe that the reactor would be used to make nuclear weapons since oil-rich Iraq had no need for nuclear power to generate its electricity or other fuel needs; and that the nuclear weapons might be targeted against what the Saddam regime proclaimed was the Zionist enemy. The day chosen for the attack was a Sunday when the French engineers building the plant were expected to be absent. So the attack was launched. One French technician who had returned unexpectedly to the site was killed. There were no other casualties.

The attack was universally condemned at the time, including by the US and UK.[22] But, in retrospect, it could be argued that it was a justified attack. The threat

---

[21] Grotius, *De Iure Belli ac Pacis*, Book II, Chapter XXII, section V in Reichberg, Syse and Begby, *Ethics of War*, p. 410.

[22] UNSCR 487, passed unanimously, was 'deeply concerned about the danger to international peace and security created by the premeditated Israeli air attack on Iraqi nuclear installations on 7th June 1981.'

posed by Iraq's acquisition of nuclear weapons was not imminent but there were good grounds for supposing it to be serious, as judged by both the damage that could be caused and high probability of its occurrence. The opportunity for dealing with the threat was also time limited. Although – as Nick Ritchie argues in Chapter 12 – such an attack could not remove the Iraq nuclear threat altogether, it could – and did – seriously delay and degrade the programme. So, it could be argued that there was just cause and that the action was undertaken for the sake of that cause.

A just cause does not on its own justify military action since all the other just war conditions need also to be met. For military action to be justified, it needs not only to have (and be undertaken for) a just cause, but also to be undertaken only as a last resort, with competent authority, with more good than harm judged likely to ensue, and in its conduct compliant with the principles of proportion and non-combatant immunity.

Given the intransigent nature of the Iraqi regime, the Israelis could reasonably maintain that there were no alternative options available, while military action would be too risky once the nuclear reactor had gone live. So the condition of last resort was met. There was at the time little prospect of the United Nations, its deliberations in 1981 still immobilised by Cold War rivalries, taking any effective action. The Israelis could thus claim that they had competent authority. They could also argue that, with an attack on a Sunday when nobody was expected to be present and before the reactor had gone live, casualties would be minimal, so enabling the conditions of proportion and non-combatant immunity to be met. So, overall – with Iraq's nuclear programme set back with minimal casualties – the attack might appear justified.

This example suggests that a sufficient threat can provide just cause even if it is not imminent. But the rather exceptional chain of circumstances in this case also show how difficult it may be, in practice, for pre-emptive action to meet the just war conditions. The threat must be sufficiently serious to justify military action. The military means selected must be appropriately fashioned so that any harm caused is not disproportionate to the harm averted. For, otherwise, we risk the action causing more harm than good. Intelligence that a one-off attack was to be mounted by terrorists to destroy a prestigious architectural monument might justify a pre-emptive raid on the house where the plotters were at work. It would not justify a military invasion of the country from which the attack was planned. Crucially, there should be very strong and reliable grounds for believing in both the gravity of and high probability of the threatened event's occurrence. There should also be no alternative means available to counter the threat. Such grounds for confidence in the threat, as well as the lack of alternative means to counter it, are much more likely to be justified, if the threat is imminent than if it is distant. 'Fear', as Grotius stressed, 'is not enough.' What matters is 'the degree of certainty.'

It has been argued that a further objection to pre-emptive attacks is that because they take place before war has started and before military action has commenced, they will necessarily be aimed at the innocent. Such attacks would thus be indiscriminate and breach the just war principle of discrimination or non-combatant immunity. A pre-emptive attack would thus be unjust. It is on such grounds that pre-emption should be ruled out. Jeff McMahan, for example, argues that the people attacked are likely to be the ordinary soldiers, not the generals and politicians plotting the harm.[23] Since the ordinary soldiers do not share moral responsibility for an unjust threat they should not be liable to attack.

But this objection is too strong. For if such desert is a requirement before attacks can legitimately be undertaken, it would be not just pre-emptive but any military action that would be ruled out since the ordinary soldiers engaged in non-pre-emptive military action are also unlikely to share responsibility for initiating an unjust attack and so do not deserve to be attacked. Soldiers are liable to be attacked not because they are guilty and deserve to be attacked but simply because they are posing a threat, they are, in that sense, not innocent but *nocens*. The appropriate grounds for distinguishing between the combatants that can legitimately be attacked and the non-combatants who are to be spared are that the former, but not the latter, are posing a threat and so in that sense are judged to be not innocent. The just war tradition does not require that those attacked are at the moment they are attacked engaged in hostile military action. The tradition permits attacks against military forces not engaged in action in recognition that they may be so engaged at a later date and so may still be judged to present a threat.

Nonetheless, these considerations clearly constrain who can legitimately be attacked by pre-emptive action. The only legitimate targets of attack are those who are posing the threat. The threat needs to be evidenced, as Grotius insists, not merely by capability or power but also intent. Such intent could, for example, be reasonably inferred if there were good grounds for believing that terrorists were actively planning an attack to kill innocent civilians; while the capability would be judged by evidence of the weapons at their disposal. Taken together, such evidence of intent and capability would help support the belief that a serious threat existed, as judged by both the damage threatened and the probability of its occurrence. Pre-emptive action to counter such a threat, and so to save many innocent lives, could be judged discriminate, if it were launched against those posing the threat: the terrorist plotters and those actively assisting the planned attack.

So, if there had been firm and reliable intelligence prior to 9/11 of the planned Al-Qa'ida attacks on New York and Washington, this could have justified pre-emptive action against the terrorists plotting the attacks, and their immediate supporters amongst the Taliban, in order to prevent the attacks and the substantial loss of civilian life they would cause. This might, for example, have justified an attack, suitably underpinned by reliable intelligence, on a terrorist training camp in Afghanistan or an attack such as that launched in October 2002 in the Yemen

---

[23]   Jeff McMahan, 'Preventive War and the Killing of the Innocent' in Sorabji and Rodin (eds.), *Ethics of War*, p. 186. David Rodin similarly argues that the problem with prevention is that, 'In preventive war, one attacks and kills those who have not yet committed a wrongful aggression against you'; Henry Shue and David Rodin (eds.), *Preemption: military action and moral justification* (Oxford, 2007), pp. 164–5.

when an armed US surveillance drone launched a missile that killed six al Qaeda suspects travelling in an automobile. What it would not have justified would have been a bombing raid on Kabul aimed at killing innocent civilians in advance retaliation for the murder of New Yorkers.

Conclusions

A doctrine of pre-emption to prevent the mass killing of civilians, even where the threat is not imminent, could, in principle, be justified according to just war teaching. But, in practice, meeting the just war criteria in such circumstances is extremely difficult. For the just war criteria require that we have 'a degree of certainty' about the threat. Such certainty is unlikely to be available with threats that are not imminent. In the real world there was no actionable intelligence of the 9/11 plot before it happened. The concatenation of circumstances surrounding the Israeli attack at Osirak, where an emergent threat was certain, was exceptional.

The doctrine of pre-emption was launched in September 2002. It is salutary to recall that on its first outing – the invasion of Iraq in March 2003 – the requirement that there should be strong and reliable grounds affording a degree of certainty about the threat was not satisfied. The US and UK Governments believed Saddam had retained significant stocks of weapons of mass destruction and so posed a serious threat to regional stability. But, as the Iraq Survey Group subsequently discovered, Saddam did not possess such weapons at the time of the invasion and so did not constitute such a threat.[24] The invasion and its chaotic aftermath also led – again unlike the Osirak raid – to substantial civilian and military casualties.

Pre-emptive military action against a sufficiently serious threat can be justified within the just war tradition. But it is very difficult, in practice, to meet the conditions and, particularly so where the threat is not imminent. That difficulty stems not from some obduracy on the part of medieval just war schoolmen. But rather from the fact that the future is, of its nature, usually uncertain and the more distant it is, the more likely to be uncertain. We may, occasionally, be granted reliable glimpses into the future and so, occasionally, we may be justified to act to forestall disastrous events, such as the mass killing of innocents. But such glimpses are rare. More often, our knowledge of the future is uncertain and speculative. Our confidence in our ability to predict the future needs then to be tested and tried, not least through the critical mutual examination of our friends and allies. This underlines the wisdom of a multilateral approach that allows for such consultation rather than an over-confident unilateralism. There is, moreover, likely to be time for such consultation with a threat that is not imminent. It was the failure to pursue such a multilateral approach that contributed to the widespread criticism of the pre-emptive military action undertaken against Iraq.

---

[24]   *Iraq Survey Group Final Report*, 30 September, 2004.

Pre-emption may exceptionally be justified. But pre-emptive military action will cause certain harm. It can, therefore, only be justified, if we have very strong grounds for believing that more good than harm will result. In view of the uncertainties of the human condition, such confidence over the course of future events where a threat is not actual or imminent is likely only rarely to be justified. There is, accordingly, a strong moral presumption against pre-emptive military action against a threat that, however serious, is not imminent. We should be very wary of the claims of those advocating pre-emptive action to counter such threats. Just war teaching would, therefore, not support the kind of unqualified right of pre-emption – a right to be exercised, if necessary, unilaterally and against a very wide a range of threats – that the US National Security Strategy arrogated to itself in September 2002.

Chapter 8

How Much of Our Liberties and Privacy do We Need to Give Up for Public Security?[1]

David Omand

What the Crevice, Overt and Rhyme Cases Revealed

On 30 April 2007 five young men stood in the dock of the Old Bailey in London to receive sentences of life imprisonment for their part in a bomb plot linked to Al-Qa'ida that could have killed hundreds of people. The convictions came after the jury had deliberated for 27 days, a record in British criminal history. Two and a half years later, three more young British Muslims stood in the dock of Woolwich Crown Court to receive life sentences (the ringleader receiving 41 years in prison) for their part in an Al-Qa'ida bomb plot to bring down several airliners over the Atlantic in an attempt to achieve an impact comparable to 9/11. In the airline case the convictions came after a retrial, the original jury having failed to reach a verdict on the most serious charges. These trials, the investigations that led up to them (Operations Crevice and Overt respectively) and the controversy that the cases provoked in the media, illustrate well both the nature of the terrorist threat itself and the dilemmas facing the intelligence and security authorities as they attempt to reduce the risk to the public that the threat represents.

The most obvious point to emerge at the time of the Crevice trial, and one that was powerfully reinforced in Operation Overt, was further confirmation that within our society there were disaffected young people who were prepared to commit mass murder for their cause, and who had made the shift from extremist rhetoric to violent action. This would have added to the public anxiety following the murderous attacks on London transport on 7 July 2005. The trials revealed how the gangs had made preparations for assembling home-made bombs and that, significantly, the gangs had been in contact with high-level Al-Qa'ida planners in Pakistan close to what remained of bin Laden's network. In the case of the Crevice plotters they were put in touch with a Canadian-based extremist to help them construct the detonation mechanism for their bombs. Evidence at their trial

---

[1] A full account of the case for the ethical code described here can be found in D. Omand, *Securing the State* (London, 2010) and *idem* 'Ethical guidelines in using secret intelligence for public security', *The Cambridge Review of International Affairs*, vol. 19, number 4 (2006).

also came from a witness in US custody. In the case of the airline bomb plotters it was during terrorist training in Pakistan that they appear to have learned how to make homemade liquid explosives that could be smuggled onboard airlines in soft drink bottles and with disposable cameras hiding their detonators. These two cases, therefore, could be clearly seen by the public to exemplify the new type of international terrorism that had eroded traditional boundaries between domestic and overseas spheres of security and intelligence operations. The cases illustrated how British authorities had had to work with US, Canadian, Pakistani and European services in order to frustrate the plots and to assemble evidence to bring those responsible to trial through intelligence and detective work on a scale never experienced before. Without that pre-emptive co-operative intelligence work by intelligence and police services enabling the plots to be uncovered, thousands would have lost their lives.

More alarmingly still, but surprisingly less publicly remarked upon, the Crevice gang had pursued an Al-Qaʿida plan to acquire from the Russian Mafia a radiological dispersal device, or 'dirty bomb', a possibility that turned out to be a scam. Although they were not successful in obtaining a radiological device the evidence at the trial left little doubt that they had had that intention and that had they succeeded they would have used such a device, with devastating consequences. 2006 also saw the conclusion of another major terrorist case, Operation Rhyme, with the sentencing of Dhiren Barot to 40 years of imprisonment, later reduced to 30 years on appeal, after pleading guilty to planning attacks on buildings in the United States and the UK. His terrorist cell also considered using a radioactive bomb. That ever-present fear, of terrorists acquiring a viable means of committing mass murder and causing long lasting disruption to life in a major city, haunts Western security authorities. It distinguishes the present terrorist campaign from any previous and it conditions the counter-terrorist responses of governments. It does not, however, yet seem to be fully reflected in public perceptions of the threat. We should not be surprised, therefore, that there have been continuing tensions between Government, Parliament and public over what security measures should be considered both necessary and proportionate.

Convictions in court may have been the end of the criminal justice process but it has not been the end of the debate.[2] In a statement attacking the security authorities read out by their lawyer after the trial, the Crevice defendants declared that, 'This was a prosecution driven by the security services, able to hide behind a cloak of secrecy, and eager to obtain ever greater resources and power to encroach on individual rights. There was no limit to the money, resources and underhand strategies that were used to secure convictions in this case. This case was brought in an atmosphere of hostility against Muslims, at home, and abroad. One stoked by this government throughout the course of this case. This prosecution involved

---

[2]   For example, the blog of the '7th of July Truth Campaign', http://j7truth.blogspot. com/2007/05/imran-khans-post-crevice-trial.html, accessed 18 April 2009.

extensive intrusion upon personal lives, not only ours, but our families and friends. Coached witnesses were brought forward. Forced confessions were gained through illegal detention, and torture abroad. Threats and intimidation were used to hamper the truth. All with the trial judge seemingly intent to assist the prosecution almost every step of the way. These were just some of the means used in the desperate effort to convict.'

There is a ready audience for such harsh views: from subsequent comment on blogs and web-sites it does appear that conspiracy theories swirl around these trials, as they do around the attacks on 7/7, and as they still do over 9/11. A Channel 4 News survey of 500 British Muslims, carried out by GFK NOP, found that nearly a quarter did not believe the four men identified as the July the seventh London bombers were responsible for the attacks.[3] And a similar number said the government or the security services were involved. Nearly six in ten of those polled believed the government had not told the whole truth about the 7/7 bombings – and more than half said the intelligence services had made up evidence to convict terrorist suspects. The evidence brought out at the Overt trial of the airline plotters, including video surveillance footage of the suspects and their pre-prepared suicide videos, may have shaken some of this denial of reality, but conspiracy theories continue and controversies continue to be sparked off by police actions, for example the arrests of suspects who are then later released without charge.

The questions impose themselves therefore: can the minority communities from whom the terrorists might hope to seek support be persuaded of the reality of the threat (the terrorists attack Muslims and non-Muslims indiscriminately)? Can they be reassured that their community is not being stigmatized or discriminated against domestically, at the same time as vigorous and effective intelligence-led action is taken to uncover the existing terrorists hiding within the community? This need for reassurance extends to being able to demonstrate that the methods being used by our allies and partners in the wider fight against terrorism overseas are in keeping with the underlying values of a democratic state ruled by law.

Most of the ethical problems associated with measures to counter terrorism, including facilitating intelligence-gathering, thus centre on how one might arrive at the appropriate mix for the circumstances in question of individual categories of rights, such as the right to life – with the expectation of both being protected by the State from threats to oneself and ones family – and the right to privacy of personal and family life. There is an obvious danger that security concerns are somehow thought always to trump consideration of human rights with the desire for immediate security gain as having automatic primacy. It is a balancing act within rights that should be sought and not a trade-off between rights and a separate public good called security.

---

[3]   Channel 4 web-site 4 June 2007, http://www.channel4.com/news/articles/society/religion/survey+government+hasnt+told+truth+about+77/545847 accessed 18 April 2009.

After 9/11, the British Government entered a derogation from the Human Rights Act 2000 justified on the grounds that 'There exists a terrorist threat to the United Kingdom from persons suspected of involvement in international terrorism. In particular, there are foreign nationals present in the United Kingdom who are suspected of being concerned in the commission, preparation or instigation of acts of international terrorism, of being members of organizations or groups which are so concerned or of having links with members of such organizations or groups, and who are a threat to the national security of the United Kingdom.'[4] When, however, the point was tested in the House of Lords during the appeal in the case of the Belmarsh prisoners detained under immigration powers, one Law Lord, Lord Hoffman, (admittedly in a minority opinion and before the Crevice trial reached Court) held the derogation unlawful on the ground that there was no 'war or other public emergency threatening the life of the nation' within the meaning of Article 15 of the European Convention on Human Rights.[5] Public sentiment at the time seemed to share the sceptical judgment of Lord Hoffman about the British Government's attempts to use immigration legislation so that, in his words, 'The real threat to the life of the nation, in the sense of a people living in accordance with its traditional laws and political values, comes not from terrorism but from laws such as these. That is the true measure of what terrorism may achieve. It is for Parliament to decide whether to give the terrorists such a victory.'

The aim of UK counter-terrorist strategy, as it is of UK national security strategy more generally, is to reduce the risks to the UK and its interests overseas so that people can go about their lives freely and with confidence. That aim seems to have been met over the years since the strategy was conceived in 2002/3. A number of serious plots have been disrupted, keeping down the level of violence, and the public has shown much stoicism (and for example tourism to the UK has continued) despite a number of failed or actual attacks. In part precisely because of this success in keeping down the level of actual violence, sections of the press question what the fuss has been about. When it comes to judging the proportionality and necessity of measures to uncover and disrupt terrorist planning there remains continuing tension between public perceptions of the degree of seriousness of the current terrorist threat, as evidenced by the number and type of attacks that have actually occurred, and the fears of government over the potential for mass casualties from attacks in public places and for violent extremism to gain ground among radicalized and disaffected sections of Muslim youth in the UK and by right-wing extremist groups seeking to capitalize on that situation.

---

[4]   *Human Rights Act 1998* (Designated Derogation) Order 2001, No 3644, which came into force on 13 November 2001.

[5]   House of Lords SESSION 2004-05 [2004] UKHL 56 Judgments - A (FC) and others (FC) (Appellants) v. Secretary of State for the Home Department (Respondent).

As far as concerns the current level of threat, well-publicized statements by successive Directors General of the Security Service,[6] backed by evidence from subsequent trials of other individuals charged with terrorist offences, have gone some way to remind the public of the extent to which the authorities do have reason to believe that the threat remains substantial. Despite the evident successes eroding Al-Qa'ida leadership overseas and in bringing terrorists to trial in the UK, it remains the case that extremely violent jihadist views are shared by a significant number of radicalized individuals within the United Kingdom and elsewhere in Europe.

Greater efforts have been made by the UK Government in 2009 in the publication of the refresh of the counter-terrorism strategy, CONTEST 2, to provide explanatory background to the origins of Al-Qa'ida and its ideology and to the reasons for its global appeal.[7] CONTEST 2 contains an analysis of the thinking of these extremists, and seeks to counter their justification for their actions as defensive on the basis that they consider that the West has been conducting a war on Islam itself. It has become tragically evident that for the extremists the concept of an 'innocent' Western civilian in this struggle has no meaning since it is in the nature of democracy that the people have chosen their government and have thereby, in the eyes of the extremists, allowed their governments to wage war on Islam. The senior official responsible for counter-terrorist policy in the Home Office has explained publicly how such radicals see themselves as the vanguard of a wider global movement whose ultimate aim is to establish what they regard as genuine Islamic states ruled by Islamic law.[8] And how, following the lead given by bin Laden and his deputy Al Zawahiri, these radicalized groups have come to regard the West itself as a necessary target, standing in the way of their objectives of remodelling the world of Islam by overthrowing the regimes in the Middle East, Gulf, North Africa and South East Asia to which they take exception.

One very disturbing feature of attacks in the UK and overseas that has added to concerns over public safety has been the use of suicide bombings. The willingness of terrorist leaders to sacrifice their own lives in the name of religious belief (or to be more accurate often the lives of their followers or even as seen in Afghanistan innocent children duped into carrying bombs) makes the task of protecting the public considerably harder. This threat leads for example to the presence of armed police as a routine in many public places and to extreme precautions with officers in

---

[6]   Speeches by Dame Eliza Manningham-Buller of 10 Nov 2006, and Jonathan Evans of 5 Nov 2007 and 7 Jan 2009, accessed on 18 April 2009 at http://www.mi5.gov.uk/output/news-speeches-and-statements.html.

[7]   The UK Government Counter-Terrorism Strategy (CONTEST 2), Cm 7547, (London: Home Office, 24 March 2009).

[8]   See the analysis of Charles Farr, Director General of the Office for Security and Counter-Terrorism in the Home Office in his Colin Cramphorn Memorial Lecture, (London: Policy Exchange, April 2009).

full protective gear being deployed for searches or arrests.[9] The traditional British unarmed 'bobby on the beat' has become an endangered species in central London. Special rules of engagement have had to be issued to armed police (Operation Kratos) which provide in extreme circumstances for an armed officer to shoot a suspect in the head if intelligence suggests that he is a suicide bomber who poses an imminent danger to the public or police and this action is necessary to avoid his setting off any explosives that might be attached to the suspected bomber's body. All of these developments, explicable given the actual police experience of this form of terrorism, has added to public unease about 'heavy-handedness' in the security response. Tragic accidents, such as the shooting by police of the Brazilian electrician, Jean Charles de Menezes, in the intelligence-led follow-up to the 21/7 attempted attacks on the London Underground heighten public concerns over the conduct and oversight of intelligence and security work

Contingency planning for the possibility of future low probability but potentially highly catastrophic events, such as might follow the acquisition by a terrorist group of serious means of mass destruction through radiological, chemical or biological means, has always been hard to explain publicly without running the risk of creating an alarmist climate of fear. But some events would be so devastating both in their immediate impact and in their longer-term political and social implications for the normal life of the nation that they justify significant attention by government. How amenable, for example, would such a future threat be to the processes and provisions of conventional criminal justice, and how far would in those circumstances legislation have to provide for further extraordinary measures, beyond those already introduced such as new offences of encouraging terrorism or committing acts preparatory to terrorism?[10] The very heated debate in 2008, in which the UK Government's proposals for extending the time that suspects may be held in police custody to 42 days before charge were heavily defeated in the House of Lords, demonstrated the absence of consensus on how seriously to judge the threat from extremist jihadist terrorism and on what tools should be available to the security authorities to combat it.[11] In the same way, the UK Government was forced in September 2009 to order an independent review of the working of their Control Order regime (involving electronic tagging and movement restrictions on suspects) following adverse judicial judgments. In assessing how far to act in anticipation of such developments governments have to draw on the assessments of their intelligence communities, but are constrained in how much of that intelligence material can safely be put in the public domain and how.

---

[9]   PC Stephen Oake of Manchester Police was murdered during the arrest of the main suspect, Kamel Bourgass, in the so-called Ricin plot.

[10]   In the Terrorism Act 2006, http://www.opsi.gov.uk/acts/acts2006/ukpga_20060011_en_1, accessed 18 April 2009.

[11]   Culminating in the House of Lords vote against the extension of the time limit to 42 days, http://news.bbc.co.uk/1/hi/uk_politics/7666022.stm accessed 18 April 2009.

The intelligence and security services therefore find themselves not just in the front line in the fight against terrorism, where they would want to operate, but also in the associated front line of political and media controversy where they have no wish to be. Their actions, and the intelligence justification for those actions, are constantly under media scrutiny. In addition, the intelligence community in the UK, as in the US, has faced heightened media scepticism harking back to the problems of intelligence assessments on Iraqi Weapons of Mass Destruction (WMD), and their use by government to make the case for the intervention in Iraq. The case of the 2002 Iraqi WMD dossier in particular showed the difficulties governments face when they decide to justify policy by putting intelligence into the public domain.

Public tolerance of security measures (including tough counter-terrorism laws) is most likely to come from an understanding of the necessity for them that rests on an appreciation of the dangers terrorism poses – and that in turn depends upon a belief in the integrity of the assessments of the threat that government and police make publicly available. Intelligence assessment and policy advocacy do not comfortably coexist. Yet that is in essence the everyday dilemma facing the police, security authorities and Ministers after every controversial counter-terrorist operation or new security measure or legislative proposal that has to be justified to a curious and possibly sceptical public. Government can, of course, as we have seen make the situation worse by appearing to be using the need to act tough on terrorism as a political device for outflanking the opposition. It is remarkable, and depressing, that unlike the long struggle against terrorism in Northern Ireland and the search for peace there, no British inter-Party consensus has existed on policy towards international terrorism.

Government has, therefore, struggled to justify the tougher aspects of its counterterrorist legislation and to explain new security measures such as the ban on liquids being carried by airline passengers. The police have equally found it hard to explain their operations such as the large scale raid on a suburban house in Forest Gate, London that failed to find evidence of the suspected existence of terrorist cyanide dispersal devices or the hasty arrest of 12 suspects, none of whom was then charged, in what the Prime Minister declared to be the stopping of 'a major terrorist plot'. There is also pressure on government from the prosecutors and from many politicians to legislate to allow more secret intelligence to be used in securing convictions for terrorist offences in court that also creates a dilemma: bringing terrorists and their supporters to justice depends upon the deployment in court of highly sensitive material from secret sources such as human agents or electronic bugging or from overseas liaisons with countries whose methods differ from those of the UK. Due process has to be balanced by the need to protect intelligence sources, methods and effort. An ages-old dilemma has been heightened in a modern context of how much of the hidden in a world of secret intelligence to reveal for the honest purposes of public safety and education and in the interests of justice.

It can be deduced from the tone of majority public reaction after terrorist-related incidents that there is nevertheless an expectation that terrorist activity will be frustrated through effective security action, not just that there will be effective law enforcement after an attack leading to the arrest and successful prosecution of those responsible. It is likely that given good pre-emptive intelligence even if the threat were to worsen significantly it would be possible to manage down the level of risk to the public without government being driven to consider extreme measures affecting criminal justice, such as changing the rules of evidence, introducing house arrest or detention without trial for suspects, courts sitting without a jury or introducing further new classes of offence such as association with known terrorists. Armed with good pre-emptive intelligence, counter-terrorist operations can also be designed and focused on legitimate targets without dislocating the normal life of the community and without creating a sense of discrimination in the application of security measures. Operation Overt that uncovered the airline plotters was the largest ever joint Security Service and police covert investigation. And good intelligence can also inform the understanding of the reasons for the violence (the Prevent part of the British Government's counter-terrorism strategy, CONTEST2) and thus guide the search for strategy that can address the roots of the problem as well as its symptoms.

The risk of this line of thinking, correct though I believe it to be, is that it leads to unreal public expectations about the certainty of pre-emptive intelligence being available in every case and of the ability of the intelligence analysts invariably to assemble fragments of intelligence in a timely way into the right jigsaw picture. Popular fictional cinematic accounts of hi-tech espionage conceal the hard truth that such feats are indeed normally 'mission impossible' and set an unrealistically high standard for the gathering of pre-emptive intelligence. Again, this danger is illustrated by the media coverage following the verdict on the Crevice trial. Media attention very quickly shifted from condemnation of terrorism following the conviction of those who had plotted mass murder to serious criticism of the Security Service for failing to follow up all the potential suspects with whom the Crevice gang were seen to be in contact and two of whom subsequently went on to take part in the murderous attacks in London on 7/7. Some 2,000 individuals were said to have been logged by the investigators of the Crevice conspiracy, of whom 50 were judged worthy of further interest and 15 classed as essential targets. Surveillance resources did not allow all 50 cases to be fully followed up, and a possible opportunity to uncover the 7/7 plot could therefore be said at least in theory to have been thereby missed. As the Director General of the Security Service has commented: 'Every decision to investigate someone entails a decision not to investigate someone else. Knowing of somebody is not the same as knowing all about somebody. And it would be perverse for my Service to avoid knowing of somebody for fear of being held to blame if they later become involved in an attack.

I think we should be very careful to bear this in mind when talking about so-called intelligence failures.'[12] Reasonable operational judgments were no doubt made at the time, in the light of the information available at the time, but the media were looking to allocate blame and to use this case to argue for much greater openness of security activity to outside scrutiny and in particular to question the effectiveness as overseers of the Intelligence and Security Committee of parliamentarians. It was argued in *The Guardian* that, 'counter-terrorism is one of the most important areas of government activity, yet it is one of the least scrutinised – and the latest revelations suggest that what scrutiny there is does not work', under the headline, 'The Crevice trial exposes the fatal lack of scrutiny under which the security services are operating.'[13]

Revolutionary jihadism represents in practice a very hard target for the intelligence community to penetrate, since it is organized around tight cells of dedicated extremists with linkages that rely on kinship, personal relationships and recommendations built on shared experience such as attendance at Al-Qaʻida training camps overseas. The intelligence agencies and the police will therefore continue to be under pressure to generate more actionable intelligence by extending the range of methods judged acceptable in the pursuit of public safety, and to use the product more aggressively to strike more directly at the terrorists themselves.

Pre-emptive intelligence is a good example of a public good, adding considerable public value, indirect as well as direct, through helping provide domestic security. It comes largely from two directions: information volunteered from within the community in rejection of the extremists and their ideology; and modern, professional intelligence gathering using all the human and technical tradecraft of which the Agencies are capable – including information which they may acquire from intelligence allies and liaison services. The desire to provide more useful intelligence creates real dilemmas for governments, and for their intelligence agencies, in defining what are acceptable boundaries of their conduct. One such area relates to the use of modern information technology to access and exploit information about individuals and their associations and movements that can help narrow down the search for terrorist networks. Another area relates to the consequences of the international nature of the threat, and therefore the depth and breadth of international cooperation between intelligence agencies that has to be developed in order to identify terrorists and their networks.

The Use of Information Technology

As demonstrated in the Crevice and Overt cases, terrorists are living and working amongst the general population. There is no simple profile that can be used to

---

[12]   Jonathan Evans, Address to the Society of Editors, 5 Nov 2007 http://www.mi5. gov.uk/output/intelligence-counter-terrorism-and-trust.html accessed 29 April 2009.

[13]   Vikram Dodd, 'Preventable Errors', *The Guardian*, London, 1 May 2007.

identify someone who holds extremist views and has decided to become an active member of a terrorist network. There are essentially three types of source to which intelligence analysts working on counter terrorism can go in order to access information that could help identify their targets.

The first type of source consists of the product of the various traditional intelligence activities: recruiting human agents, carrying out surveillance, examining the telephone and other communications of suspects, and so on. This category includes information volunteered from sources within the community, thus reinforcing the point that the community must have confidence in the integrity of the intelligence and security authorities and confidence that the rights of individuals will be protected when action is taken on information provided.

The second type of access goes under the broad description of 'open source' material, including the huge amount of information that is available openly on Internet websites. Additionally, study of the thousands of extremist internet websites, used by jihadists for recruitment and propaganda, and of the public statements and videos emanating from terrorist leaders, can produce useful insights into the causes, extent and nature of extremist activity.

The third type of access consists of data-protected personal information relating to individuals of interest (which I label with the acronym PROTINT by analogy with human intelligence, HUMINT and signals intelligence, SIGINT). Such information is nowadays held on electronic databases such as mobile telephone call data, airline reservations and advance passenger information, banking and credit card transactions, biometric border and passport data and so on. Some of this personal information will be held on UK government databases, some within the UK on private sector company databases, and some will be held offshore by foreign governments or companies (a developing justification for extending intelligence liaisons with other nations). Modern computer technology provides sophisticated ways of analyzing and correlating such information and identifying clusters of associated data for further investigation by more traditional police methods. It is in the nature of such data bases that they will contain mostly information on the ordinary citizen, thus information on the innocent as well as the guilty will have to be scanned electronically to identify any patterns of interest. It has of course always been the case that authorized investigators can with probable cause obtain access to personal information about named suspects, but now the associations and connections of the suspect can be identified leading to new lines of investigation. The modern world provides countless electronic traces of the passage of an individual that can certainly have intelligence value but which require the modern techniques of information technology and data mining to uncover.

Another area of technology that has already been exploited for counterterrorism is the availability of cheap camera and video-recording technology through extensive CCTV systems installed inside and outside public and commercial buildings, and in public spaces. Such capability has been of enormous use in the investigation of terrorist attacks such as 7/7 and the subsequent attempts to bomb the London underground on 21/7 as well as high-profile murder, abduction and assault cases. Future CCTV systems will employ active rather than passive technology, alerting operators to unusual behaviour. In future, we may well see the widespread application of advanced pattern recognition technology to provide automatic warning of anomalous or suspicious behaviour (such as leaving bags unattended) that can be detected on such systems. It is now feasible to use in future such technology to tag the image of a suspect so that the individual can then be tracked through a transport system and even, as the technology improves, to recognize wanted individuals. Automatic vehicle number plate readers have over the last few years been widely installed in the UK on main roads, and provide the basis for congestion charging systems, such as that which covers central London. Such developments can then effectively identify the presence and location of any suspect vehicle. The prevalence of miniaturized video capability in mobile phones has however also generated a different phenomenon, that of the citizen reporter – able to send to the media real-time footage, for example of a police raid or the policing of a public demonstration.

A further cause for public concern has been the spread of the use of techniques of surveillance into other parts of government, for example by local authorities and by civil government agencies of the powers to authorize surveillance, at least at the less intrusive levels, provided for in the Regulation of Investigatory Powers Act 2000. Thus, some local authorities have conducted surveillance operations on families to check whether they live within the catchment areas of their chosen schools, to catch fly-tippers and environmental polluters and even to reduce dog fouling on tourist beaches. The authority granted by Parliament through the provisions of RIPA 2000 was designed for the purposes of national security and the detection and prevention of serious crime, and in response to public concerns the Home Office has proposed to raise the rank of those in local authorities who are allowed to authorize use of RIPA techniques, and is asking the public to consider whether or not it is appropriate for those people to be allowed to use those techniques to conduct investigations into local issues.[14]

These developments in the possibilities of new technology, lumped together, have been criticized as evidence that the UK is heading to become a 'surveillance society'.[15] The total impact of individually justifiable measures may add up to an unwelcome capability of the State to access information on its citizens for undefined purposes, and thus to provide an unconscious chilling effect on everyday behaviours, freedom of association and expression. I would describe this nightmare as 'the Panoptic State': the all-seeing State where surveillance is so widespread as

---

[14] Home Office Consultation Paper, April 2009, http://www.homeoffice.gov.uk/documents/cons-2009-ripa accessed 29 April 2009.

[15] House of Lords Constitution Committee (2009), *Surveillance: Citizens and the State*, HL 18; Home Affairs Committee (2008) *A Surveillance Society?*, London: HC 58; Richard Thomas and Mark Wallport, Data Sharing Review Report (2008); Surveillance Studies Network, A Report on the Surveillance Society (2006), Report for the Information Commissioner.

to provide a new form of social control. In his 1785 description of the design of his ideal prison, the Panopticon, Jeremy Bentham wrote of it providing 'a new mode of obtaining power of mind over mind, in a quantity hitherto without example'[16]; what the French philosopher Michel Foucault much later saw as a powerful metaphor for how modern societies exercise unconscious social control through surveillance.[17] The future danger comes from the combination of expanding technology of 'access', scale of effort and especially mission creep outwards from legitimate national security to the provision of joined up service to the citizen and the protection of public expenditure from fraud. As a vocal critic, Henry Porter has described his fears: 'Who knows what conclusions will be drawn from innocent web searches, phone calls and emails? Who dares to predict the kinds of abuse by the government, which is already tracking legitimate protestors in real time with automatic number recognition cameras and infiltrating environmental groups with informers and spies?'[18]

There are counter-arguments that such developments are not an inevitable consequence of current trends in policy provided that adequate safeguards are put in place. As former Home Secretary John Reid has put the case for government access to communications data:

> Used in the right way, and subject to important safeguards, communications data can play a critical role in keeping us safe. It helps investigators identify suspects and solve life-threatening situations. It can assist the emergency services locating vulnerable people. And it is critical to protecting national security against terrorism. Maintaining this essential capability will become more complex in the future in the face of technological change…it is clear to me that the way we collect communications data needs to change so law enforcement agencies can continue to do their job; to tackle serious crime and gather evidence to fight terrorism and prosecute criminals. Of course, there must be stringent safeguards to control how data can be obtained.[19]

The nature of those safeguards is going to need to be reviewed in line with the developments in the technologies concerned. The security case to be made is that – as in Operations Crevice and Overt – intelligence and security agencies will need access to personal information and have the ability to reveal patterns of interest if they are to protect society from the most serious threats of modern international terrorism and serious crime. Limiting the access of the intelligence and security services to these sources of personal information and the technologies to exploit it,

---

[16]   Jeremy Bentham, *The Panopticon* (Dublin: Thomas Byrne, 1791), Preface.

[17]   Michel Foucault, *Discipline and Punish: the Birth of the Modern Prison* (Paris: Gallimard, 1975; London: Vintage Books, 1995).

[18]   Henry Porter, *The Guardian*, (28 April 2009), p. 31.

[19]   http://www.guardian.co.uk/commentisfree/libertycentral/2009/apr/27/surveillance-data-protection accessed 1 Nov 2009.

and surrounding their use with excessive regulation, will probably result in greater risk to the public. There is thus a trade-off between personal privacy and security that has to be weighed for each technique, accepting that intrusions into personal privacy can and should be limited to the most serious challenges to security, from terrorism and serious crime and not from the multitude of minor misdemeanours that authority must therefore find less intrusive ways to prevent – and Parliament must legislate where necessary to ensure that is the case.

As already noted, to encourage the provision of information to the authorities requires maintaining public confidence in the actions of the State, including in the protection provided for minority communities by the framework of human rights and the quality of justice. The actions of the security authorities therefore must be – and be seen to be – both necessary and proportionate. Modern intelligence access will also often involve intrusive methods of surveillance and investigation. Being able to demonstrate proper legal authorization, stringent safeguards and appropriate oversight of the use of such intrusive intelligence activity becomes even more important for the intelligence community, if the public at large is to be convinced both of the desirability of such intelligence capability and of the necessity of paying heed to its threat assessments. This aspect of security policy deserves more attention that it has so far been given.

The Implications of International Relationships

Another area where the demands of providing intelligence for public protection can clash with public expectations of desirable standards of conduct is over the maintenance of intelligence liaisons with States that have very different standards of conduct from those of the UK in tracking down and dealing with terrorist suspects. The UK has incorporated human rights protection into the fabric of domestic law through the Human Rights Act 1998 and has always been clear that it will not condone, let alone allow, the practice of torture. The memory is still strong of the dire consequences of the brief use in 1971 by the British Army in Northern Ireland of coercive interrogation methods, found by the European Court of Human Rights to have amounted to inhuman and degrading treatment and subsequently banned by Prime Minister Heath from use by any British personnel for all time. [20] The fall-out from that episode polarized attitudes in Northern Ireland and overseas for many years. By no means all countries affected by terrorism provide equivalent protection for their citizens, nor do their intelligence and security agencies have standards of conduct towards suspects comparable to those of the UK. Practices range from extra-judicial killing to extraordinary rendition. The UK's principal ally, the United States, authorized under the Bush Administration rendition and

---

[20]   The 5 techniques of hooding, sleep deprivation, wall standing, restrictions on food and water and white noise that were banned by the UK following the adverse finding of the European Human Rights Court: Ireland v United Kingdom, 25 Eur. Ct. HR (ser.A) (1978).

interrogation practices by its intelligence community that were outlawed for members of UK agencies and service personnel. As the Parliamentary Intelligence and Security (ISC) oversight committee recognized, the UK agencies were slow to detect the emerging pattern of US extra-ordinary renditions and slow to apply greater caution in their dealings over cases of mutual interest.[21] The injunction to apply greater caution, however correct, does not, however, eliminate the dilemma for intelligence agencies seeking pre-emptive intelligence.

Terrorism is an international problem, and sharing intelligence on terrorists, their networks and their modus operandi was recognized after 9/11 by the United Nations Security Council as an imperative for nations 'to assist each other to the maximum extent possible, in the prevention, investigation, prosecution and punishment of acts of terrorism, wherever they occur.'[22] Intelligence and police services have therefore since 9/11 been steadily deepening and expanding their range of international contacts. In the case of the United States, the key partner in the NATO operation in Afghanistan in which UK forces are so heavily engaged, intelligence exchanges continue at a high level. Another very important relationship for the UK in tackling terrorism is the newer but very important links to Pakistani intelligence, security and police agencies. So was it therefore acceptable to receive actionable intelligence from those and other liaison services about whose practices there was legitimate doubt? Was it right to pass information from UK investigations on a suspect of interest to those countries? If, as happened in some cases, UK investigators were authorized to question suspects held by liaison services was that tantamount to collusion in their prior or subsequent ill-treatment?

Typically, an overseas service will want to offer their UK liaison agencies information that relates to terrorist threats that have links back to the UK, in the expectation that the UK will reciprocate. Such information exchanges are the main rationale for intelligence liaisons. Most of the major terrorist plots, and most of the actual attacks, that have been uncovered in the UK certainly have links overseas, often to individuals in Pakistan. The information provided to the UK may be as little as an address or a telephone number with a request that it be checked out, or a warning that a British embassy or consulate, company or tourist destination in the overseas country is known to be the subject of a terrorist plot. Or it may be an offer to allow follow-up questions to be put to a suspect being held who has admitted to plotting against UK interests. Such exchanges are central, as the UN Security Council recognized, to the prevention of terrorism. In return, liaison services will expect information from UK agencies that will assist their own investigations, for example whether a suspect had associations with terrorists in custody in the UK.

As with the 'ticking bomb' scenarios used in ethics classes to illuminate the nature of human agency, the 'blood on the report' scenario is not how in practice the problem presents itself. Intelligence agencies guard their sources, and typically it

---

[21] Intelligence and Security Committee, *UK Agencies and Rendition*, (London: Cabinet Office, July 2007).

[22] For example in UNSC Resolution 1456 (2003).

will simply not be apparent whether a piece of information has come from a human agent, from a technical operation, a combination of these or from the interrogation of a suspect – and in the last case it will certainly not be apparent on the face of the information whether it has been extracted through a voluntary confession, by some form of plea bargain or covert deal with the suspect (something the agency concerned will be most anxious to conceal if the individual has agreed to work as a double agent for the authorities) or by coercive interrogation. Questions to the liaison service on that last point will simply not be answered (or if answered not answered truthfully).

Procedures and safeguards already in place, for example to report cases of suspected ill-treatment of suspects, can reduce the risk that UK intelligence officers will find themselves caught up in appearing to condone ill-treatment or torture by countries overseas. It should be made clear to all British officials who may become involved in liaison work that they must in good faith ensure, both generally and in individual cases, that there are no misunderstandings on the part of the country concerned that the UK in any way expects its requests for information to be met through mistreatment of detainees or suspects. Such messages can be reinforced by the continuing work that UK security and justice officials and military staffs are conducting with liaison partners to raise standards and professionalism in these areas. It is already the case that such liaison support is making a positive difference.

The real risk remains that in the eyes of defence lawyers, the media, and thus the public, the very existence of a liaison relationship with such a country will be seen as collusive. The only way to avoid that risk would be not to have external diplomatic or intelligence links with nations known to have, or suspected of having, lower standards for detention and interrogation than in the UK. However, that is simply not an option that would be diplomatically feasible or could be responsibly regarded as being in the public interest in relation to counter-terrorism. Intelligence exchanges are, as the ISC recognized, critical to UK security. It is the case that information from such exchanges has disrupted attacks planned against the UK and has thus saved lives. There was no way of knowing at the time whether information received came from torture, or whether sources were otherwise tainted, and there is no sure way of knowing now. The furore after the deaths of British tourists in the terrorist bombing in Bali in 2002 showed that the public does expect its intelligence services to provide forestalling intelligence of such attacks, however hard that may be. It is, I believe, a fundamental duty of those charged with the protection of the public to pay heed to information that may directly bear on public safety. The protecting state must make its own standards of conduct clear and its officials must abide by them; but it cannot shun the rest of the world if it wishes to manage, as the public would wish it to, the risks to its citizens at home and when abroad.

Some Principles of Ethical Conduct in the World of Secret Intelligence

The oversight committee for the British intelligence services, the ISC, has already recognized the importance for public confidence of demonstrating that there is adequate oversight of the management of intelligence activities. In exercising such oversight it would help to sustain confidence if there were recognition that the legislation and administration governing the intelligence community does embody ethical principles set firmly within the framework of human rights, including the important tests of necessity and proportionality. The limitations society should place on the methods to be employed as these capabilities are unleashed can be regarded, by analogy with just war principles, as *jus in intelligentia*.[23] It would also help develop sensible debate on the use of intrusive intelligence methods to recognize that there is also a recognized principle governing the purposes – the potential intelligence requirements and types of target – for which government should seek to acquire such capabilities, *jus ad intelligentiam*. Public support in the UK, and agreement at a European level, for necessary future developments in intelligence collection and use in reducing the risk from terrorism may come to depend upon such an understanding.

I would suggest six headings, the first relating to the restrictions laid down by Parliament on the scope of the work of the UK intelligence agencies, the remainder relating to the use of intelligence capabilities methods used in individual cases:

1. There must be sufficient sustainable cause

This is a check on any tendency for the secret world to encroach into areas unjustified by the scale of potential harm to national interests that is to be prevented or advantage to be secured, for example in the use of the RIPA 2000 powers to use highly intrusive methods. If intelligence capability is to be developed and maintained in being there has to be a sufficiently compelling purpose that can then be reflected, in British usage, in an approved set of intelligence requirements. With such considerations in mind, in the legislation that placed the Intelligence Agencies on a statutory footing the UK Parliament limited the purposes for which intelligence activities are allowed.

2. There must be integrity of motive

Following this guideline should involve public assurance that there is proper concern with the integrity of the whole system throughout the intelligence process, from collection through to the analysis, assessment and presentation of the resulting intelligence. Governments are too often accused these days of having

---

[23] M. Walzer, *Just and Unjust Wars* (New York, 1977) and M. Quinlan, 'Just Intelligence: Prologomena to an Ethical Theory', *Intelligence and National Security*, (Feb 2007), vol. 22, no. 1.

hidden agenda, not least in their presentation of the terrorist threat to the public. Any guidelines for the intelligence community must, for example, make clear that there is no possibility of political authority being misused. Whatever the arts of deception (the 'trade-craft' in the jargon) the reader of an intelligence report must have complete confidence in the integrity of the system that delivered it. Negative results must be reported as well as positive scoops, and every result must have associated with it the error estimate and the degree of reliability. Such issues were central to the independent Review (the Butler Inquiry) set up by the British Government in 2004 into intelligence on weapons of mass destruction.[24]

3. The methods to be used must be proportionate

Is the likely impact of the proposed intelligence-gathering operation, taking account of the methods to be used, in proportion to the seriousness of the business in hand in terms of the harm that it is sought to prevent, for example by using only the minimum intrusion necessary into the private affairs of others, and taking account of the nature of agent recruitment and inducements, the physical risks involved, and the moral hazard to agent and handler alike particularly where participating informants are being run? The Regulation of Investigative Powers Act 2000 (RIPA), for example, already embodies the principle of proportionality through differing levels of request and approval. In other words, the test for those approving bugging and eavesdropping operations is of minimum necessary intrusion[25] comparable to the common law doctrine of 'minimum necessary force'.

4. There must be right authority, including upholding of the universal ban on torture[26]

This principle ensures that there is sufficiently senior sign off on sensitive operations and accountability up a recognized chain of command to permit effective oversight. A senior judge is appointed as Intelligence Services Commissioner under RIPA 2000 to keep under review the issue of warrants by the Secretary of State authorizing eavesdropping and interference with property and the use by the Security Service of covert human intelligence sources in accordance with the requirements of the law.[27] In addition, RIPA 2000 provides for another senior judge to act as Interception of Communications Commissioner with responsibility

---

[24]   *The Review of Intelligence on Weapons of Mass Destruction* (the Butler Report), (London: House of Commons: HC 898 14 July 2004).

[25]   R.V. Jones, *Reflections on Secret Intelligence* (London: Mandarin, 1989).

[26]   Convention against Torture and Other Cruel, Inhuman or Degrading Treatment or Punishment, Dec 10, 1984, 1465 U.N.T.S 85.

[27]   The Commissioner's annual report is presented to Parliament – see http://www. official-documents.co.uk/document/hc0506/hc05/0548/0548.pdf accessed 10 August 2009.

to keep under review the issue of interception warrants by the Secretary of State.[28] Even in hypothetical 'ticking bomb' scenarios such a firm rule of right authority cannot have a *force majeur* let-out clause to be invoked to allow torture when the stakes are high enough without vitiating the role of ethical guidelines. We cannot have ethical guidelines that cease to apply when it could be argued they are most needed. We have to recognize that individuals still retain the freedom to guide their own actions as free moral agents. If individual police or intelligence officers choose to operate outside their guidelines on interrogation they know they will be answerable at law as would any citizen. They would not be entitled and should not expect to be allowed to use the secrecy of their profession to evade accountability or to have pre-emptive legal absolution.

5. There must be reasonable prospect of success

Intelligence operations carry risks, and before approval is given there has to be a judgement that the impact if the operation were to be exposed or otherwise go wrong is acceptable. Even if the purpose is valid (guideline 1) and the methods to be used are proportionate to the issue (guideline 3) there needs to be a hard-headed risk assessment of risk to the operatives and those assisting them and of collateral damage to others, and not least the risk to future operations and to institutional reputations. And the authorizing authority has in weighing the risks of collateral damage to consider the likelihood of unintended consequences, or of political or diplomatic damage if exposed, and judge them acceptable – including applying the golden rule 'do unto others as you would be done by.'

6. Recourse to secret intelligence must be a last resort if there are open sources that can be used

There should be no reasonable alternative way of acquiring the information from less sensitive or non-secret sources, thus avoiding the possible moral hazards and trade-offs that collecting secret intelligence may involve. In another sense, of course, collecting open information and, where justified, secret intelligence should always be the first, and resort to armed force the last, resort of government. Secret intelligence is also expensive – and makes demands on very scarce human resource – and on those grounds alone, even without invoking ethical considerations, should not be sought if there are open ways of obtaining the information needed.

---

[28]   Report of the Interception of Communications Commissioner, London: 2004, http://www.archive2.official-documents.co.uk/document/deps/hc/hc883/883.pdf accessed 10 August 2009.

Conclusion

Security comes at a price. There is an opportunity cost in terms of resources not available for other public goods such as education or culture. The threat of terrorism imposes restrictions on individual liberty, as the gates to Downing Street mutely remind us. And there is a price in terms of personal privacy to allow the authorities to generate the pre-emptive intelligence on which much of the effort to maintain public security rests. By definition, secret intelligence concerns information that someone is trying their utmost to prevent you acquiring. Accessing useful intelligence is therefore going to involve rather different ethical rules than we might hope would govern private conduct as individuals in society. If the secrets of terrorists and criminal gangs are to be uncovered, therefore, there will be inevitable intrusions into their privacy and that of their associates. These intrusive methods are powerful and they get results. So public trust that this machine is only to be used for public protection against major dangers will continue to be essential. If the intelligence community is to access the full range of data (and meta-data) relating to individuals of interest, their movements, activities and associations in a timely way then the rules of engagement need to be clear and unambiguous. Those rules need to be ones acceptable in a democratic and free society and their application needs to be subject to the appropriate oversight and with means of independent investigation and redress in cases of alleged abuse of power.

The potential intrusion into personal privacy due to intelligence activity thus needs to be regulated and overseen according to well-defined principles as I have suggested in this chapter, and, in particular, applying the principles of necessity and proportionality. There does not, however, have to be a populist choice presented to the public between security on the one hand and the framework of human rights on the other, with the evident danger that the former will be expected to trump the latter. The balance is one to be struck within that framework, including proper weight being given to the right to life that is central to public security. The public needs to be reassured that Parliament will find the proper balance of measures to provide security within the framework of rights (and the absolute ban on torture). At one extreme there may again be times of great public danger to the life of the nation when some rights have to be curtailed, as they were in 1939 and derogations entered from our international human rights obligations. At other times, such as the use of 'Diplock' courts sitting without a jury during the emergency in Northern Ireland because of the prevalence of witness intimidation, Parliament may have to legislate very specific derogations to ensure the rule of law is upheld. So there is no simple answer to the question posed in the title of this paper. The balance will need to be struck and then adjusted when necessary in the light of assessment of the level, type, and persistence of the threat to public security and weighing heavily in the scales the knowledge that human rights and the rule of law are crucial components of the very security that is being fought for.

What all this adds up to in current circumstances is the need for a 'grand understanding' between Government and public on security and intelligence that results from a serious political process of rational Parliamentary debate in which the public is asked to accept that:

- there is no absolute security on offer and chasing after it does more harm than good. Providing security is an exercise in risk management. Security is a state of confidence that the major risks are being managed so that normal life can continue;
- pre-emptive secret intelligence is key to reducing the risk from terrorism to achieve the aim of security;
- there will always be unexpected events and gaps in intelligence, but overall the work of the intelligence and security services shift the odds in the public's favour, sometimes very significantly;
- intelligence gathering for the purposes of national security must include surveillance and accessing protected personal data (PROTINT), properly authorized;
- there is no general public 'right to know' about intelligence sources and methods, but the public has a right to oversight of the work of intelligence agencies by cleared Parliamentary representatives on the public's behalf, and should expect judicial oversight of the exercise of statutory authorities for intrusive investigation, with the right of investigation and redress in cases of abuse of these powers.

The Government, on the other hand, should commit the security and intelligence community to operate in turn on the basis that:

- ethics matter: there are 'red lines' that must not be crossed. So some intelligence and security opportunities have to be passed over;
- principles such as proportionality, necessity and due authority have to be followed in accordance with a published code of ethical principles;
- the effectiveness and efficiency of the intelligence community has to be subject to Parliamentary oversight including adherence to a set of ethical principles and judicial oversight of the use of Statutory powers;
- the aim in counter-terrorism is the protection of the public, and when apprehended terrorists will be prosecuted through the criminal law;
- processes must be sufficiently open to build confidence in the integrity of all involved, such as recruitment to the intelligence community; the Agencies are entitled to keep their sources and methods secret;
- Government, its agencies, and the public accept that values will be upheld, including the rule of law and working within the framework of human rights, including the fundamental right to life.

I have described public security as a shared state of mind, a state of confidence, that the major risks are sufficiently under control and can be managed so that people can go about their normal life, freely and with confidence. Life is full of surprises, sometimes unwelcome. Some level of insecurity has to be accepted day to day and lived with. There are also going to be times when due to the overwhelming pressure of events public security in general cannot be assured. Working to keep those risks to a minimum is a primary duty of government, part of the implicit contract between people and their government. Fulfilling that duty is thus integral to good government. Failure to try hard enough to do so is a likely indicator of poor government.

PART THREE
New Ways to Counter the Threat

Chapter 9

Just Wars, Just Outcomes – Reconciling Just Outcomes in Military Intervention

Shenaz Bunglawala, Rosemary Durward and Paul Schulte

The broadly conceived and repeatedly broadcast aims of the interventions in Afghanistan and Iraq – to improve peace, stability and human welfare – stand in marked contrast to the traditional purpose of victory in war that has pertained since humankind first picked up weapons. These new aims expand the already challenging Just War criteria of success following consideration of the balance of consequences. For long-term peace and stability are conditional on justice both being done and being seen to be done. Yet satisfying the contradictory concepts of justice held by all the protagonists may well be an impossibility.

Successful peace building through nation building and good governance will go some way to delivering justice. But effort must be made, too, to understand and improve the substance of relationships between individuals and groups of individuals, whether identified by political interest, tribe, sect or religion and find a common moral ground. To engage with the moral dimension, the West needs to understand better the roots of its own moral assumptions, both religious and philosophical, and the moral assumptions of the people for whom it is trying to bring stability. This points to the need for a very serious engagement with religion in peace building, not just by religious actors, but by strategists in planning and conducting future interventions.

Just War and the 'Likelihood of Success'

Contemporary Just War doctrine can be traced to St Augustine (354–430 CE) and St Thomas Aquinas (1225–1274 CE). Just War's *Jus ad bellum* requirements are that: military intervention must be for a right and necessary cause and for no other reason; intervention must be under lawful authority; there must be due consideration given to the balance of consequences, including the likelihood of success; all other options other than war must have been explored before embarking on war; and, intervention must adhere to *Jus in bello*.

Jus in bello, affecting the conduct of war, requires that military action be proportionate; that it discriminate between combatants and non-combatants; that decision-making on lethal force be based on military necessity and not convenience; and that the means and methods of warfare be limited.

Behind early Just War thinking was the need to reconcile the early Christian pacifist impulse that rejected violence, based on the Beatitudes in Matthew's Gospel (Matthew 5: 3–12), with the reality of violence and aggression in war. In its original form, Just War involved the promotion of good to avoid a lesser evil, placing importance on right motives for intervention. St Augustine listed *'The passion for inflicting harm, the cruel thirst for vengeance, an unpacific and relentless spirit, the fever of revolt, the lust of power, and such like things, all these are rightly condemned in war.'* St Augustine argued, instead, that: *'True religion looks upon as peaceful those wars that are waged not for motives of aggrandisement or cruelty, but with the object of securing peace, of punishing evil doers, and of uplifting the good.'*[1] The inward disposition of the soldier was significant in St Augustine's concept of Just War, and likewise the motives of the state. Rather than endorse self-defence, St Augustine affirmed an obligation to defend neighbours.

St Thomas Aquinas, in *Summa Theologiae IIaIIae*, Q. 40:1, mirrored St Augustine when he rejected motives of anger and revenge in war, going further by insisting on the right of self-defence, the duty of 'proportionality' and the 'balance of consequence'. On the latter, right intentions were sufficient to justify warfare, even where innocent bystanders were injured and killed.[2]

Just War has become an international norm over centuries signifying legitimacy of military intervention across cultures and states.[3] The doctrine does, nonetheless, face difficulties in its encounter with the Islamic tradition of Holy War, or *jihad*. The shaping of the Just War doctrine in Western theological, philosophical and legal thought, and its progressive shift away from religious to temporal authority, in determining just cause and defining the legitimate authority to wage war, demurs from the Islamic tradition past and present.

The progressive secularisation of Just War theory in Western culture renders the concept of *Jihad* as Holy War, or war for religion, difficult for those that have shifted the basis of their reasoning and justification for war away from religion and religious authorities. James Turner Johnson argues that the rejection of war for religion by the West early in the modern period has made it 'especially difficult for Western culture to accept and make sense of the ongoing presence of the phenomenon of *jihad* as war for the faith in modern Muslim societies.'[4]

---

[1]   Quoted in Charles Reed, *Changing Society and the Churches: Just War?* (London, 2004), p. 39.

[2]   Major Jennifer B. Bottoms, 'When Close Doesn't Count: An analysis of Israel's jus ad bellum and jus in bello in the 2006 Israel-Lebanon War', *The Army Lawyer*, DA PAM 27-5-431, (April 2009), pp. 27–30.

[3]   See Paul Robinson (ed.), *Just War in Comparative Perspective* (Aldershot, 2003).

[4]   James Taylor Johnson, *The Holy War Idea in Western and Islamic Traditions* (Pennsylvania, 1997) p. 15. But on this point see above, Chapters 2 and 3, by Tim Winter and Ahmad Achtar.

The problem is amplified by the complications that arise from the divergence of the contemporary situation of sovereign Muslim states and the structure of international society from the classical juridical writings on *Jihad* in Islam, which are formulated on the presumption of a single, unitary Islamic state and a single religio-political authority at its head – the Caliph-Imam.

While Just War in the Western tradition has supplanted religious authority with the primacy of the temporal authority of the secular state, and secularised the reasoning behind *jus ad bellum* and *jus in bello*, so that war becomes a function of the state and not of religion, religion, by contrast, continues to resonate heavily in Islamic thinking on jihad.

The disparity on the prominence of religion aside, Just War does provide Western and Muslim governments and military strategists with some common ground, thus offering some scope for successfully engaging religion in promoting justice and peace-building in post-war situations.

The Just War doctrine provides an important check-list for governments, but as a check list not an exact science, involving judgement in its interpretation. For example, Just War doctrine could not prevent an intervention in Iraq based on mistaken judgements of possession of illicit weapons of mass destruction rather than an immediate and direct threat.

Indeed, the debate over the Iraq intervention tended to focus on the legality of the decision at the expense of other Just War criteria. Intervention in Afghanistan was judged legal by the Security Council of the United Nations based on self-defence following 9/11. The intervention in Iraq was judged legal not by the UN but by the governments of the intervening forces. It was widely criticised for bypassing the UN Security Council, with intervention piggy-backing onto historic resolutions that preceded and followed the expulsion of Iraq from Kuwait. In this case, where the intervention could not be proven to be manifestly illegal, other Just War principles such as the balance of consequences were overridden by political and military necessity, concerns about the future enforceability of global controls over the most dangerous weapons technologies, and even expediency.

Subsequent difficulties in Afghanistan and Iraq highlight the importance of satisfying Just War criteria in all dimensions prior to intervention. To judge the balance of consequences and likelihood of success, in particular, there must be some clarity about prospects for Just Outcomes. St Augustine understood that there cannot be a lasting peace without justice, nor can there be justice without peace. At the same time, justice requires more than peace.[5] The failure to consider Just Outcomes means that the conditions that contribute to violence will remain, if not worsen. Here strategic prudence coincides with morality.

---

[5] St Augustine, trans. H. Bettenson, *City of God* (London, 2003), p. 869.

Just Outcomes and the Moral High Ground

An internationally accepted check-list of principles underpinning Just Outcomes does not exist. Traditionally, the main aim of war has been victory and the focus in international law has been on the right and humane treatment of the vanquished by the victor, rather than the duty to build peace and a capacity for stable independence.

The dictionary definition of 'just' is: *'acting or done in accordance with what is morally right or fair'*; with justice relating to 'fairness', and 'the maintenance of authority in the maintenance of right'. But what, after all, is 'fair' and 'right'? In the case of Afghanistan and Iraq, answers are likely to be determined not by some objective and universal measuring rod, but by local and regional norms underpinning relationships within the political, social, economic, judicial and security realms.

Attitudes to peace and war, the relationship between the individual and the law, the nature of society, the relationship between the individual, ethnic or religious group and the state, attitudes to conquest and outside interference influenced by historic memories and contemporary experience, preferences between short- and long-term goals, attitudes to violence, pain, life and death, belief in God and the kind of God believed in, will all influence judgements about 'fair' and 'right'. The chaos in the wake of the interventions in Afghanistan and Iraq and the violence perpetrated against Western forces and internally organised groups and militia, reflects the diverse range of answers to these questions.[6] Religion and history will be significant in shaping the answers, but it is important to stress that Islam and history can only be viewed through contemporary eyes and Islam's expression, whether fundamentalist or liberal, today is both a feature of and reaction to modernity.[7]

Building Peace and Liberal Interventionism

Building peace depends on effective nation-building. This aims to deliver for each individual the basic necessities of life – food, water, fuel, and shelter, as well as negative freedoms – from fear, violence, hunger, powerlessness; and to enable the exercise of positive freedoms – to make use of new opportunities for the benefit of the individual and community. It aims to achieve strong, accountable civilian controlled armed forces, with a capacity to defend the state against internal and external security threats; an effective and accountable police force and judiciary,

---

[6]   See Ahmad Achtar's analysis in Chapter 3 of typologies of Islamic responses to the challenges of modernity and how the varied ideological orientations of contemporary Islamic movements influence Muslim reactions to Western intervention in Iraq and Afghanistan.

[7]   See Katerina Dalacoura, *Islam, Liberalism and Human Rights: Implications for International Relations* (London, 2003/1998), p. 67.

capable of upholding the rule of law and protecting the citizenry; a strong and vibrant economy and society; and representative central and local government structures with a vigorous civil sector. These pillars are inter-related and underpinned by security. Hence, economic activity cannot take place effectively without the protection of people and property. Stable government and an independent judiciary are co-dependent and also rely on the provision of security.[8]

At the base of liberal interventionism is the assumption that intervention can liberate subjugated or politically misled peoples, who will immediately or in time (as with Germany or Japan after 1945) come to welcome and flourish under their new freedoms.[9] Elections made possible by the interventions in Afghanistan and Iraq have demonstrated a strong swell of popular support for the political and economic possibilities of freedom. However, the interventions have also provoked tribal, nationalist and, in particular, religious opposition to the presence and projects of foreigners, allowing a resurgence of the Taliban in Afghanistan after initial defeat. In Iraq, in addition to attacks on the Coalition Forces, religious violence was sparked between Sunni and Shia sects, where Saddam had previously kept latent resentments under repressive control. The difficulties in unifying ethnic, religious and tribal groups in Afghanistan and Iraq have turned nation-building into Contested State Building.

The Religious Dimension

Religiously motivated violence within Afghanistan and Iraq feeds Western anxiety about the global rise of violently intolerant religious fundamentalism, which provided the original case (Afghanistan) and context (Iraq) for the interventions. At the same time, violent Islamist fundamentalism is fuelled by the physical presence of Western forces and the perception of malign intent behind Western interference. Al-Qa'ida has exploited global communication mechanisms to point to the illegitimacy of the West's presence in the Muslim world, based on the historic legacy of injustice in the crusading and colonial periods. After 9/11, Bin Laden launched an ideological assault on the West which was anti-American and anti-Israeli, and interspersed with references to Islamic teaching to support the idea of a Holy War against infidels. Bin Laden's claim to be able to speak on behalf of the Islamic world is strongly contested by other Muslims, as Ahmad Achtar explains with devastating clarity in Chapter 3. Nonetheless, until Afghanistan and Iraq have achieved full independence and created states that are flourishing economically, politically and socially, the heavily armed presence of the West in those countries, will give ammunition to Al-Qa'ida's assertion that the West has perpetuated a

---

[8] See Francis Fukuyama (ed.), *Nation-Building: Beyond Afghanistan and Iraq* (Baltimore, 2006).

[9] See Ian Clark, *The Post Cold War Order: The Spoils of Peace* (Oxford, 2001).

situation of inequality which allows it to dominate the Muslim world. On that basis, success in the peace building project is vital.

Success will also impact on domestic security within Western states as those involved in terrorist attacks in London and elsewhere have frequently referred to the same 'grievance narrative' in their suicide video messages.

But the overall narrative also emphasises the double standards employed by the West in applying international law. For example, Israel's non-compliance with UN resolutions is used by extremists to depict the West as upholding selective justice; one that sees it turning a blind eye to the transgressions of its allies (Israel *and* authoritarian Muslim states) whilst pressing others, like Iraq, to comply with international law or face invasion. The narrative has enabled the extremists' simplistic duality of the 'West' and its visceral hostility to the 'Muslim world' to gain currency and considerable support.

There is, among large swathes of Muslim opinion, a deep rooted sense of bias in the West's application of law and policy, with Israel often cited as the most blatant example of Western states' willingness to acquiesce to powerful lobby groups and divert from the moral aim of impartially brokering peaceful relations between antagonistic parties, particularly in the Middle East. There is a pervasive sense amongst Muslims of an influential Zionist lobby advocating uncritical support of Israel and so overwhelming moral purpose and neutrality in Western policy on the Middle East. Success of the projects in Afghanistan and Iraq might go some way towards exonerating principled Western interventions by removing major current grievances. But it is unlikely that it could by itself expunge that now deeply culturally entrenched story.

Violent Islamist extremism has been ascribed to many causes. There has been a visible post-colonial failure of Muslim elites to build inclusive, just and effective nation states, leading to a lack of popular political participation and *rentier* states, uneven economic development and cultural erosion.[10] On this reckoning, the interventions (which occurred years after the first Al-Qaʻida attack on the World Trade Center in February 1993 or the East African Embassy bombings in August 1998) merely exacerbated an existing problem rather than created it. Historic animosities reaching back beyond the Crusades, and the perception of contemporary double standards ('selective justice') in international law and Western hypocrisy in preaching democracy but supporting authoritarian but conveniently well disposed Muslim regimes, have been powerful, mutually reinforcing, motivators for terrorism. Given the underlying frustration against the West and its relationship with the Muslim world, particularly in the post-colonial period and beyond, it is hard to disentangle resentment against intervention as a cause of violence from generalised anger with the West and its perceived culpability in the problems of the Muslim world.

---

[10]   S. Sayyid, *A Fundamental Fear: Eurocentrism and the Emergence of Islam*, (London/NY, 2003). pp. 18–22.

Political expectations of justice and subsequent disappointments have underlined religious and cultural differences. Western perceptions of the needs of modern representative government in plural societies based on tolerance, consent and the separation of power, for example, have not yet been reconciled with Islam's insistence that there can be no separation of religion from politics. At first sight, religion divides the participants in nation building by virtue of the existence of two distinct traditions amongst the indigenous people and intervening forces, Muslim and Judeo-Christian, and within the indigenous communities, between Islamic sects that differ in their commitment to a return to fundamentals. The co-opting of religion by sects to justify cultural practices that contravene human rights sharpens this division and highlights tensions between the intervening force and the host state.

Muslim identity has become a more potent political issue. Thus, Israel's occupation of territory beyond its 1967 borders has done much to strengthen Muslim identity as a bulwark against Zionist fundamentalist objectives. In addition, cultural practices ascribed to Islam have shaped patriarchal societies in Afghanistan and Iraq in which laws flowing from democratically endorsed constitutions have been flouted in favour of the subordination and widespread abuse of women, including a tolerance for 'honour killings'. Western calls for women's freedom, in turn, have turned the limits on the freedom of women into an identity issue for some traditionalist Muslims. In this sense, too, religion is reacting to modernity.

In another twist linking actions abroad with domestic consequences, we see the status of women in Iraq and Afghanistan interspersed in debates in Europe and North America over Muslim women and the public sphere. The issue of 'liberation through military intervention' in Iraq and Afghanistan and its positive and negative effects on female emancipation is reproduced in the Muslim diaspora in debates on Islam and women's rights.[11] The 'Western' project of gender equality thus becomes an issue not of Western imposition of foreign values but of supporting Muslims in their battle against a patriarchal traditionalist minority in both interventionary and domestic contexts. It is a project more complicated than one of imposing alien norms. The project itself is increasingly shaped by the contributions of Muslims, particularly women living in the West, of ideas on gender equality in Islam.[12]

---

[11] See Yasmin Ali Bhai Brown, 'Who'd be female under Islamic Law?', *The Independent*, (4 May 200) and article response on *Engage*, 'On women and women's rights under Islam', http://iengage.org.uk/component/content/article/1-news/325-on-women-and-womens-rights-under-islam. See also Nuseiba, 'Mona Eltahawy on Afghan women', http://nuseiba.wordpress.com/2009/04/28/mona-eltahawy-on-afghanistan/, accessed 8 and 16 May respectively.

[12] See Asma Barlas, *Believing Women in Islam: Unreading Patriarchal Interpretations of the Qur'an* (Austin, Texas, 2002).

The Decline of Intervention and Moral Responsibilities

The post 9/11 interventions in Afghanistan and Iraq may mark the climax but also – some predict – the beginning of the end of the era of intervention that began with NATO's intervention in Bosnia and Kosovo. A major factor may be the impossibility of achieving peace with justice. Controversies about the legality of the invasion of Iraq, accusations about the conduct of the intervention forces, particularly over the treatment of detainees, the material and human cost, the failure to alleviate the threat from Islamist terrorism and insurgency have raised doubts about the sustainability of the operations. A related uncertainty is, if a Just War has to be conducted in the interests of a just peace, whether a war that is manifestly unjust can produce a just peace?[13]

There are accusations that such stabilisation operations amount to neo-colonialism and that they exacerbate interreligious tensions and the terrorist threat, born of an existing deep sense of injustice in the Muslim world. By interfering in the internal affairs of states, established norms of respect for sovereignty are loosened, encouraging international anarchy. Above all, critics stress the human costs, to local populations and Western troops, of anti-occupation insurgencies and general lawlessness. From this perspective, containment and diplomatic engagement, with all their limitations, rather than intervention will generally appear a more prudent and morally attractive strategy.

The arrest warrant issued in March 2009 by the Chief Prosecutor of the International Criminal Court (ICC) against President Omar Hassan al-Bashir, President of Sudan, for alleged crimes of genocide in Darfur draws the prospect of an effective international judicial process against transgressors of international law a little closer, and with the possibility of making the likelihood of war a little more remote. If Saddam Hussein could have been effectively prosecuted for genocide and war crimes in Halabja in 1987, then he would not have posed a threat to Kuwait, and the course of Iraqi history, and that of the international community would have been different. In reality, the United States was still opposing the ICC right up to its establishment in 2002. After Saddam Hussein's capture by American troops, it was the Iraqi government that insisted on justice being done, a kind of justice by the death penalty, that, although consistent with US and Iraqi law, is increasingly viewed internationally as violating human rights law on the rights to life, to protection from cruel, inhuman and degrading treatment, contained in the Universal Declaration of Human Rights.

This has been speculation in hindsight. The risks and costs of military intervention, and even interventions where just cause is debated, do not negate the argument that, once mandated, there are strong moral and strategic reasons for continuing to engage and give appropriate support to emergent governments.

---

[13]   Michael Walzer argues 'manifestly unjust wars waged for conquest or economic aggrandizement are unlikely to foster a just peace since both these types involve acts of theft.' Michael Walzer, 'Just and Unjust Occupations', *Dissent*, (winter, 2004), p. 61.

On moral grounds, there is a responsibility to 'make good' the job that was begun, since the consequences may otherwise be a still worse security situation with un-reconciled animosities and continued human tragedy, so long as there is some expectation that it can be made good. On prudent strategic grounds, there is a case for continuing comprehensive engagement in support of modernisers because failure to do so means that whatever military outcomes might be achieved, are temporary. And such failures would betray local allies and encourage the spread of expressions of Islam, which are avowedly antithetical to the West's interests and inimical to the interests of large swathes of the indigenous populations.

These arguments do assume that the benefits of engagement outweigh the disadvantages. The dilemma remains that Western military engagement within the Islamic world is a double- edged sword which can both stimulate surges of violent, religiously-based extremism and protect and enable reformers, modernisers and moderates. Until Afghanistan and Iraq are flourishing economically, politically and socially, with governments that are not seen as either criminally corrupt or subservient Western clients, (and which could certainly include fundamentalist parties, hostile to democratic changes induced by intervention, providing their opposition remained peaceful) the presence of the West in Afghanistan and Iraq will give ammunition to Al-Qa'ida's assertion that the West has perpetuated a situation of inequality which allows it to dominate the Muslim world. But to conclude that all military interventions, even those guided by Just War principles and backed by development assistance,[14] by non-Muslims in countries with Muslim majorities are morally unjustified would have perverse and undesirable results. Such a principle would reduce the constraints against externally aggressive or internally tyrannical behaviour. It would therefore increase tendencies towards international or internal disorder, which would ultimately damage the interests of Muslims in those states.

The level of conflict in Afghanistan and Iraq is likely to increase rather than diminish, without external involvement. Over the next 30 years, demographic trends in much of the Muslim world will lead to a significant increase in population. Unless opportunities for economic growth are at least preserved, and if at all possible, enhanced, the result will be a widespread reduction in standards of living and widespread human misery. The avoidance, or minimisation, of internal and external conflict will be a vital precondition for improved economic growth. The major trends of globalisation will continue and may well accelerate. This means that flows of ideas, migrants, refugees, aid, investment, energy supplies and commodities, including drugs, illicit weapons, or components of WMD proliferation, will extend and intensify all across the world, offering unprecedented opportunities for prosperity, knowledge and mutual understanding but also increasing risks to security.

---

[14] As set out in current UK doctrine on *The Comprehensive Approach*, 2006, Joint Discussion Note 4/05, Ministry of Defence, Shrivenham, available at: http://www.mod.uk/NR/rdonlyres/BEE7F0A4-C1DA-45F8-9FDC-7FBD25750EE3/0/dcdc21_jdn4_05.pdf.

Given the increasing penetration of interests, concerns and international public sympathy for human tragedies in areas like Darfur or Somalia, it would be historically anomalous to insist now that the non-Muslim forces could never justifiably intervene in the Muslim world. But, that said, the balance between the use of force and other methods to transform situations of instability, failing states and poor governance must remain open to debate.

Typically, priorities following interventions that are primarily imposed by force or levered through threats, denial and coercive inducements tend to favour structures to maintain stability rather than to achieve justice. If there is any justice at all in the outcome, it may be punitive and partial, there for some and not for others, leaving room for resentment to build up opposition which then attains a momentum that is difficult to halt. The United States insistence in Iraq that detentions under Multinational Force (MNF) Authority should not take account of human rights law but only the laws of war is one example. The result is that detainees have not had access to defence counsel. The United Nations Assistance Mission for Iraq (UNAMI), set up to promote and protect human rights and the rule of law in close collaboration with Iraqi and non-governmental sectors, under UNSCR 1770 (2007), reported in 2007 that:

> procedures in force have resulted in prolonged detention without trial, with many security internees held for several years with minimal access to the evidence against them and without their defence counsel having access to such evidence.[15]

In March 2007, the total number of detainees held across Iraq stood at 37,641. The highest proportion of that related to MNF detainees, at 17,898, according to UNAMI. In the period from March to June 2007, that figure increased to 21,112, attributable to arrests carried out under the Baghdad Security Plan.[16] Overcrowding and poorly trained security forces left prisoners exposed to inhuman conditions, including torture.

The continued deployment of Western troops in Iraq and Afghanistan, building up and supporting the local security forces, would serve no purpose once adequate security had been achieved. They have remained because the rule of law and norms of consultation in politics and economic activity have been compromised by internal violence and cross-border attacks that local security forces cannot deal with alone. Although the use of force by local and interventionary Security Forces can intensify resentment, this must be set alongside the certainty that force as a last resort is necessary at times, for the provision of security and stability, necessary for the furtherance of good governance in the political, economic and judicial realms.

---

[15]   UN Assistance Mission for Iraq (UNAMI), *Human Rights Report*, (1 April 30 June 2007), p. 25.

[16]   UN Assistance Mission for Iraq (UNAMI), *Human Rights Report*, (1 April 30 June 2007), pp. 20–21.

For the moral use of force, there must be an assumption that its utility is provisional, and there must be substantial investment in training along with high levels of discipline to ensure it is used proportionately and discriminately for militarily necessary purposes only. The experience of the Bosnian army after the Dayton Accords indicates that it is possible, through development of an *esprit de corps* and professional training to turn an army divided by ethnic origin and religion into a cohesive force. However, even the best-trained forces are challenged to abide by the principles of proportionality, military necessity and limitation when confronted by suicide bombers who wage 'war amongst the people' with deliberate and programmatic lack of pity.[17]

Investment and the creation of opportunities for the ordinary people of Iraq and Afghanistan are intended to achieve peace. But a fledgling market economy cannot develop without protection, and the task of reconstruction is made deliberately harder without security. Trust necessary for peaceful human interaction is destroyed by anarchy which, in the extreme, can only be returned to a situation of order through the threat or use of force. Each Iraqi and Afghan death impacts on friends, neighbours, and relations making reconciliation, recovery and conflict resolution harder. The Geneva Conventions have universal application in constraining the use of force. But to Al-Qaʻida's supporters, there are no constraints because the ultimate goal blesses the means.

The challenge for forces attempting to contain their brand of terror is to uphold the standards set by the Geneva Conventions and maintain the moral high ground. Observance of international law is an important aspect of building and maintaining a consensus on the aims of just outcomes. Internal investigations into allegations of criminal and other activity by occupation forces need to be rigorously pursued, as in the case of the Abu Ghraib prison abuses. It is imperative to demonstrate to both the local Muslim society and the wider Muslim world, that moral standards are strictly observed and equally applied. In respecting and complying with the Geneva Conventions, occupation forces undermine the terrorists' narrative that law and morality are selectively observed by the West in its encounter with Muslims.[18]

By the same token, it is critical that difficult questions in the moral realm are not ignored in favour of sustaining hierarchies of power that encourage only short term stability. Whilst the Security Forces work to provide stability to support the pillars of good governance, including the judiciary, the political system, civic society and the economy, there remain many instances where international norms are being ignored. Women's rights constitute perhaps the most prominent issue, where Islam is quoted to justify practices which are abhorrent by any objective or universalist measure of human worth. From Afghanistan, in particular, there is

---

[17] See General Rupert Smith, *The Utility of Force: The Art of War in the Modern World* (London, 2006).

[18] See also Ahmad Achtar's discussion in Chapter 3 of Dr Sayyid Faḍl's challenge to Al- Qaʻida's narrative on the principle of reciprocity and the onus on Muslims to observe the moral high ground in their reactions to alleged abuses.

a litany of cases of state sanctioned abuse of women reported in the newspapers. In a woman's prison on the outskirts of Kabul, for example, women can be charged and imprisoned over 'moral crimes', including running away from an abusive husband and being the victim of rape, some by the police who detain them.[19] When deliberately tolerated by the official legal system, this amounts to subverting the constitutional and legal arrangements voted for by the great majority of the Afghan population (including, of course women) in order to accommodate the passionate self-interested prejudices of a proportion of violent men. Similar systematic abuses are reported in Iraq. It is not enough for the West to take a morally relativistic position and 'turn a blind eye'. Moral relativism in this case ignores the fact that the abused have no voice to express their cultural, moral or religious preferences. It also erodes the possibility of principled international support for future interventionary campaigns.[20]

Engaging with the Moral and Religious Dimension

The difficulties in Afghanistan and Iraq of achieving good governance are complex, involving former regime elements – resentful supporters of displaced elites – and criminals, not motivated by ideology or 'belief' but by mercenary payment to snipe at soldiers or place Improvised Explosive Devices. In addition, there are real disputes and anxieties relating to inter-ethnic, religious and tribal conflict that are persuading people to take up or maintain arms, as well as a prevailing insecurity in parts of Afghanistan and much of Iraq that makes possession of weapons seem essential for survival.

The attractions of stability based on traditional hierarchies and structures – patriarchal structures, for example – make the 'good' in good governance vulnerable. At the same time, though progress over women's rights and roles may hold the key to the transformation of Afghan and Iraqi society, almost by definition, lasting and transformative progress can only be made in ways which are regarded as legitimate and consistent with local traditions and religious attitudes. It is hard to promote 'good' without reference to Islam, for it provides the moral reference point for the majority of Afghans and Iraqis.

Long-term stability requires laws and constitutional relationships that have a moral underpinning. Religious discourse is significant in defining goals and also in finding solutions amongst the Afghan and Iraqi people and amongst political elites. Peace building, as defined by the United Nations, involves reconciliation, apology and forgiveness of past harm. These are concepts with religious roots and their relationship to concepts of justice and resort to force needs to be explored by

---

[19]   Tim Albone, 'New Afghan Women MPs pledge to roll back the tyranny of men', *The Times* (2 October 2005).

[20]   See also 'Silence is Violence: End the abuse of women in Afghanistan'. UNAMA and OHCHR (July 2009).

all faiths.[21] Where deeply rooted differences arise in the moral realm, they need to be addressed, rather than ignored.

Here, religion has the potential to unite, in a way that politics has not succeeded in doing, through the connection of the three Abrahamic faiths with one God, understood as a God of justice. The first step should be a humble acknowledgement of the strands in Christian, Jewish as well as Muslim traditions that commend violence and war. This should lead to a search for self understanding and a genuine search for mutual forgiveness and reconciliation of past injustices, as well as a mutual commitment to reject violence and anarchy.[22]

There are verses of the Qur'an that are instructive in this regard:

> It may be that God will grant love (and friendship) between you and those whom you (now) hold as enemies. For God has power over all things; God is Forgiving, Most Merciful. God forbids you not, with regard to those who fight you not for (your) Faith nor drive you out of your homes, from dealing kindly and justly with them: for God loves those who are just.[23]

The next step should be consideration of how that deepened self-understanding can relate to the modern world which both glorifies violence but yet no longer sees war as heroic, but a source of human misery and suffering. This step must, at risk of acting in an illiberal fashion, discredit fundamentalist reasoning that treats religious texts, their own and others' as though they are car manuals with 'bolt-on' rules, rather than as a discourse through which truth can be found.

Finally, religion needs to challenge the myth perpetuated by the Enlightenment that there must be a separation of religion from politics. That may be desirable if religion is assumed to be trying to impose a higher authority, interpreted by humankind in the name of God, which is authoritarian. But it is not the reality, given that religion provides the meta-narrative for progress and lack of it for the vast majority, even in late modernity, as well as the context and basis for a great deal of ethical thinking today. Hence, religion has a role in the development of human rights law, international justice and in their implementation.

Just as moral principles should not be used to club religion and culture, so, as the Indian Supreme Court once commented, religion and culture should not be used to club morality. The failure to address morality, and concentrate solely on the provision of security for good governance leads to confusion. Beyond the immediate goals of defeating the Taliban, finding bin Laden, eliminating security

---

[21]   See Andrew Rigby, 'Forgiveness and Reconciliation in Jus Post Bellum', in Mark Evans (ed.), *Just War Theory: A Reappraisal* (Edinburgh, 2005), pp. 177–200.

[22]   See Rosemary Durward and Lee Marsden (eds.), *Religion, Conflict and Military Intervention* (Aldershot, 2009) which explores Christian and Islamist attitudes to violence, war, reconciliation and peace in Afghanistan, Iraq and Pakistan.

[23]   The Qur'an, translated by Abdullah Yusuf Ali. (Hertfordshire, UK: Wordsworth Editions, 2000), chapter 60, verses 7–8.

threats, and ending high-profile non-compliance over WMD, the interventions have been sustained in the longer term by the hope of achieving 'good' through the reinforcement of international law, which includes human rights law, and the rehabilitation of black holes of poverty, misgovernment and desperation. It is vitally important not to confuse practices which are universally unacceptable (for example, unprosecuted rape) with those which, although undesirable in Western culture, nevertheless reflect Afghan choices.[24] But total unwillingness to bring religion or morality into interventionary discourse on security, ignoring areas in the moral realm that are considered taboo, justified by moral and cultural relativism and driven by concern about inconvenient consequences for short and medium term stability, could well jeopardise long-term stability.

Conclusion and Recommendations

A pessimistic view might be that Islam and the Western world are so incompatible that there can be no agreement on common values and goals and where power should lie. That would also be the view of local insurgents who try to prove it by their violence. This chapter proposes, however, that there are sufficient areas of commonality and overlap, shared experience and values in the moral realm, to suggest a workable platform from which to build. Basic human needs and welfare are broadly the same across religious communities but we must be tentative on such a complex subject. We could say that the Just Outcomes to be sought should be perceived as legitimate, based on perceptions of fairness and justice from all sides, from the West, with its Judeo-Christian heritage, and from the Islamic world, especially in relation to the local traditions of the country concerned. All this is very likely to require a psychological shift away from punitive justice and towards justice based on fairness, human dignity and security. This chapter proposes some possible criteria for Just Outcomes that reflect the importance of constitutional and legal but also moral criteria. They are that Just Outcomes should, at a minimum:

1. accord with and uphold international law;
2. bring fewer human and economic costs than those of not intervening;
3. neutralise or prevent a recurrence of the precipitating threat or violence;
4. ensure a fairer distribution of power;
5. enhance security with good governance;
6. restore human dignity.

The objective must be to move from a position of victor in which there are also losers, to a position where benefits are shared. It may be that Just Outcomes have to be 'just good enough', given the strength of internal tribal or ethnic divisions

---

[24]   See Anila Daulatzai, 'The Discursive Occupation of Afghanistan', *British Journal of Middle Eastern Studies*, vol. 35, issue 3, (December 2008), pp. 419–435.

and the regional context in which Afghanistan and Iraq are situated. Afghanistan faces instability on its borders with Pakistan and Iraq has Iran, Syria and Saudi Arabia vying for dominance, as well as the nearby Arab-Israeli conflict that transfixes, unites and divides. It is axiomatic that the achievement of Just Outcomes becomes more difficult where Peace Building is contested and civil war exists or is imminent. War is the domain of tragedy and it is unsurprising therefore that there may have to be tragic choices in accepting many imperfect arrangements to end or diminish murderous conflict as a precondition for autonomous state building, normal politics and effective development.[25]

For planning and operational purposes, nevertheless, there needs to be a clear view of Just Outcomes, to determine what to aim at and to judge when objectives have been achieved. In addition, the overall vision of intended outcomes needs to be shared by the majority of the indigenous populations, and not be one-sided and imposed from outside.

Christianity, Islam and Judaism all point to a heavenly peace. The hope for peace on earth is symbolised by the statue in front of the United Nations building in New York underwritten by Isaiah's injunction, '*They shall beat their swords into ploughshares and their spears into pruning hooks.*'(Isaiah 2:4 and Micah 4:3). Some fear that divisions between Islam and the West at a moral level run so deep that there can be no prospect of peace founded on a shared view of just outcomes. This is, from the liberal or cosmopolitan perspective, a message of global despair.[26] For the sake of long term peace and stability, rather than short-term gain, it is important to address, debate and seek agreement on the moral dimension of Just Outcomes across cultures and between religious sects, at all levels of engagement, even though the questions involved are sensitive and sometimes incendiary.

To shy away from debate is to undercut the nation and state building project in its infancy, leaving a legacy of dispute and disagreement that will return in the long term to destabilise and disrupt the peace. If the perpetrators of xenophobic violence succeed in halting the project of reconstruction and nation building, it would be an example of the thwarting of Just Outcomes. The temporary success of violence in preventing the achievement of rightly intended actions and Just Outcomes is

---

[25]   This is not a novel predicament: '*It is the logic of our times, No subject for immortal verse – That we who lived by honest dreams defend the bad against the worse.*' As Cecil Day Lewis observed in 1941 in *Where Are The War Poets?*

[26]   As discussed by David Fisher and Brian Wicker in the Introduction, Bernard Lewis and Samuel Huntingdon are among those whose works on Islamic culture and politics posit the notion of an ideological incompatibility between Islamic and Western countries on political values and processes. Their views are echoed by and influence the work of neo-conservatives who similarly believe in entrenched and insuperable differences that make consensual decisions on state building and moral values between Muslims and Christians impossible. Paradoxically, such works reinforce the binary world view and discourse of Al-Qa'ida, a discourse that sees assimilation or domination as the only means of dealing with value pluralism.

hardly unprecedented in human history. The consequences of violence are tragic, but peace cannot be at any price.

That said, the significance of the moral realm in achieving Just Outcomes means that the balance between the use of force and other methods to transform failing states such as Afghanistan and Iraq must remain open to debate. The Christian and Islamic perspective is that peace is the only way to construct a more just and solid society. Success needs to be measured against winning the peace, as much as winning the war. The lesson of peace building is that campaigns need to be comprehensive and not end simply when the main shooting stops. In the violence confronted today in Afghanistan and Iraq, that does not mean reducing the role of the armed forces in providing security, but it may mean considerably more effort in the other pillars of good governance, with effort to ensure a moral dimension to considerations of Just Outcomes.

But it is also important to remember that responsibilities for achieving Just Outcomes do not intrinsically rest only with Western interventionary states – at least once post-interventionary nation building has been endorsed by the United Nations. It would be easier to reach Just Outcomes in Iraq and Afghanistan if the process were assisted by the direct involvement of Muslim states that have, through democratic processes, more successfully managed religious, ethnic or sectarian differences; for example Turkey or Malaysia. Part of the violent opposition to intervention enacted by Al-Qaʿida and others is that it reproduces the Manichean split between good and evil, or religious virtue and technocratic militarised and oppressive power on which they insist. An important way of subverting that simple, easily assimilated and profoundly destructive binary representation of the world would be to strengthen and expand the contributions of Muslim countries themselves in the usually dangerous and painful business of contested state building by contributing armed forces as well as money and influence. There are useful precedents in this regard, for example, the contribution of troops from Jordan, Malaysia and Pakistan to UNPROFOR in Bosnia and Turkey's contribution of troops and aid to Lebanon (2006) and Afghanistan.

While state building exercises in Iraq and Afghanistan can suffer from disputes over the conduct or legality of the military interventions, the issue to be faced now, and one which involves Muslim states, is the future of the people of Iraq and Afghanistan, although the requirement will differ according to local circumstances. Justice is often not achieved without human loss and those, worldwide, who yearn for it, or denounce its absence, should ask themselves what actions might lie within their power to extend, reinforce and guarantee it.

Chapter 10

'Eating Soup with a Knife' – Counterinsurgency and Just War.

Hugh Beach

'To make war upon rebellion is messy and slow, like eating soup with a knife.'

T.E. Lawrence, *Seven Pillars of Wisdom: a Triumph.*

This chapter examines the way in which Just War principles can be applied to the theory and practice of counterinsurgency. It is relevant to the 'War on Terror' for two reasons. The first is that, at the level of *in bello*, counterinsurgency provides the best-fitting framework for addressing strategic problems in defeating campaigns of terror.[1] Given the aims and capabilities of those who wage such campaigns, their defining strategy, in the early stages at least, is bound to be one of insurgency. Only rarely can they advance to the type of set-piece confrontation that amounts to civil war. Thus it is no surprise that the more 'warlike' excursions of the United States in recent years, in Afghanistan and Iraq, have morphed seamlessly into counterinsurgency, because insurgency is the default mode which their opponents are bound to adopt. Sarah Sewall, one of the influential co-authors of the recent American Field Manual of Counterinsurgency, puts the point as follows:

> Increasingly, analysts argue that the Al-Qaʿida-inspired Salafist terrorism network is functioning as a modern-day global insurgency. Any effective campaign against terrorism must include paramilitary, political, economic, psychological and civic actions along with military efforts. There are important differences … between counterinsurgency and an effort to defeat Al-Qaʿida and its allies, but the overall strategic problem is uncannily parallel.[2]

The second reason is that the way in which a nation tackles the very difficult task of counterinsurgency, and its success in that effort, is bound to affect future decisions *ad bellum* in the campaign against terror. The American failure in Vietnam cast a long shadow. Similar doubts are now re-surfacing. To quote Sarah Sewall again:

---

[1]   David Kilcullen, 'Counterinsurgency *Redux*' *Survival*, 48/4, (winter, 2006–07), p. 111.

[2]   US Army and Marine Corps *Counterinsurgency Field Manual, FM, 3-24* (Chicago, 2007). See Introduction by Sarah Sewall, p. xlii.

Americans yearn to understand a world in which old assumptions and advantages no longer seem relevant. They wonder if it is possible to secure the Somalias, Afghanistans and Iraqs, let alone advisable to try. [Counterinsurgency] doctrine raises fundamental questions about the legitimacy, purposes and limits of U.S. power. ... In explaining what "fighting well" requires, the doctrine raises profound questions about which wars the United States should fight.[3]

Origins

It is a useful exercise, if boring, to start with definitions. Logically 'insurgency' comes first. An insurgency is a struggle to control a contested political space, between a state (or group of states or occupying powers) and one or more popularly based non-state challengers. 'Counterinsurgency' covers all measures adopted to suppress an insurgency. Insurgencies seldom succeed in overthrowing established states, though they may play a part in dismembering or ravaging failed ones as in Somalia and East Timor. Sometimes governments or invading coalitions have initiated campaigns to which the insurgents simply reacted – Iraq and Chechnya are examples. In Pakistan's campaign in South Waziristan some, at least, of the insurgents, so far from being revolutionaries, are tribesmen fighting to preserve their traditional culture against an intruder.[4]

The classical theory of counterinsurgency developed as a response to the wars of national liberation following World War II, though it had deeper roots in works like that by T.E. Lawrence quoted at the head of this chapter.[5] Among the more important exponents were David Galula, a lieutenant-colonel in the French army, who served in China, Greece, Indochina and Algeria, and wrote a book while on sabbatical at Harvard which has been very influential,[6] and two British authors: Robert Thompson, a civilian administrator who drew on experience in Malaya to advise the American forces in Vietnam,[7] and Frank Kitson, a soldier with extensive field experience in Kenya, Malaya and Northern Ireland.[8] All these were writing in the 1960s. But the American army resisted their ideas. As the then Chief of Staff of the US Army wrote in 2002: 'The organisational culture of the US Army, predisposed to fight a conventional enemy that used conventional

---

[3]   Ibid., p. xxi.

[4]   David Kilcullen, 'Counterinsurgency *Redux*', p. 112.

[5]   This was an autobiographical account of the efforts by 'Lawrence of Arabia' to organise Arab resistance to Turkish rule in World War I.

[6]   David Galula, *Counterinsurgency Warfare: Theory and Practice* (Westport CT, 1964).

[7]   Robert Thompson, *Defeating Communist Insurgency: Experiences from Malaya and Vietnam* (New York, 1966).

[8]   Frank Kitson, *Low intensity Operations: Subversion, Insurgency and Peacekeeping* (London, 1971).

tactics, overpowered innovative ideas from within the army and from outside it.'[9] The reason was not hard to find. As a former Vice Chief of Staff of the US Army explained, speaking of Iraq in 2003: 'We put an Army on the battlefield that I had been part of for 37 years. It doesn't have any doctrine, nor was it educated and trained to deal with an insurgency. ... After the Vietnam War we purged ourselves of everything that had to do with irregular warfare or insurgency, because it had to do with how we lost that war. With hindsight, that was a bad decision.'[10] It was indeed. Nor had the humiliating failure of interventions in Beirut (1983) and Mogadishu (1993) done anything to whet the appetite for drawing lessons from these disasters. It has been said that in 2003 most officers knew more about the American Civil War than they did about counterinsurgency.[11]

A New Start

As the insurgency in Iraq developed, the Combined Arms Centre at Fort Leavenworth, Kansas, belatedly recognising the problem, set to work generating a doctrine. This work only took wing in October 2005 with the arrival in command of General David Petraeus. This remarkable officer, the son of a Dutch sea-captain, is an infantryman who has spent much of his service with airborne forces. He was the top graduate of the Army Command and Staff College in 1983 and gained a doctorate in international relations from Princeton University, where his thesis concerned the influence of the Vietnam War on military thinking. He served with the United Nations Military Staff in Haiti in 1995 and with the NATO Stabilisation Force Bosnia in 2001–2, in both places being directly concerned with the problems of nation-building. He commanded the 101st Airborne Division in the initial invasion of Iraq (2003) and became responsible for governing Mosul. His division employed classic counterinsurgency methods from the outset. They used force judiciously, jump-started the economy, built up local security forces, staged elections for the city council, oversaw a programme of public works and launched several thousand reconstruction projects. In June 2004, still in Iraq, he was promoted and put in charge of the Security Transition Command with responsibility for creating and developing Iraqi Forces. At Leavenworth Petraeus made counterinsurgency the top priority. He personally led the effort to write an up-to-date Field Manual on this subject, calling on the skills and knowledge of Marine Corps and Army officers as well as academics with a track record in the field. As soon as a complete draft was available, in February 2006, it was

---

[9]   General Peter J. Schoomaker, in the Foreword to John A. Nagl, *Learning to Eat Soup with a Knife:*

Counterinsurgency Lessons from Malaya and Vietnam (Chicago, 2005), p. ix.

[10]   General Jack Keane, on the *Jim Lehrer News Hour* 18 April 2006, quoted in Counterinsurgency *Field Manual, FM 3-24*, p. xiv.

[11]   John A. Nagl, Foreword to *Counterinsurgency Field Manual FM 3-24*, p. xv.

exposed to a vetting session at Leavenworth, which included practitioners and academics along with journalists, human rights activists and other NGOs. During that summer revisions were accepted, not only from the military, academics and politicians, but also by the press, using an early draft leaked on the internet. The finished Manual was released on 15 December 2006 to great acclaim. In the first two months after publication the internet version was downloaded 2 million times. It was widely reviewed, including by several *Jihadi* web sites, and copies have been found in Taliban training camps in Pakistan. No military doctrinal manual has been so eagerly anticipated or so well received. The reason is clear. At a dark moment the Manual sought to realign America's strategic requirements with its ethical principles; to reconcile the imperatives of counterinsurgency – 'the most complex and maddening type of war' – with the demands of Justice.[12]

What the Manual Says

The Counterinsurgency Field Manual FM 3-24 is a formidable book, running to 420 pages, replete with Tables, Figures, Vignettes, Source Notes, a Glossary and – uniquely for a military manual – an Annotated Bibliography. It has Appendices dealing with Social Network Analysis, the handling of Interpreters, the Laws of War, the use of Air Power and a 'Guide to Action' at company level. The Manual goes into extraordinary detail – for example: 'Do not teeter on the lectern while the interpreter is translating.' One of the most intriguing and useful sections is called 'Paradoxes of Counterinsurgency' presenting a series of Zen-like contradictions.[13] This chapter can do no more than give the gist, the prevailing atmosphere in which the whole textbook is drafted.

The first and overarching point is that the Manual expressly rejects the normative American approach to counterinsurgency in favour of what the authors themselves call traditional British (or Anglo-French) principles. Whereas the American approach typically aims at destroying the enemy hidden in the population – as with free-fire zones and carpet bombing – the Manual adopts the opposite aim, focusing primarily if not exclusively on the civilians. The reasoning is simple. The civilian population is the deciding factor in the struggle; their support must be won, or all is lost. The question then becomes who will help them most, hurt them least, stay the course and earn their trust? Protecting the civilian population becomes by far the most important part of the counterinsurgents' mission. This has important strategic implications. The number of enemy killed (the body count) is no longer the measure of success. And killing civilians can no longer be discounted as collateral damage – dismissed as unintended – because any such damage materially undermines the counterinsurgent's goals. 'An operation that kills

---

[12]   Sarah Sewall, Foreword to *Counterinsurgency Field Manual, FM 3-24*, p. xxi.

[13]   *Counterinsurgency Field Manual FM 3-24*, pp. 47–51.

five insurgents is counterproductive if it leads to the recruitment of fifty more.'[14] Conversely, even when insurgents cause civilian deaths, the population may blame the counterinsurgents for failing to stop the killings. Inability to protect not just government officials and supporters but citizens at large will ultimately mean strategic failure. The balance of military effort shifts accordingly. It is a complete departure from the Powell doctrine of overwhelming and decisive offensive force, and has radical implications for the size of forces needed. Instead of calculating these in relation to numbers of the enemy – which in an insurgency are normally small – the Manual calculates the force requirement in relation to the number of inhabitants, suggesting a minimum of twenty counterinsurgents per 1,000 people. For Iraq this would imply a figure of 535,000 for the security forces. The current total of coalition and Iraqi forces is well above this figure.[15] It is illuminating that in February 2003, General Shinseki, Chief of Staff of the US Army, testifying on Capitol Hill, when asked for the size of the army's force requirement for the post-war occupation of Iraq, gave an estimate of 'several hundred thousand soldiers'. Paul Wolfowitz then said that the troop level by mid-summer would be around 35,000. Scorned by his political masters Shinseki retired a few months later.[16] Providing security for the population creates needs in other areas of business such as intelligence, which drives every operation, linguistic capabilities, weapons, equipment, tactics and the training of host nation security forces.

A second important implication is that, in order to win, counterinsurgents must assume more risk and – in the short term at least – accept higher casualties. This is in direct contradiction to the traditional American concern with force protection, with troops living in fortified bases and travelling everywhere in heavily armoured vehicles. Moreover it is counterintuitive and seemingly unfair. Insurgents fight dirty, dress as civilians, hide behind women, use children as spotters, store weapons in schools and hospitals, operate out of mosques, make extensive use of mines and booby-traps and kill civilians precisely to provoke over-reaction from the counterinsurgent forces and thus discredit them. The Manual tells troops to move out and about among the population, not only to protect them but to gather intelligence. Every action, including use of force, must be 'wrapped in a bodyguard of information'. It also emphasises the need to use minimum force and comply with the Laws of Armed Conflict. Of the nine 'Paradoxes' in the Manual, four bear on this point: 'Sometimes doing nothing is the best reaction,' 'Sometimes the more you protect your force, the less secure you may be,' 'Sometimes the more force is used, the less effective it is' and 'The more successful the counterinsurgency is, the less force can be used and the more risk must be accepted.'[17] This seems to

---

[14]   Ibid., p. 45.

[15]   Coalition forces 120,000, Iraqi armed forces 190,000, Ministry of Interior 386,000: total 696,000, as at November 2009.

[16]   Thomas E. Ricks, *Fiasco: the American Military Adventure in Iraq* (London, 2006), pp. 97 and 156.

[17]   *Counterinsurgency Field Manual, FM 3-24*, pp. 47–51.

give a free pass to the insurgents' foul play and to be ethically perverse. But it is inescapable.

In the normal civil-military tradition elected political leaders decide when to use force and to what ends: military leaders apply their professional skills to the conduct of war. This division of labour usually brings success. In counterinsurgency, matters can stand differently, and this is a third implication of the Manual. Since the struggle is above all for legitimacy, civilian involvement is called for at almost all levels of operations. It will fall to the political leadership to deliver 'victory' in the form of a negotiated settlement. And civilians are best able to advise host-nation governments on how to enhance their legitimacy. Moreover, success depends on providing jobs, water, electricity and a functioning judicial system – human security in its wider sense. These activities become in effect the soldiers' exit strategy. So another of the Manual's paradoxes is that 'Some of the best weapons for counterinsurgents do not shoot.'[18] Dollars and ballots will have more effect than bombs and bullets. Clearly these functions belong properly to civilian agencies and in the post-Vietnam era the US Army had explicitly disavowed nation-building. But this is not how matters always work out. 'If these other instruments of national power don't show up, can't stay or aren't effective, the buck then passes back to the military forces. In the aftermath of combat operations, the Army repeatedly has found itself "holding the dripping bag of manure."'[19]

The Manual recognises military responsibility for these tasks if all else fails, assuming for example the role of mayor, trash collector and public works employer.[20] We have seen that General Petraeus did this in Mosul, as early as the summer of 2003 when he became known as *Malik Daoud* (King David). A realistic division of labour in counterinsurgency involves preparing military forces to fill this gap.[21] This can bring obvious advantages in terms of unity of command, but is ultimately a cop-out. Counterinsurgency requires effective civilian-led effort to strengthen economies, political and administrative institutions and social infrastructure and services. Because legitimacy of the host nation government is what matters in the long run, civilian authorities should not abdicate their responsibilities to the military. It is a third radical implication of the Manual that the risks and costs of counterinsurgency should not be confined to the Pentagon but spread across the whole American body politic.

---

[18]   Ibid.

[19]   *Counterinsurgency Field Manual, FM 3-24*, p. xxxi.

[20]   General Peter Chiarelli, when commanding 1st Cavalry Division in Baghdad emphasised what he called SWETI operations: sewage, water, electricity, trash, and information.

[21]   *Counterinsurgency Field Manual, FM 3-24*, p. 55.

Afterthoughts

About six months after the Manual was published, the University of Chicago Press produced an edition containing an Introduction by Professor Sarah Sewall which is in some ways the best part of it.[22] Having summarised what she regards as the most innovative aspects of the doctrine she goes on to explore two main lines of criticism. The first is that the Manual is in fact a charade, no more than a marketing campaign for a type of war that is inherently brutal and lawless, promising a better counterinsurgency only to assuage the public conscience. During Vietnam Americans spoke of winning hearts and minds even as they carpet-bombed rural areas and attacked villages with napalm. She defends against this charge by recalling the way the Manual was written, being co-sponsored by a human-rights centre (her own) and exposed to extensive consultation with other Non-Governmental Organisations (NGOs), academics, politicians and press as described above. The military authors pledged full endorsement of the Geneva Conventions, devoted a full chapter to Leadership and Ethics and included in an Appendix an *Aide-mémoire* on Legal Considerations. Sewall says that a touch of idealism, buttressed by an extraordinary faith in the US soldier and marine, coursed through the workshop and materialised in the Manual.

But she has doubts whether the armed forces as an institution and a culture can live up to these promises. Innovations do not come easily to large institutions and these are 'paradigm shattering.' Doctrine, organisation, training, materiel, leadership, personnel and facilities all have to change, in a co-ordinated and mutually supportive fashion. Resources have to be devoted to it. Can the army become more intelligence-driven at the expense of combat power? Will it provide specialised counterinsurgency units or simply more training in this type of war for general purpose units? Where the military culture is concerned there remain deep layers of scepticism and any lasting outcome is still to play for. We return to this point later.

She next tackles the obverse concern: namely that the US Army will, indeed, put the Manual into practice only to find itself hamstrung in dealing with barbaric opponents. On this view the only way to win is by unabashedly adopting harsh methods, erasing the distinction between insurgents and civilians, destroying a village or a city in order to save it. The Russians in Grozny have been an example of this strategy, and of its apparent success. It is an approach that rejects the central view that counterinsurgency is above all a political exercise. As Sewall comments, 'It also demands that Americans abandon their core values. To save ourselves we would destroy our souls. History can be a harsh judge of such choices.'[23] A more nuanced version of this concern bears upon the aversion to casualties in which the Americans have cocooned themselves. With a Defence budget equalling that of the rest of the world put together and unrivalled technology, Americans can inflict

---

[22] Ibid., pp. xxi–xliii.

[23] *Counterinsurgency Field Manual, FM 3-24*, pp. xxxvi–ii.

casualties grossly disproportionate to their own. Since Vietnam, in which more than 48,000 US military were killed in combat, the figures for subsequent conflicts have been: Beirut 256, Gulf War 148, Grenada 18, Panama, 23, Somalia 29, Kosovo nil. The Field Manual threatens this immunity. Combat deaths in Iraq since 2003 have reached 3,680 and the American public has become uneasy. Sewall's question is, will Americans keep enough forces there, accept the casualties (running at about 25 killed every month in 2008), fund serious nation-building and stay many long years to conduct counterinsurgency by the book? 'The costs are not unbearable. Willingness to bear them is a choice.'

Sewall then points to an ugly dilemma in which America can find itself. Counterinsurgency favours peace over justice. The US can be harnessed to a beast it may prove impossible to tame. America tries to enhance the host government's legitimacy and help it to become independent. But what if that government is not good or brave or wise? It is seldom America's faith in a host government (often by definition weak when threatened internally) that drives the US into supporting it. More often it will be self-interested fear of the insurgents. But what if legitimacy involves abandoning equal rights for all citizens, centralising the economy or eliminating due process? Imposing a revolution from the outside provides a weak and illegitimate basis from which to defeat an insurgency. Fostering stability can be a valuable principle in both the choice and conduct of a campaign, but entails its own costs. The American decision about which insurgency to fight, and hence which government to support, shapes how US forces will fight and thus the chances of success. The difficulty of establishing just outcomes is further explored in Chapter 9 of this book.

Sewall points out that military doctrine ought to flow from a broader strategic framework, but none has been provided. 'The doctrine is a moon without a planet to orbit.' The very word 'counterinsurgency' has become so linked with Iraq and a strategy of regime change that many public servants do not want to consider themselves part of it. Lack of clarity about when and why America will conduct counterinsurgency undermines the likelihood that they will ever do it well. Her conclusion is daunting but inspirational. As the leading power in a fragmenting international order, the strategic challenge for America is stabilisation. This means not simply buttressing a government in order to legitimise a state, it must buttress multiple failing states to legitimise the interstate system. As this requires helping governments to control internal threats it can endorse US efforts to defeat terrorism. Likewise, antiterrorism efforts can support the stabilisation and governance aspects of a counterinsurgency campaign. The strategic objective is to enable local authorities to contain threats to security, forcing terrorism back into a criminal box. The Field Manual offers insights that should inform this stabilisation strategy: the primacy of politics, seeing the largely undecided middle as the campaign's centre of gravity, the need for restraint in the use of force, and greater willingness to spread the risks and costs.[24]

---

[24]   *Counterinsurgency Field Manual, FM 3-24*, pp. xlii–iii.

At much the same time David Kilcullen's further thoughts were developed in an article called 'Counter-insurgency *Redux*' in the IISS Quarterly *Survival*.[25] He was concerned first with the consequences of globalisation and the effects of the internet. This empowers not only Al-Qaʻida's very professional media handling, but internet-based financial transfers, training and recruitment, coded communication, planning and intelligence, all providing an electronic 'virtual sanctuary' for insurgents. Cyber-mobilisation or 'electronic *levée en masse*' is deeply entwined with the insurgency in Iraq. This has given modern insurgency a trans-national character, leading to real time co-operation and cross-pollination among insurgents in many countries. Members of Al-Qaʻida pass messages between and among Pakistan, Afghanistan, Iran and Iraq. Iranian improvised explosive technology appears in Iraq and Pakistani extremists operate in Afghanistan and India.

Kilcullen says that modern insurgents operate 'more like a self-synchronising swarm of independent but co-operating cells than like a formal organisation. Even the fashionable reference to networks and nodes may imply more structure than actually exists.' Almost any tactical action can have immediate strategic impact, making statistical trends less important than a general sense of how things are going. The demeanour of a single soldier (like Lynddie England) can communicate more about the state of a campaign than any amount of official information. And it is not unusual for the insurgents to be wealthier than the population at large. In Afghanistan the fruits of extortion, corruption and the trade in heroin are great engines of the Taliban campaign.

Based upon these reflections, Kilcullen has come up with some new 'paradigms' for counterinsurgency. Success, he thinks, will depend less on establishing legitimacy at the local level than on mobilising the home population, the host country and the global audience of allied and neutral countries. Counterinsurgents are attempting to control a complicated 'conflict ecosystem' rather than defeating a single adversary, and trying to impose some order on a chaotic and unpredictable environment. Paradoxically, a common diagnosis of the problem may be more important than formal unity of effort. International aid agencies, global media, NGOs and religious leaders are critical to success but cannot possibly be brought under the counterinsurgent authority's control. While Galula described counterinsurgency as 80 per cent political, today it may make more sense to think in terms of 100 per cent. Comprehensive and almost instantaneous media coverage can make even the most straightforward combat action a political engagement. Even at the lowest tactical level the military need to see their task as a form of political warfare in which perceptions and political outcomes matter more than battlefield success. Likewise, secret intelligence may matter less than information that is not classified by any government but is located in denied areas. This is not to play down the importance of human and signals intelligence, but detailed knowledge of physical, human, and cultural factors, based on open-source research and the tribal currents in no-go areas may be even more important. Lastly,

---

[25]   David Kilcullen, 'Counterinsurgency *Redux*', pp. 111–130.

in counterinsurgency victory may never be final. It may have to be redefined as the disarming and re-integration of insurgents into society, coupled with popular support for permanent institutionalised anti-terrorist measures that damp down the risk of terrorist cells re-emerging. This might be described as a post-modern concept of counterinsurgency.

Walking the Walk

Within a month of the publication of the Manual, General Petraeus was back in Iraq, with the rank of four-star general, commanding all the coalition forces there. He held the post for the next 21 months, and how the campaign fared during that time provided a good test both of himself and of the doctrine.

One of America's justifications for invading Iraq in 2003 was that Saddam Hussein was supporting Al-Qa'ida. That claim, like the one that he had weapons of mass destruction, has been discredited. In fact, it was the invasion of Iraq that revived Al-Qa'ida after its eviction from Afghanistan in 2001. By early 2006, America's National Intelligence Assessment on terrorism concluded that the Iraq conflict was 'breeding a deep resentment of US involvement in the Muslim world and cultivating supporters for the global jihadist movement.' Al-Qa'ida grafted itself onto a local Sunni insurgency and carried out many of the bloodiest suicide-bombings that wrecked the prospect of an early political settlement and provoked a sectarian war. In June 2006 American forces tracked down the Al-Qa'ida leader in Iraq, Abu Musab al-Zarqawi, and killed him in a bombing raid on his hideout north of Baghdad. His decision to bomb three hotels in Amman in November 2005 had backfired badly, causing a wave of revulsion, and his death seemed to have removed the main impetus behind exporting Iraq's violence. Even so, a bleak Marine Corps intelligence report found that American and Iraqi troops were 'no longer capable of militarily defeating the insurgency in Anbar.'

When Colonel Sean MacFarland of the 1st Armoured division took charge of Ramadi, Anbar's capital, in early 2006, he felt that the city was in 'enemy hands'. To retake it he needed more Iraqi recruits, so he decided to woo local Sunni tribal leaders who had *wasta*, or influence.[26] His first task was to protect those sheikhs who had moved over to the Americans. They became the conduits of American humanitarian assistance. In neighbourhoods where security was improving, the Americans also got the infrastructure repaired and the machinery of government restored. The Americans and their new Iraqi allies pushed into Al-Qa'ida's strongholds, retaking Ramadi neighbourhood by neighbourhood, combining American firepower with Iraqi knowledge. This started a virtuous circle in which Sunni tribal sheikhs felt secure enough to join, in turn increasing security. This

---

[26] 'British Armed Forces: Losing their Way?' *The Economist*, (31 January 2009), p. 32.

'Awakening' then spread beyond the original province of Anbar, pushing Al-Qaʻida further northward.

At this time a high-level study group recommended that the US should wind down its combat role in Iraq as soon as possible and engage with Syria and Iran. President Bush, advised by General Petraeus, decided to do the exact opposite. His plan called for a troop reinforcement of some 30,000 soldiers, most of which would be deployed in an effort to secure Baghdad and clear it of sectarian forces, with new, more aggressive rules of engagement, using both US and Iraqi troops embedded in the capital's nine districts. There would be a parallel effort in Anbar province, using 4,000 of the extra troops there. The Iraqi government was to take control of all provinces by November 2007 and to share the country's oil wealth with the Sunnis. By linking military and host nation governmental actions, this plan followed one of the principles of the Manual, although the 'quick-fix' approach went against it. This plan, generally known as the 'Surge', went into operation at the same time as General Petraeus assumed command.

In the month of February 2007, 81 US troops were killed in Iraq. The number rose to a high of 126 in May, as more troops poured in and the general ordered them out into Iraqi villages and neighbourhoods to engage a variety of insurgent groups. In July 2008, only 13 American soldiers died in Iraq, the lowest level since the invasion began. The civilian death toll, which had hit 5,000 a month in 2007, was down to 387 according to the Iraqi authorities (other estimates were a bit higher, at around 500). Iraqi security forces were now in command of ten of the country's 18 provinces and Iraq's government had gained in stature and confidence. Thanks to the then soaring oil prices it was flush with money. It was standing up to Iraq's assorted militias and asserting its independence from both America and Iran. The overlapping wars – Sunni against American, Sunni against Shia and Shia against Shia – had abated. The country no longer looked in imminent danger of breaking apart or falling into permanent anarchy. A few Sunnis, motivated by Islam or simple resentment of foreign military occupation, continued to attack American forces. But many Sunni tribes, repelled by the atrocities committed by their former and often foreign allies in Al-Qaʻida, had joined the Sunni 'Awakening', and crossed over to America's side. At the same time, Sunnis and Shias had stopped killing each other in the vast numbers that followed the blowing up of a Shia shrine in early 2006. One reason for this was that after the previous year's frenzied ethnic cleansing fewer neighbourhoods were still mixed. But many Iraqis, having waded briefly into the horror of indiscriminate sectarian slaughter, had for the present made a conscious decision to step back. The conflict between Shias and Shias had also died down. In August 2007 Muqtada al-Sadr, the vehemently anti-American Shia cleric, declared a cease-fire. In the summer of 2008 Iraq's prime minister, Nuri al-Maliki, sent the army to take control of the port city of Basra and the Baghdad slum known as Sadr City, both strongholds until then of the powerful militia run by Mr Sadr. The fact that Sadr considered it wise not to resist, suggests not only that the army was now strong enough to out-face private militias but also that the state had acquired far greater political legitimacy, in Shia minds at least.

General Petraeus's handover of command brought a harvest of praise. Defence Secretary Robert Gates said: 'General Petraeus is clearly the hero of the hour, but I think all of us would say there are an awful lot of heroes working for him that have actually made this happen'. Michael O'Hanlon of the Brookings Institution, an early sceptic of the new strategy and the troop surge that went with it said: 'We have to start by saying it's simply remarkable, it's the latest, greatest comeback in American military history, perhaps since the Civil War.' Andrew Bacevich of Boston University also credits General Petraeus with helping to avoid defeat in Iraq.[27] But he is less sure just how much of the credit the general himself deserves. The surge as such, in terms of an additional increment of 30,000 or so US troops, probably was not decisive. More important, probably, was the change in tactics, or doctrine, that Petraeus introduced. Bacevich thinks that Petraeus was good, but also lucky, with the cease-fire declared by the main Shiite militia, and the change of allegiance among Sunni tribal leaders from Al-Qa'ida insurgents to the new Iraqi government. And the success of the overall strategy is still in question.[28]

Under a recent agreement the Americans have promised to leave within three years. Their forces withdrew from the cities in the middle of 2009. All military operations now require the assent of Iraqis. Americans will be barred from using Iraq as a launch pad to attack other countries. But there is, in fact, considerable wiggle-room in the agreement. The timing can be extended by mutual consent. Even the requirement for American troops to withdraw from city centres may be open to an elastic interpretation. The Joint Security Stations, where American troops are entrenched in mini-forts scattered across the cities, have been an essential part of the plan especially in Baghdad. Already they are jointly manned by Americans and Iraqis. Iraq's generals may well be loath to remove the Americans, perhaps re-labelling them as 'advisers'. The Iraqi security forces have improved out of all recognition in the past two years and now number about 577,000 (including the armed forces and those controlled by the Ministry of the Interior) not to mention the so-called 'Sons of Iraq' militias formed under the 'Awakening' by the mainly Sunni tribal councils.[29] Even without the Americans this is already slightly more than the number that the Manual prescribes. But even the best Iraqi units still rely heavily on the Americans for air support, not least the helicopters that are crucial in counterinsurgency, and for other technical skills, including communications, intelligence and logistics.

General Petraeus himself has repeatedly said that the gains remain 'fragile and reversible'. National elections in March 2010 failed to give a clearer picture of Iraq's future balance of power. A potentially devastating lack of consensus among the main political groups and their leaders still prevails. Corruption is rife. Many ministries are still fiefs of patronage. Family and tribal ties are what count in

---

[27] Andrew J. Bacevich, 'The Petraeus Doctrine', *The Atlantic Online*, October 2008.

[28] Al Pessin, 'Gates Hails "Hero of the Hour" ', *Voice of America*, Baghdad, (15 September 2008).

[29] *The Military Balance 2009*, IISS (London, 2009), p. 247.

getting jobs. Intrigue and deceit seem to dog the management of just about every political party. No culture of tolerance or pluralism has yet emerged. A fundamental three-way split still prevents Iraq from coming together as a country. Though it is hopeful that the Sunni Arabs, probably some 20 per cent of the population, seem set to be drawn back into the heart of parliamentary and provincial politics, few of their leaders seem willing yet to acknowledge that they have lost the power that they had always held. Perhaps the biggest division is between Arabs and Kurds, who control most of the east and north of Nineveh, and account for about one-third of its population.

Jus in Bello

Just War principles *in bello*, of proportion and discrimination, run like a golden thread through the new Manual. To repeat, there is a clear focus on protecting the population as against protecting one's own troops ('force protection') or killing the insurgents ('body count'). The tactical battle is judged not in terms of territory lost or won but for its political effects. The aim throughout is to gain legitimacy for the host nation government, not to win in the traditional military sense. Every action, including uses of force must be 'wrapped in a bodyguard of information'. It is crucial to use minimum force and comply with the Laws of Armed Conflict. The way that General Petraeus handled his command in Mosul in 2003 (p. 138 above) could stand as a model of proportionate and discriminate handling of military force.

The British in Basra have been condemned for fecklessness. According to this view the British, having been forced by constant attack to abandon one base after another, were finally forced to retreat to Basra airport. The Iraqi government and the American army, frustrated by the failure of the British to carry out their responsibilities, launched the 'Charge of the Knights'. Entering Basra in overwhelming force they routed the Mahdi army and restored the city to peaceful normality. It was made clear to the British that their presence in Iraq was no longer relevant.[30] But there is a completely different way of looking at this story: that it was the result of a plan of action based on the precepts of FM 3-24. Consider some of the paradoxes that form the centerpiece of this doctrine. 'Sometimes doing nothing is the best reaction.' 'Tactical success guarantees nothing.' 'The host nation doing something tolerably is normally better than us doing it well.' The last of these is particularly a propos. As the Chief of Defence Staff has explained: 'Operation Charge of the Knights at last provided a clear political lead that had up to then been absent in Basra and that was a prerequisite for success. The Iraqis deserve congratulations for that. And so do our forces that provided air, aviation (*sic*), armoured, artillery, logistic, medical and other support. Of course the Charge of the Knights was not a British affair. It was not intended to be. But it was

---

[30]   C. Booker, 'Our Army failed its test in Iraq', *The Sunday Telegraph*, (4 January 2009).

the culmination of a long term plan and we played our part in its execution.' While not a wholly convincing explanation, it hews closely to the spirit of the Manual. And there had been success of a sort. In January 2009 the Chief of Defence Staff was able to claim that: 'As a consequence of its success, British forces are now back on the ground in Basra completing the mentoring and training of Iraqi forces that have security responsibility for the city.'[31] But he also conceded that Britain had become too complacent and smug about its experiences in Northern Ireland and Bosnia. 'You're only as good as your next success, not your last one.'[32] New doctrine has been published in 2009 drawing upon American experience. Equally worth remembering is another of the Manual's paradoxes. 'If a tactic works this week it might not work next week: if it works in this province it might not work in the next.'[33]

Jus ad bellum

The new Field Manual concerns implementation. As Sarah Sewall observes at the end of her Introduction: 'It is not a guide for deciding which insurgencies to squelch. It is neutral regarding the choice of war.' But this is not the last word. She continues:

> Ironically, though, the Manual's ultimate value may lie in better informing the nation's *jus ad bellum* decisions. The Manual offers an honest appraisal of what it takes to fight a counterinsurgency campaign well. In so doing the manual has the potential to shape America's choice of war for years to come. But it must first overcome profound institutional and political obstacles. This will require much more than a new field manual.[34]

Her comment has been illuminated in a recent article by Andrew Bacevich.[35] He says that within the American military a great debate is unfolding which focuses on two large questions: first, why, after its promising start, did the campaign in Iraq go so badly wrong? Second, how should the hard-won lessons of Iraq inform future policy? The protagonists fall into two camps which he calls Crusaders and Conservatives. Crusaders see the Army's problems in Iraq as self-inflicted, because rigidly conventional senior commanders, determined 'never again' to see the Army bogged down in a Vietnam-like quagmire, ignored unconventional warfare and were poorly prepared for it. Crusaders vow that 'never again' shall

---

[31]   Air Chief Marshal Sir Jock Stirrup, *Defence Daily Update*, 5 January 2009.

[32]   Ibid.

[33]   *Counterinsurgency Field Manual FM 3-24*, p. 50.

[34]   Ibid., p. xliii.

[35]   Andrew J. Bacevich, 'The Petraeus Doctrine', *The Atlantic Online*, (October 2008).

the officer corps fall victim to this kind of wilful amnesia. The events of 9/11 showed that political conditions abroad will pose the greatest threat to the United States. Denying terrorists sanctuary in rogue or failed states becomes a national security imperative, hence winning battles becomes less urgent than pacifying populations and establishing effective governance. This will require the US military not just to dominate land operations but to change entire societies; to get better at building structures that can stand on their own. This means buying fewer tanks, while spending more on language proficiency; curtailing the hours spent on marksmanship, while increasing those devoted to studying foreign societies. It implies changing the whole culture of the officer corps. Instead of a battle-oriented warrior ethos, it will emphasise the intellectual tools to foster the political and economic development of host nations. In the 1990s the Powell Doctrine, with its emphasis on overwhelming force, assumed that future wars would be brief, decisive and infrequent. According to the emerging Petraeus Doctrine, the Army (like it or not) is entering an era in which armed conflict will be protracted, ambiguous and continuous, with the application of force becoming a lesser part of the soldier's repertoire.

Conservatives dispute this *mise-en-scène* and do not regard Iraq as a harbinger of things to come. A leading voice in this camp is Colonel Gian Gentile, a Berkeley graduate with a doctorate in history from Stanford, who is teaching at West Point.[36] He has served in Iraq twice, commanding an armoured reconnaissance squadron in Baghdad in 2006. He attributes the improvements during the Petraeus era less to new tactics than to a 'cash-for-cooperation' policy that put 100,000 Sunnis, many of them former insurgents, on the government's payroll. But his deeper concern is that an infatuation with stability operations will lead the army to reinvent itself as a constabulary, shorn of adequate ability for conventional war fighting. The Army's National Training Centre at Fort Irwin is now focusing exclusively on counterinsurgency. Its trainees now learn about spending money rather than blood, and negotiating the cultural labyrinth through rapport and rapprochement. Three former brigade commanders declare that the Army's field artillery branch may soon be all but incapable of providing accurate and timely fire support; it has become a 'dead branch walking'.

There is a deeper worry here. Calling for an army configured mainly to wage stability operations is to affirm the Long War (formerly the War on Terror) as the organising principle of post-9/11 national-security strategy, with US forces called upon to bring light to those dark corners of the world wherever terrorists flourish. There is room for doubt whether the underlying motive is democratic transformation or imperial domination. Did America invade Iraq to liberate the country or control its oil reserves? Both perhaps? Time will tell. But it is certain that the Long War implies a vast military enterprise on a global scale and likely to

---

[36] Gian P. Gentile, 'Misreading the Surge Threatens US Army's Conventional Capabilities' *World Politics Review*, 4 March 2008; Judah Grunstein, 'The limits of the Surge: An Interview with Gian Gentile' *World Politics Review*, 1 April 2008.

last for decades. In this sense the FM 3-24 agenda, if implemented, would serve only to validate and perpetuate the course set by President Bush after 9/11. Dick Cheney, Donald Rumsfeld and Paul Wolfowitz would be vindicated after all.

Gentile points out that, historically, expectations that the next war will resemble the last one have seldom served the military well. He believes that the choice of an alternative to the Long War should remain a possibility. The effect of the new Manual will be to preclude that possibility, allowing second-order questions (How should we organise the Army?) to crowd out the more fundamental one (What is the Army for?). And he picks up on Sarah Sewall's point that the new doctrine is a 'moon without a planet to orbit'. The prospect that President Obama will advocate alternatives to the Long War appear slight. The power of decision may well devolve upon soldiers by default. This choice should not be for the Army to make. To put the point another way, considerations of *jus in bello* should not predetermine decisions regarding *jus ad bellum*. In this light perhaps the new Manual is just a bit too clever for its own good? But, as Sarah Sewall points out, the most prescient critics are ahead of themselves, since the US military has by no means internalised the new Field Manual as yet.[37] Gentile's objection is not to the doctrine as such, which he strongly supports, claiming that he was operating this way in Basra in 2006, even before the Petraeus era. His quarrel is with the use that he fears will be made of it to unbalance the American army in the service of an impermissible world view, as embodied in the concept of the Long War.

The wider question remains, of deciding which insurgencies to crush when there is a choice among so many. For the existing rulers of a country in which insurgency breaks out there may be no other option. In the mid-twentieth century the British had been ruling Kenya for fifty years, Malaya for a hundred and Northern Ireland since the seventeenth century. When insurgencies broke out there was little choice but to suppress them. This is not to deny that in some cases the insurgents may have justice on their side. (The question of Just Rebellion is a much wider one and is a matter for another book). And, of course, there exists the option to cut and run. The British, having demanded the Palestine Mandate in 1923, surrendered it ignominiously twenty-five years later in the face of intractable terrorist activity on the part of both Arabs and Jews. Sixty years later still the fruits of that debâcle are only too painfully obvious; it is not a course anyone would wish to have chosen.

But the situation is very different when the counterinsurgency is being conducted by an intervening power in support of a host government. This applies to all American counterinsurgent operations (and to the British since Northern Ireland). It is a far more difficult task and failures are frequent. It is harder still when the intervention has been undertaken for other reasons and has in turn generated the insurgency – as recently in Iraq. The *ad bellum* criterion of likelihood of success is obviously relevant, but very difficult to apply, not least where a coalition or supra-national bodies like the UN Security Council are involved in the decision making.

---

[37]   *Counterinsurgency Field Manual, FM 3-24*, p. xlii.

Afghanistan

Afghanistan provides an even more difficult example. It is a country half as large again as Iraq, landlocked, mountainous and inhospitable. Its population is of similar size, equally tribal and much more widely dispersed, mainly in villages. With its reserves of oil, gas and minerals undeveloped, it is one of the poorest countries on earth, with up to a third of its small GDP deriving from trade in drugs. Its politics has historically consisted of power struggles, bloody coups and unstable transfers of power. The government of President Karzai has been dysfunctional and massively corrupt. The 2009 presidential election was characterised by lack of security, low voter-turnout, widespread ballot-stuffing and intimidation. America and its allies have been in occupation for eight years and it is generally agreed that during the past year security has only been getting worse. The insurgent Taliban enjoy the massive advantage of a sanctuary across the eastern border with Pakistan, where a part at least of the establishment regard them as providing strategic depth against their real enemy India. Nor has anyone the faintest idea where Osama bin Laden and the Taliban leader Mullah Omar are hiding.

The American commander General Stanley McChrystal is a true believer in the Petraeus doctrine, but he has been dealt an impossible hand. The theoretical force requirement for true counterinsurgency (as in FM 3-24) would be around 600,000. When the reinforcement now planned is complete the sum total of security forces will amount to barely three quarters of this figure.[38] Even if the extra forces were available, it could take decades and many billions of dollars remaking Afghanistan as a fully functioning democratic state complete with civil society, equal rights for women and so forth. Given the ambivalent state of public opinion towards the war this would be a wholly unrealistic endeavour. McChrystal inevitably opted for a modest 'surge' in troop numbers and President Obama, after long deliberation, found that he had no choice but to go along. To cut and run would have been to hand a huge propaganda coup to the Islamists – and the Republican Party. The status quo was plainly not working. A strategy of 'counter-terrorism', based on decapitation and containment, as reportedly favoured by Vice-President Biden, contradicted the very premises on which this chapter is based and would have done little to help the Afghan people. It is, however, the US strategy in Pakistan where the number of American un-manned strike aircraft is being stepped up for this purpose.

In Afghanistan the President has opted for a much faster build-up than originally planned, coupled with an undertaking that American troops would 'start leaving' in July 2011. The aim is to prevent Al-Qaʿida from returning to Afghanistan and keep Taliban insurgents from toppling the government there. 'Nation-building' is explicitly ruled out. The new American troops will focus on securing certain

---

[38] American forces 100,000; ISAF allied forces 45,000; Afghan army expanding to 171,600; Afghan police to 134,000; total 450,600 by 2011. A further expansion of the Afghan Army and Police to 400,000 has been mooted.

population centres, such as Kandahar and Khost where the Taliban are strongest, and pair up with specific Afghan units with the aim of building them into an independent fighting force. The rate at which American troops withdraw will depend on progress made and some troops will remain as a 'light footprint', in a supporting role, probably for years to come.[39]

Assessed against the criterion of 'probability of success' the strategy is a huge gamble. It depends on 'carving away at the bottom' of the Taliban's strength by reintegrating less committed members into tribes and offering them paid jobs in local and national military forces. It requires big advances in the competence and reliability of those local forces. Success also depends largely on President Karzai providing at least half-decent governance and rooting out corruption. It hinges, above all, on a renewed relationship with a Pakistani government whose military and intelligence services distrust the United States and whose willingness to take on elements of the Taliban remain unproven. It is to be hoped, for all our sakes, that the project is successful.

Whatever the outcomes in Iraq and Afghanistan, intervention will sometimes be necessary to defend allies, stop mass killings, shore up fragile states, close down terrorist havens and relieve suffering. These jobs should not be left to America alone or to the poor states that contribute most to the UN. The new Manual has great value as a way of doing counterinsurgency which is more ethically centred and more likely to be effective than any that the Americans have had before. The rest of the world, including Britain, has much to learn from it.

---

[39] David E. Sanger and Peter Baker, 'Obama to accelerate deployment of troops', *International Herald Tribune*, 2 December 2009.

Chapter 11

Going Off the Reservation into the Sanctuary–Cross-Border Counter-Terrorist Operations, Fourth Generation Warfare and the Ethical Insufficiency of Contemporary Just War Thinking

Paul Schulte

'My bottom line is that we cannot allow Al-Qaeda to operate. We cannot have safe havens in that region.'

President Barack Obama – Press Conference, 10 February 2009

'Israel's aim was to provide a strong blow to the people of Gaza so that they would lose their appetite for shooting at Israel.'

President Shimon Peres, speaking to a delegation from the American Israel Public Affairs Committee, February 2009

'No insurgency has ever been destroyed as long as the sanctuaries remain alive.'

Western Military Spokesman, Pakistan, quoted in *The Guardian*, London, 21 March 2009

Introduction and Definitions

The aim of this chapter is to consider key ethical issues raised by military action by state-controlled armed forces against terrorist sanctuaries across international boundaries dividing them from the territories where those forces originate or are based. Distinctive and recurrent aspects of these operations are discussed against a common set of Just War principles. Finally, certain implications for international moral judgements and consequent political responses are suggested.

For these purposes, a sanctuary is considered to be 'a secure base area within which an insurgent or terrorist group is able to organise the politico-military infrastructure needed to support its activities.' Military operations against sanctuaries may today involve artillery bombardment, aerial attack, insertion of ground forces, including unacknowledged, or plausibly deniable, operations by Special Forces, and open (usually temporary) ground occupation. Invasions and long-term occupations leading to regime change and nation building are not covered, and it is not implied that there is a moral distinction between the kinetic actions of Intelligence agencies (e.g. CIA/Mossad) and militaries (e.g. Special Forces Command). Similarly, 'terrorist' or 'insurgent' are not used as intrinsically derogatory terms implying that operations against them are always automatically justified – though many commentators would feel at least a presumption against tolerating illegal violence, especially when it is used indiscriminately .

Examples

Recent and Current

This chapter was written against the background of Operation Cast Lead, the Israeli Armed Forces operations against Hamas in Gaza between 27 December 2008 and 18 January 2009, together with the continuing American drone strikes against Muslim extremist targets within north-west Pakistan connected with the insurgency in Afghanistan. If only for reasons of space, it cannot pretend to give a full account of these two operations, but it has set out to examine key arguments and accusations encountered in public commentary.

Historical

Historical comparisons are also worth bearing in mind. Previous examples over the past 50 years of this category of military action would include:

- Commonwealth action against Indonesian forces in 1964–5 (Konfrontasi – Operation Claret);
- US bombings and incursions into North Vietnam, Laos and Cambodia during the Indochina Wars between 1964 and 1973;
- apartheid South African attacks on African liberation movements in Angola and Mozambique in the 1980s;
- the Turkish Army's repeated incursions into Iraqi Kurdistan;- US UAV or gunship strikes in Yemen and Somalia as an acknowledged part of the global war on Terror;
- previous Israeli incursions, raids, commando actions, targeted killings, and air attacks on neighbours especially Lebanon, the West Bank, and Gaza.

Counterfactual

But it is important to remember that military reactions to externally mounted provocation are not necessarily inevitable. In many cases risks and costs are seen to be prohibitive. Examples of restraint and prolonged acceptance of cross-border terrorist activities would include many campaigns which have *not* taken place, due to decisions such as by the UK not to venture into the Irish Republic during the Northern Ireland troubles, or into Yemen during the Dhofar insurgency, by America not to embark on any sustained ground incursion into North Vietnam, by the Soviet Union not to cross the border into Pakistan during its Afghan campaign, and by India not to attack Pakistan despite prolonged terrorist violence in Kashmir and elsewhere.

Examination against Just War Criteria

Just War theory is Latin and Christian in origin. But it has been developed by open international debate. Its fundamental positions are not contradicted by other civilisation traditions.[1] It is the closest equivalent to a shared global framework for moral evaluation of conflict. Its categories recur endlessly (and unsystematically) in worldwide commentary and denunciation. The following examination of aspects of attacks on terrorist sanctuaries is conducted principally against the analytical categories in Guthrie and Quinlan's authoritative recent treatment.[2]

I: *JUS AD BELLUM*

To resort, justly, to war, all of the following tests must be satisfied.

Just War Requirement 1: Just Cause

'The initiating side must have a proper reason for going to war, such as protecting the innocent, restoring rights wrongfully denied, or re-establishing just order. Revenge, punishment for its own sake or upholding a ruler's prestige are insufficient.'

Discussion

Cross-border operations generally occur well into clearly established and challenging low-intensity conflicts. Thus they seldom raise *new* questions about the overall justice of the dispute. They will always depend upon the case for the survival of the state regime under attack.

They can usually also be more immediately justified as assisting the *protection* of friendly civilians and soldiers against future violence, by inflicting direct

---

[1] Vesselin Popovski, Gregory Reichberg and Nicholas Turner, *World Religions and Norms of War* (Tokyo, New York, 2009).

[2] Sir Michael Quinlan and Sir Charles Guthrie, *Just War – The Just War Tradition: Ethics in Modern Warfare* (London, 2007).

attrition on enemy combatants, weapons, infrastructure and supplies (*decapitation, damage, and disruption*). They may also have a wider psychological intent, to re-establish *deterrence* in order to stop or mitigate attacks within the conflict, as claimed by the Israeli leadership as a recent objective in Gaza, as previously in South Lebanon in 2006.

Success in this would continue even when the enemy had succeeded in restocking and replacing casualties after the attacks had ceased.

Achieving deterrence by reasserting national military credibility are more reasonable collective objectives than simply '*upholding a ruler's prestige*'. But the determined actions which they inspire may look very similar.

Just War Requirement 2: Right Intention

> 'The aim must be to create a better, more just and more lasting subsequent peace than there would have been without going to war.'

Discussion

Single Intention?

Discerning, and then judging, the true underlying strategic intention of a cross-boundary military operation is seldom easy. There may be no single simple answer. Governments responding to terrorist actions may be motivated by outrage, and an imprecise long-term hope of contributing to conditions which will eventually remove the threat or assist a satisfactory settlement. (Aggressive military operations, despite appearances, governmental rhetoric and dramatic media commentary, do not necessarily rule out back-channel negotiations). Cross-border actions may have been launched to be capable of branching out in various directions in response to unforeseeable developments.

Their objectives may include the less openly admitted and more ethically disputable aim of *reassurance* of friendly civilians. For democratic states, where the reassured and protected civilians are also electors, decision-making over war and peace raise special questions about the justice of the intervention.

Collective Willpower and Consciousness?

Issues of willpower are inescapable in these situations.

In the Clausewitzian tradition '*War is a contest of wills conducted with physical means*' and its object is a better peace, from one's own point of view. Within intractable long-running low-intensity conflicts, the only realistic near term objective practically available for decision-makers may be a somewhat better truce or lull (or Arabic: *hudna*; Hebrew: *tahdiyeh*):

Both sides try to dominate the opponent's will, while protecting their own. The respective wills of the people, government and military are potentially vulnerable. Protecting one's own will is as important as attacking that of the opponent. The military is responsible for its will (morale) – politicians are responsible for the wills of both the government and the people.[3]

But targeting willpower is difficult, especially with highly committed non-state actors. Information operations are complex, uncertain and limited in effect on their own. Kinetic action – bombing, shelling and physical occupation of territory – may, therefore, seem an essential means of eroding enemy will, by physically eliminating human and material resources required for victory. Yet to avoid committing war crimes (and violating Just War Requirement 8 below on Discrimination) this needs to stop short of direct attack on the civilian population and of causing excessive collateral damage.

There are serious disagreements over which categories of physical objects and human beings remain legitimate targets. Sporadic aerial strikes against widely dispersed leadership targets in Pakistan have inherently limited physical consequences. Destroying infrastructure in Gaza on the grounds that it is being militarily utilised by Hamas will have wider and more lasting effect on the civil population. And forcibly changing the consciousness of an opposing ethnic, cultural or religious group, so that its members conclude that they are so irrevocably beaten that they have to relinquish intensely held previous aspirations, may seem to be incompatible with human dignity and national autonomy.[4] Yet how much dignity and autonomy does a conventionally stronger side owe to opponents who interpret in them an obligation, or even a religious duty, for endless resumption of the conflict?

---

[3]   This formulation is from a chapter entitled 'A Theory of Victory' from the semi-official *US National War College Guide to Security Issues* (vol. 1, third edition, edited by J.B. Bartholomees Jr., US Strategic Studies Institute, 2008), page 93.

[4]   I am indebted to Professor David Yost for pointing out that this was in fact exactly the intention of the allies in World War II, as the only long-term foundation for lasting subsequent peace with Germany and Japan. The harshest recent statement of this kind was misattributed to the Israeli Chief of Staff, now Vice Prime Minister, Moshe Yaalon, in 2002: '*The Palestinians must be made to understand in the deepest recesses of their consciousness that they are a defeated people*'. This was repeatedly re-quoted in various media sources until definitively refuted by the Toronto Star in August 2009. But soon afterwards the pro-Israeli controversialist Daniel Pipes insisted that the statement '*sums up my understanding of the Arab-Israeli conflict and accurately represents my views. The world may quote me on it without fear of contradiction.*' Predictably enough, there were numerous expressions of support on his website - and denunciations on others.

Just War Requirement 3: Proportionate Cause

> 'To warrant engaging in war, with all its likely evils….those deciding must have a reasonable expectation that the outcome will entail enough good (over and above what might be achieved in any other way) to outweigh War's inevitable pain and destruction.'

Discussion

There is evidently widespread confusion in recent public commentary about whether what should be balanced against immediate and painful human consequences is *actually experienced* or *eventually intended or possible* levels of harm.

Predicted harms will rest on intelligence judgements about future terrorist operational capability and intent. Forecasts may include the introduction or extension of methods such as suicide bombers, longer range, more accurate ground-to-ground rockets, Man Portable Air Defence Systems capable of shooting down airliners, or more sophisticated Improvised Explosive Devices (IEDs) now capable of destroying main battle tanks. (Concerns that Hamas were acquiring longer range rockets capable of threatening a much larger area were part of the Israeli rationale for Operation Cast Lead. This insisted that the immediate human consequences had to be considered against Hamas's demonstrated willingness to fire 3000 rockets and mortar shells in 2008, doubling the number in the two previous years, and to make threats that 'Israel would be hit in a way that it had never been before.'[5]) Worst cases might be effective and deployable chemical, biological, radiological or nuclear weapons (frequently and indiscriminately called WMD).

Estimating and balancing alternative politico/military consequences is inherently uncertain. But that seems less a *moral* uncertainty than the intellectual intractability of strategic prediction. In this, governments and militaries may possess important information unavailable to the public or even to expert commentators. They may, however, also be lying, blinded by professional prejudice, exaggerating, suppressing evidence, or distorting their claims – and they may certainly be sincerely mistaken.

Just War Requirement 4: Right Authority

> 'The decision to go to war must be made by those with proper authority for so grave a step. Historically, this has usually been the ruler or government of a sovereign state, as opposed to an internal warlord or faction. …Now, new and

---

5   *Hamas rockets* at http://www.globalsecurity.org/military/world/para/hamas-qassam. htm

complex questions arise about how far, and when, international authority may be required.'

Discussion

International authority

There is deep disagreement about which authority can give sufficient legitimacy today to authorise these actions. Only the UNSC? Or regional organisations such as NATO (as in its 1999 armed intervention over Kosovo) or perhaps, in future, the African Union? Or legitimately elected sovereign national governments under evident attack exercising their inherent right of individual or collective self-defence under Article 51 of the UN Charter? Without unanimous international approval, which (often for self-interested geopolitical reasons) will be rare, attacking other states' territories will always tend to undermine lawful world order. Such attacks represent 'states of exception' responding to 'cracks in the system' of ordered national control. While terrorists understandably try to exploit these geopolitical anomalies as far as they can, those pressing for the achievement of global cosmopolitan order will find refusal of legal constraints in itself an important reason to denounce military action projected into other states. But complete insistence upon multinational authorisation might mean that nothing could *ever* be done to counter illegal cross-border aggression forcefully at source. And, rightly or wrongly, there are recurrent statements or accusations that, in practice, the US, as global hegemon, able to impose a wide range of costs and risks, is the authority which effectively decides when, how long, and how intensively its allies or its own forces are entitled to go off the legal reservation by crossing international boundaries.

Historically, there has also been a frequent pattern of secrecy in which publics and even legislatures are not told of bombings or, especially, Special Forces' actions by their states. For example, insertion of Commonwealth forces into Indonesian territory during Confrontation was kept deliberately secret from national parliaments and the media. Secrecy was also sought, less successfully, for the US bombing of Cambodia and other incursions during the Indochina Wars of the 1960s and 70s.

Democracy

Striking at terrorists across borders is often intensely popular and can enhance the electability of those who order or loudly advocate it. On the other side of the border revanchism, as in Gaza, may also be a genuine and consistent democratic choice. Some critics, unhappy with electoral results which launch or intensify conflicts intended to change the choices of opposing communities by the deliberate infliction of painful consequences, fear that '*corrupted democracies*', '*willing to elect, with untroubled consciences, those who speak the language of torturers and terrorists'...'may increasingly prove the norm rather than the exception.'[6]*

It is far less clear now than to the mediaeval founders of Just War theory what constitutes an incontestably legitimate state. The most popular, but far from precise, contemporary criterion is democracy. Democracies can make bad choices. But if well informed and intensely involved electorates are not to be trusted to endorse these decisions by 'deliberative democracy', it is unclear where else should we look.

Just War Requirement 5: A Reasonable Prospect of Success

> 'The initiators must see a reasonable chance of succeeding in their just aim. War offers no certainties, but arms must not be taken up nor lives sacrificed if, on honest appraisal, the likely result is simply death and suffering without making things materially better than they would otherwise have been.'

Discussion

What kind of success in which aim – or combination of aims?

The difficulties in identifying *a single aim* have already been discussed. But several different possible meanings of *success* are frequently conflated in commentary:

- Total victory and security against the terrorists, their backers and supporting populations?
- Improvement of the geopolitical balance?
- Avoiding humiliation and accelerating defeat?
- Eliminating a proportion of the insurgent leadership and arsenal?
- Achieving a more satisfactory '*hurting stalemate*',[7] out of which an eventual peace agreement, or least a sullen ceasefire, might emerge?
- Establishing or re-establishing *deterrence*, through the credible threat of future punishment, as a future national resource?
- Maintaining national morale?
- Degrading the will of the enemy organisation – or its 'civilian' supporters?

---

[6]   See Pankaj Mishra, 'Behind the violence in Gujarat, Gaza and Iraq is the banality of democracy', *The Guardian*, (11 February 2009), which links a critique of Israeli electoral choices after Cast Lead with the re-election of Gujarat's ultra nationalist Hindu Prime Minister.

[7]   This is a frequently encountered term of art in conflict resolution analysis, and is connected with the notion of 'ripeness': that stage in a conflict when both sides might be willing to consider transformative concessions to escapefrom a mutually intolerable situation.

What is 'reasonable'- and to whom?

A significant moral question here is perhaps *who* is entitled to judge the possibilities of success – and who is then entitled to second guess their assessment?

- The political or military leaderships of the initiating state?
- Opinion polls or the anticipated electoral verdict of its national electorate?
- A virtual international consensus of academia, campaigning NGOs and commentariat?
- General international public opinion – the ordinary man, profoundly influenced by available media coverage, in how many different streets?
- Historians, exploiting hindsight, after decades of journals and conferences, and access to previously secret documents?

Special Features

Some critics insist that attacking sanctuaries is intrinsically likely to fail because these situations have recurrent special features:

- damage inflicted will be offset by the rage which is ignited, especially if the ratio of non-combatant civilians killed to terrorists eliminated as a result of UAV strikes is in the order of 50:1 – a figure apparently provided by Pakistani officials, frequently quoted in Pakistani papers and contested but not yet disproved by authoritative alternative official US statistics;[8]
- well-disposed governments will be undermined and hostile ones driven into more extreme resistance;
- losses will be rapidly replaced;
- it is anyway futile to attack *territory* when terrorist networks now rely upon far-flung, diverse, dispersible nodes, using cyber and international urban spaces. (In early 2009, for example, Al-Qaʿida/Taliban were said to be moving eastwards, deeper into central Pakistan, to avoid US drone strikes, and this seems to have been one cause of the subsequent large-scale and destructive internal hostilities with the Pakistani Army. By late 2009 there were repeated reports that extremist Islamist leaders had further relocated to the urban sprawl of Karachi, where 'droning' was not politically feasible.)

On the other hand, there are indications of severe and far-reaching attrition inflicted on senior Al-Qaʿida and Taliban leaders by American aerial attacks in Pakistan since CIA drone strikes started there (apparently with secret Pakistani government complicity) in 2004 and were significantly expanded in 2008 and 2009. '*In addition to killing over a dozen mid-level Taliban leaders, the strikes*

---

[8]   See for example David Kilcullen's Congressional Testimony: 'U.S. drone attacks in Pakistan "backfiring," Congress told', *Los Angeles Times*, (3 May 2009).

have taken out ten of al-Qaeda's top twenty leaders ... one of America's greatest successes in the war on terror.[9] The most important was the killing, in August 2009, of the leader of the Pakistani Taliban, Baitullah Mehsud, responsible for numerous suicide bombing outrages and accused of the assassination of Benazir Bhutto. (His successor, Hakimullah Mehsud, publicly swore vengeance but was himself reported killed in a drone strike on a compound in Waziristan on 14 January 2010. The Taliban immediately denied it and five months later he was widely reported to be issuing further threats.) The elimination of a single key leader can evidently have far reaching effects. Pakistan's President, Ali Zardari, assessed that '*due to his* (Baitullah Mahsud's) *death the Taliban leadership is in disarray, the major suicide bomb network and Taliban patronage has been disrupted. Acts of terror have considerably decreased in the border area.*'[10] There are reports that many of the strikes have been made possible by agents on the ground placing infrared homing chips, often for money, and sometimes possibly for personal revenge.

Apart from the number and significance of senior personnel lost, there appears to have been a significant general impact on terrorist operating patterns:

> the unpredictable (UAV) attacks on convoys, hujras (guest houses), compounds, training camps and madrassas have wreaked havoc in the Taliban and al-Qaeda ranks. ... al-Qaeda members have been forced to dismantle their training camps ... (for). hidden classrooms; they no longer communicate using cell phones for fear of being tracked; they have been forced to replace trusted veterans who have been killed with less experienced operatives; and they have launched what has been described as a 'witch-hunt', killing real or perceived spies and traitors. These exacerbated suspicions may now also extend to outside aid workers.[11]

There have been consistently repeated public statements by Pakistani government figures, previously confirmed by media polling, that the drone strikes are counter-productive in creating hostility to the US. But severe fighting in 2009 between Taliban and government forces in Pakistan has been a new feature of the crisis spreading through what, after the 2001 invasion of Afghanistan, is now designated as the 'Afpak' regional theatre. The increasing loathing of intimidatory Islamist violence has apparently led to some recent Pakistani public feeling, even

---

[9]   Brian Glyn Williams 'Death from the Skies: An Overview of the CIA's Drone Campaign in Pakistan', Part 1, *Jamestown Foundation Terrorism Monitor*, vol. 7, issue 29, (25 September 2009).

[10]   *Financial Times*, London, (16 September 2009).

[11]   See Jeremy Scahill, '*Blackwater's Secret War in Pakistan*' (Democracy Now: 24 November 2009 at http://www.democracynow.org/2009/11/24/blackwaters_secret_war_in_pakistan_jeremy).

amongst Pashtun tribes, that strikes against Taliban targets should be increased. The Pakistani government is reported to be seeking armed drones of its own.[12]

Similarly, the Israeli government has repeatedly stressed that its attacks have had positive strategic consequences: there has been no recurrence of rocket attacks from Hezbollah in South Lebanon since their retaliatory offensive of 2006 and much reduced firing from Gaza since Operation Cast Lead.

Overall there seem – at least so far – to be no easy historical generalisations about either the success or the indispensability of these operations. (For example, the Western military spokesman in Pakistan quoted at the beginning of the chapter is quite certainly wrong to believe that no insurgencies have been suppressed while sanctuaries remained.) Attacks on sanctuaries frequently have very different and often limited politico military aims. Where they are aimed at averting future terrorist activity, their success has to be guessed at against counterfactuals. There are analogies here with a major dispute in World War II history. Although Nazi war production rose throughout the war, historians still disagree over how high it might have risen without Allied strategic bombing, and therefore how far that growth potential morally justified inflicting mass German civilian casualties from the air.

Just War Requirement 6: Last Resort

> 'Arms must not be taken up without trying (unless there are good grounds for ruling them out as likely to be ineffective) every other way of adequately securing a just aim.'

Discussion

Very few cross boundary interventions will be an absolute or literal last resort. There will generally be other, varyingly effective, lines of operation. These include nationally or internationally applied diplomatic, legal or economic pressure on the other government, extraditions, military assistance and training, threats of military attack on government targets, enhanced border security (e.g. surveillance, tribal bribery, walls and fences) – and/ or negotiations with the insurgents.

But these may not work alone, or at all, and might anyway be pursued synergistically in parallel – often on back channels. Again, indefinite, unconditional, forbearance would amount to a policy decision never to make a military response, and, as Walzer points out: '*It is an important principle of Just War Theory that*

---

[12] See Brian Glyn Williams, 'Death from the Skies: An Overview of the CIA's Drone Campaign in Pakistan', Part 2, *Jamestown Foundation Terrorism Monitor*, vol. 7, issue 30: October 2009.

*justice, though it rules out many ways of fighting, cannot rule out fighting itself–
since fighting is sometimes morally and politically necessary.'*[13]

II: *JUS IN BELLO*

These considerations address the justice with which war is actually waged. Just
War Requirement 7: Public Declaration (not mentioned by Quinlan and Guthrie,
but a feature of some other lists of criteria).

Discussion

General threats of intervention are frequently made well in advance, to change
adversary behaviour or to justify intended attacks. They may save civilian lives
by inducing some non-combatants to move away, though disrupting life and
livelihood. But public declarations of the *precise start date* of cross-border
operations are rarer, for political and operational reasons

In Operation Cast Lead, repeated general statements that Hamas missile attacks
would no longer be tolerated were followed by an air attack without warning,
and indeed after a disinformation campaign, to catch the maximum number of
unprepared policeman, who were judged collectively likely to become combatants
against any Israeli incursion into Gaza, on their Graduation Day. Initial US air
attacks with UAVs in Yemen and Pakistan were not publicised in advance either.

Just War Requirement 8: Discrimination

> 'War must not involve deliberate attack on the innocent i.e. those 'not involved
> in harming or helping to harm.' 'But difficult judgements remain about exactly
> who is to be regarded as not involved, or 'non-combatant.' 'Deliberate attack'
> means attack in which the harm to the innocent is the direct aim of the attack, or
> essential to achieving its purpose.'

Discussion

Whatever the ground truth surrounding non-combatant casualties, global taking of
sides over the conduct of interventions is malleable, and divisively conditioned by
ethnic or religious identification – which can be a reaction, especially in the Islamic
world, to '*mass humiliation by proxy*'. Widespread partisan external judgements
of this kind can be important, but not necessarily ethically driven, consequences
of a cross-border operation.

---

[13]   Michael Walzer, 'War Fair', *The New Republic*, (31 July 2006).

Yet discrimination (or 'distinction') is often intrinsically hard to achieve in cross-border operations because of both unavoidable, and, often, deliberate mingling of low-intensity combatants among their host (or captive) populations. Critics allege that this is leading to *'the death of the civilian'*: simply by inhabiting a territorial space that has been deemed a terrorist sanctuary, whole civil groups become military targets at inevitable risk from the inherent inaccuracies of enemy bombardment.[14] But the problem is worsened in densely populated urban environments, and, most seriously, by intentional efforts to shield combatants or military assets with innocents. Here the repeated justification from governments is that *'A Tragedy Is Not a Crime.'* The intention behind the military operation may not be criminal, and the risk to civilians may be, as in Gaza, mitigated by new and unprecedented 'technologies of warning' such as mobile phone calls or texts,[15] or warning 'knocks on the roof' by non-explosive munitions advising them to move out of targeted buildings. Nevertheless, worldwide judgements of relative guilt for civilian casualties may decisively question the Proportionality of the Cause, to the extent that anticipated international revulsion may undermine the Reasonable Prospect of Success.

In relation to the drone strikes in Pakistan, political denunciations and calls for legal investigation into civilian casualties and the responsibilities of commanders and governments have been largely confined to campaigning NGOs. In relation to Operation Cast Lead, a number of governments fiercely criticised Israel during and after the attack, and the UN Human Rights Council set up a Fact-Finding Mission to Report on the Gaza Conflict, headed by Judge Richard Goldstone. The Goldstone Report was completed in mid September 2009, concluding that *'there is evidence indicating serious violations of international human rights and humanitarian law were committed by Israel during the Gaza conflict, and that Israel committed actions amounting to war crimes, and possibly crimes against humanity.'* It also found *'evidence that Palestinian armed groups committed war crimes, as well as possibly crimes against humanity, in their repeated launching of rockets and mortars into Southern Israel.'* It judged that the Israeli military action was directed at the Gaza population as a whole and that the long-running blockade represents a continuance of an overall policy of disproportionate force aimed at collective punishment.

The Report's judgements were praised by many as requiring major Israeli soul-searching, in particular, a re-examination of the system of prosecuting military personnel, and opening possibilities of international prosecution. But world responses were characteristically divided. The Report was strongly criticised, not only by Israel but by the US Government. Criticisms included flawed mandate,

---

[14]   Michael Innes (ed.), *Denial of Sanctuary: Understanding Terrorist Safehavens* (Westport, Connecticut/London, 2007), p. 44.

[15]   Eyal Weizman 'Lawfare in Gaza: legislative attack', *Open Democracy*, (25 February 2009), available at: http://www.almanar.com.lb/NewsSite/NewsDetails.aspx?id=75861&language=en

partisan membership and witnesses, indifference to the context, and therefore the justification, of the Israeli attack, for defective methodology reliant on biased or intimidated eyewitnesses, for disputable categorisation of 'civilians' and policeman as non-combatants, and for various alleged factual errors. (Pro-Israeli commentators have also pointed out that no similar process has been instituted to examine Russian actions in Chechnya or US airstrikes in Afghanistan and Pakistan where civilian casualties may have been significantly greater, both proportionately and absolutely, than in Gaza. It is noteworthy that disputes over the effects of the continuing campaign of US drone strikes in Afghanistan and Pakistan did not prevent President Obama's Nomination for the Nobel Prize in autumn 2009).

At the time of writing there are suggestions that Israeli ministers, officials, officers and even lawyers might find themselves facing war-crimes charges in several countries on the basis of judgements in the report. Whatever the eventual consequences for state behaviour, there is consequently a near-term prospect of legal Balkanisation over the validity of the report, which will further illustrate the depth of international division over the just and legally permissible limits of military action against terrorism.[16]

Just War Requirement 9: Proportionality

> 'Action must not be taken in which the incidental harm done is an unreasonably heavy price to incur for likely military benefit. Harm needs to be weighed particularly –but not only- in relation to the lives and well-being of innocent people. The lives of friendly military personnel need to be brought into account, and sometimes even those of adversaries. The principle of avoiding unnecessary force always applies.'

Discussion

Here again, intensely committed commentators often diverge from dispassionate Just War analysis, in which Proportionality should rest on *forward-looking calculations* about future harm rather than tit-for-tat reprisals for past wrongs. Thus it creates no obligation to produce anything approaching equal casualty counts. Nevertheless, between 1,166 and 1,417 Palestinians were killed in Gaza between December 2008 and January 2009, compared with 10 Israeli soldiers and 3 civilians. Figures of this kind are invariably disputed, but the size of the disparity inevitably leads to accusations of major injustice. Operation Cast Lead is described in the Islamic world as the Gaza Massacre, and there is similar intense

---

[16] The Goldstone Report : *Human Rights in Palestine and Other Occupied Arab Territories: Report of the United Nations Fact-Finding Mission on the Gaza Conflict* (UN Human Rights Council A/HRC/12/48 September 2009) is available at http://www2.ohchr. org/english/bodies/hrcouncil/specialsession/9/FactFindingMission.htm

awareness – apparently now a theme in Pakistani popular music – that American drone strikes are costly in innocent human lives and conducted at no risk whatever to their far-off operators. What is critical in moral analysis – although perhaps not in public debate – is how many of the non-military deaths were genuinely non-combatant, and might have been avoided by a greater willingness to accept military casualties from close engagement rather than reliance on inevitably less discriminating long-range firepower.

In March 2009, the Palestinian Centre for Human Rights (PCHR) published a detailed named list of 1,417 Gaza casualties, according to which 926 were civilians – including policeman. That would imply a ratio of about 1.9 non-combatants killed for each fighter eliminated. In September the Israeli Human Rights group B'Tselem released a report concluding that Israel's military killed 1,387 Palestinians during Operation Cast Lead of whom 773 of were civilians, yielding a somewhat lower ratio of around 1.3. All these figures are strongly rebutted by the Research Division of Israeli Defence Intelligence which insists that, of 1,166 Palestinian casualties in the Gaza offensive, 709 were 'terror operatives', presumably including policeman, affiliated with Hamas and other groups. This would mean that around only 0.6 non-combatants had died for each fighter eliminated.[17] Definitions of 'combatants' therefore play a bitterly disputed part in judging how far the criterion of discrimination has been met. But the different ratios that they generate seem unlikely by themselves to determine fierce overall judgements on the justice of cross-border counter-terrorist operations in which the casualties occur.

These are operations which are almost never seen as climactic last resorts or final battles. The expectation is that the terrorism will go on and there is consequently little disposition to accept serious losses amongst conventional military forces.

In contrast, some ethicists would require governments to observe a one-for-one 'substitutability ratio' between their own citizens' lives and those which might be collaterally lost in anti-terrorist operations: '*when a country, or its army, acts in a manner that places civilians ….…in harm's way, then that country's (or that army's) responsibility to minimise the peril inflicted on those individuals ought to be the same regardless of their nationality, ethnicity, creed, etc.*'[18] This would presumably rule out bombing, or long-range fire support, in all discretionary expeditionary campaigns, including humanitarian interventions, as well as counterinsurgency and cross-border counter-terrorism, for the same reasons that it is not an acceptable tactic in domestic counter-terrorism within democracies.

It is doubtful how many governments could stay long in elected office if they adopted this approach. Their senior military officers may have even stronger professional doubts about the impact of the higher anticipated losses to their own side, on military morale and sustainability of campaigns. Such scepticism would

---

[17] 'Israeli Army Refutes B'Tselem Numbers On Gaza', *Jewish Telegraphic Agency*, *Jerusalem Wire Ser*vice, (11 September 2009).

[18] Letter from Menahem Yaari, strongly supported by Avishai Margalit and Michael Walzer, in the *New York Review of Books*, (8 October 2009).

be consistent with widespread public attitudes that national military forces should not be asked to assume unnecessary risks, that indeed it would be immoral for a military leadership not to insist on minimising the risk of injury to its own soldiers, and that the civilian governments owe those soldiers a stringent duty of care since they are essentially citizens in uniform forced into danger by others' aggression.[19]

There is no worldwide consensus on any single proper exchange rate between the lives of 'our soldiers', 'our civilians' and 'hostile civilians ', still less that it should be even approximately 1:1. Even within the security organisations of a single country, individuals may disagree profoundly about this, as illustrated in 2002 in the Israeli 'Bachelor Experiment' in which officers and officials were asked to:

> Assume that there is a terrorist in Gaza and you know that the terrorist is a Palestinian male bachelor between the ages of 18 and 45 and that tomorrow he is for certain going to kill an Israeli male aged between 18 and 45, and there is only one opportunity to kill him: by means of a missile, which will definitely succeed. How many Palestinian bachelors aged 18–45 do you agree to have die, with certainty, from the missile?

The question therefore involved immediately and completely confident pre-emptive, rather than preventative or retaliatory, counter-terrorist action, and was abstractly phrased to avoid irrelevant emotional identifications. Answers varied from zero to '*as many as needed*' (no end). Younger people, and those with families, tended to give higher numbers. The average number of permitted collateral deaths was 3.14.[20] Elsewhere, amongst populations less practised in discussing counter-terrorist dilemmas, the spread of opinions would presumably be wider.

Examining the *collateral physical destruction and economic impact* of cross-border counter terrorism can produce very large numbers. Although the drone attacks in Pakistan probably destroy, apart from human beings, mud brick houses and compounds, the cost of Operation Cast Lead was enormous. The direct damage to all aspects of the infrastructure has been estimated at some $1.9 billion,[21] and indeed some critics insist that the collateral damage was the principal purpose, as an indirect, and illegal, method of punishing the inhabitants for their support of Hamas. Against that, it has been extensively argued that the extent of physical destruction resulted from Hamas's deliberate decision to use Gaza's physical infrastructure

---

[19]   See Israel: 'Civilians & Combatants', an exchange between Walzer and Margalit, on one side and Asa Kasher and Amos Yadlin, *NYRB*, (14 May and 11 June 2009).

[20]   'Consent and Advise', Yotam Feldman and Uri Blau, *Ha'aretz*, Jerusalem, (5 Feb 2009).

[21]   Figure quoted by the President of the Palestinian Economic Council for Development and Reconstruction, Mohammad Shtayyeh, at a United Nations Seminar on Assistance to the Palestinian People in Cairo on 10 March 2009. It is undoubtedly imprecise, but lower than some initial UN estimates.

to hide its fighters, and that reconstruction will be very largely paid for by the international community, particularly the European Union and the UN, rather than the Gazans themselves. The Israeli attacks also led to the destruction or capture of weapons and war materials, which would have been of strategic importance to Hamas far above their open market value, because of the difficulty of penetrating the Israeli blockade – although smuggling has now resumed on tunnel networks.

Moral–Strategic Thought Experiments

Here it may be worth proposing two further thought experiments, postulating a future where, in conflicts with irregular opponents, governments might introduce:

1. *Offensive Technical Improvements*: advanced and miniaturised sensor, C3I, and UAV technologies coupled with extremely low yield 'humanitarian munitions', so that human nodes in terrorist networks could be rapidly identified, tracked and eliminated with minimum collateral damage ('*warheads on foreheads*') by remote or robotic targeted assassinations[22];

   and/or

2. *Defensive Technical Improvements*: completely effective walls (backed up by prolific missile defences) severing the sanctuaries from the areas which terrorists would wish to target.

Would these entirely conceivable technical developments in discrimination and proportionality represent moral improvement in the way that government forces deal with terrorist sanctuaries?

Experience suggests that critics of cross-border military responses tend to reject this. Indeed they may fear that further asymmetrical technical progress might *worsen* already unjust situations by allowing just resistance to be quietly overwhelmed by expensively precise state violence or inherently oppressive infrastructure. Whether or not such concerns are well grounded, they are not fundamentally about discrimination and proportionality.

---

[22] Some of these have already been employed, as the US GBU 39 Smart Small Diameter Bomb reportedly was in Gaza. Others are in controversial development such as the Dense Inert Metal Explosive (DIME) using tungsten powder rather than shrapnel in order to achieve a more 'focused lethality', and drones 'the size of loaves of bread', capable of flying in through windows.

Discrimination, Proportionality and International Humanitarian Law (IHL)

IHL – probably more appropriately, called Law of Armed Conflict (LOAC) – also exists largely to limit unnecessary suffering by applying *Jus in Bello* principles and creating the possibility of prosecutions for War Crimes. It designates the limit of what world opinion may consider 'tolerable'.

In relation to US drones in Pakistan, an American law professor, Mary Ellen O'Connell, has put forward a detailed argument that these limits have been breached:

> These attacks cannot be justified under international law for a number of reasons. First drones launch missiles or drop bombs … (which) … may only be used lawfully … during the hostilities of an armed conflict, and, then, only lawful combatants may lawfully carry out such killing. Members of the CIA are not lawful combatants. Members of the United States armed forces could be lawful combatants in Pakistan … (only) … if Pakistan expressly requested … assistance in a civil war … . No express request of this nature has been made. Even if it were made, drone attacks are the wrong tactic. Drones have rarely, if ever, killed just the intended target. By October 2009, the ratio has been about 20 leaders killed for 750-1000 unintended victims. … Drones are … counter-productive … . (Their) use … is, therefore, violating the war-fighting principles of distinction, necessity, proportionality and humanity.[23]

The US Government strongly denies these conclusions, and a further intensification of drone attacks is a feature of the US 'surge' in Afghanistan announced by President Obama in December 2009. None of the almost 50 states contributing forces to Afghanistan under NATO command, whose troops stand to benefit from any reduction in capacity inflicted on the Taliban, has dissented from the US position.

But there is a view that legal limits are, in any case, movable and are being widened by contemporary military practice. Operating at the margin of the law may be one of the most effective ways to expand it. As a former legal adviser to the Israeli armed forces put it, '*International law develops through its violation. An act that is forbidden today becomes permissible if executed by enough countries. .Most governments and international bodies considered... targeted assassinations illegal in 2000; but, 8 years [and one attack on the US] later it is in the centre of the bounds of legitimacy.*'[24] From this perspective, whatever intrinsic constraints might be implied by the natural law tradition are of little practical relevance.

---

[23]   Mary Ellen O'Connell, *Unlawful Killing with Combat Drones: A Case Study of Pakistan, 2004-2009* (Notre Dame Law School Legal Studies Research Paper No. 09-43, 2009) available at: http://papers.ssrn.com/sol3/papers.cfm?abstract_id=1501144

[24]   Daniel Reisner, quoted in Eyal Weizman 'Lawfare in Gaza: legislative attack', *Open Democracy*, (25 February 2009).

According to another American law professor, 'Military lawyers legally [condition] the battlefield by poring over target-maps and informing soldiers how they are entitled to kill civilians. IHL then becomes the ethical vocabulary for marking legitimate power and justifiable death.'[25]

As one officer in the Israeli Armed Forces International Law Department was prepared to describe his role: '*Our goal* [In Gaza] *was not to fetter the army, but to give it the tools to win in a lawful manner.*'[26]

This has led to complaints of 'A growing merger between 'the professional vernaculars' of military force and law' and a despairing diagnosis that 'Today, IHL is utilized only to justify the use of force [and] has ceased to exist ... one can put forward weighty and serious reasons to justify almost any action ... and ... validate the use of almost unlimited force ... Instead of legal advice and IHL minimizing suffering, they legitimize the use of force.'[27]

These criticisms fit the description, or complaint, of 'Lawfare', as a calculated strategy, increasingly employed by states and non-state actors, '*of using or misusing law ... to achieve military objectives*'.[28]

The notion that the law is losing its neutral objective ability to judge and discipline conflict fits into the larger concept of Fourth Generation War.

Fourth Generation War (4 GW)

It is impossible here to enter into dispute about the novelty or far-reaching significance of 4GW.[29] The idea is a construct (alternative terms might be Complex Irregular or Hybrid Warfare) emphasising that contemporary conflicts increasingly blur the lines between _war_ and _politics_, soldier and civilian, peace and conflict, battlefield and safety. Yet key aspects of the construct help explain the complexity of moral judgement in these situations:

- 4GW is complex and long-term, with no real breaks or boundaries.
- Terror or intimidation (however defined, and by whichever side) is a constant possible operational method.
- Non-State Actors are increasingly important – often in alliance with states.

---

[25]   David Kennedy, *Of War and Law* (Princeton University Press, 2006), quoted in Weizman, *Lawfare in Gaza: Legislative Attack*.

[26]   Quoted in 'Consent and Advise' by Feldman and Blau, *Ha'aretz*, (5 February 2009).

[27]   Professor Orna Ben-Naftali, Dean of the Faculty of Law in the Israeli College of Management, quoted in 'Consent and Advise' by Feldman and Blau.

[28]   Charles Dunlap, 'Lawfare amid warfare', *Washington Times*, (3 August 2007).

[29]   For a useful introductory discussion of 4 GW see Terry Terriff, Aaron Karp, and Regina Karp (eds.), *Global Insurgency and the Future of Armed Conflict; Debating Fourth Generation Warfare* (London, 2008).

- Bases are often non-national or transnational.
- All available networks – political, economic, social, religious, diaspora, media, legal, academic and military – are exploited.
- Attacks are threatened, and occasionally carried out, on the enemy's culture, and its symbols.
- Non-combatants are deliberately introduced or exploited to create operational dilemmas.
- Sophisticated psychological warfare is employed, especially through media manipulation.
- The *willpower* (including the moral self-confidence) of electorates, supporting populations and governments is the decisive target.

Contemporary Indicators

Various recent developments indicate how far current conflicts are approaching the 4 GW Condition. For example:

- the US Government's continued and anxious quest for effective public diplomacy;[30]
- Israel's creation of a cross-departmental National Information Directorate, in 2008, charged with '*hasbara*' or explanation;
- the Hamas Charter (1987) calling on:

> Men of letters, members of the intelligentsia, media people, preachers, teachers and educators to play their role ... Jihad means not only carrying arms and denigrating the enemies. Uttering positive words, writing good articles and useful books, support and solidarity and assistance, all that too is Jihad.

- increasingly sophisticated and web-centred methods – by various sides – to bend international public judgements;
- rigged or misleading footage;
- disinformation campaigns;
- Distributed Denial of Service attacks by 'hactivists' against websites projecting opposing opinions;
- the introduction of '*Megaphone*', a 'downloadable tool used during the Gaza crisis, ... designed to alert users to anti-Israeli editorials, giving them the chance to send rebuttals, to sway public opinion through the sheer volume of replies';
- the recruitment by the Israeli Ministry of Immigrant Absorption of large numbers of non-Hebrew speakers to influence the international balance of

---

[30] See for example the consistently illuminating 'MountainRunner' blog at http://MountainRunner.us/

opinion on the Internet;[31]
- attempts to draw younger sympathisers into cyberwar through social networking sites;[32]
- The fierce British dispute in early 2009 about the BBC's decision not to screen the Gaza Appeal for charitable funds following Operation Cast Lead on the grounds that it was excessively partial towards the Palestinian interpretation of events.

Just War theory has to imply the possibility of calm and objective judgement. But it remains to be discovered whether any international consensus can now form which is capable of reliable judgements under these calculated and technically amplified pressures.

Conclusions

The world will not stop asking questions about justice in warfare. Its questioning has, over time, been more precisely formulated by the Just War tradition than any other. There are no signs that this is going to change. Yet the closer conflicts approach the 4GW Condition, the less unifying moral grip Just War theory seems to give, and the less clear-cut its answers. Cross-border attacks on densely populated sanctuaries can come very close indeed to the 4GW state.

In this situation, attempts to apply Just War categorisations slide into '*casuistical engrenage*' in which each recurrent accusation of insufficiency is met by a characteristic counterargument. Complex questions arise about levels of knowledge, democratic accountability and entitlement to judge the prudence of complex and secret long-term strategic calculations. Legitimacy and authority are fundamentally disputed. How far are sovereign governments and even vigorously democratic electorates entitled to reach and persist in their own decisions about the wisdom of force?

By observation (testable by discussion and thought experiments) what drives much moral commentary about interventions against sanctuaries is above all, critics' prior choice of *a cause, with an inextinguishable, expansive, right of self-defence against oppression or aggression*, through their attitude to the overall justice of the status quo which the military intervention aims to restore or preserve. There are, of course, exceptions, such as Richard Goldstone, who is Jewish and describes himself as intensely devoted to Israel. But they are minority voices, and Goldstone himself has been heavily attacked as 'objectively siding' with Palestinian terrorism in the basic approach adopted in his report.

---

[31]   Cnaan Liphshiz, 'Israel recruits "army of bloggers" to combat anti-Zionist Web sites', Jerusalem: *Haaretz*, (19 Jan 2009).

[32]   Danny Bradbury, *The Fog of Cyberwar*, *The Guardian*, (5 February 2009).

Just War theory now faces problems its framers never expected, dragging it far beyond ethical assessments of separately identifiable state ventures of organised military-on-military violence. As it stands, as described by Guthrie and Quinlan, it has little to say about the relative claims of conflicting communities or the impacts of prolonged political, legal, cultural, social and economic, as well as military processes.

Simply in relation to the two cases discussed here, Just War theory cannot, for example, by itself untangle the interlocking implications of the following background aspects of cross-border counter terrorism in Palestine or Pakistan: enforced exiles and consequent demands for rights of return over hugely different timescales; profoundly disputed historical memories over entitlement to sacralised territory; implacable traditions of often suicidally murderous resistance or religious intolerance, terrorist groups disputably connected to a wider global terror threat of debatable gravity, insistently different cultural willingnesses to provoke or accept casualties; growing institutional dependencies upon long-range military technologies; governmental denunciation of foreign cross-border aerial attacks on terrorist targets in national territory, combined with covert complicity and assistance, differential standards and principles for democracy and human rights (especially for women and minorities); the polarising involvement of ethnic or religious diasporas and transnational networks; uncertain, elastic and contested definitions of 'non-combatants'; denials of the right to travel or emigrate for large groups; systematically fostered religious and ethnic hatreds, discretionary military campaigns, occupations, and counterinsurgency surges, more or less painfully and temporarily maintained by political determination; negotiated military withdrawals followed by total physical control of access to power, water supplies, and movement of goods or people generating widespread 'spatial suffering'; blockades for security or, allegedly – and nearly indistinguishably – coercive political reasons; near-complete reliance of refugee communities or nations on unconditional international humanitarian and development aid for livelihoods and infrastructure; government dependencies on US military aid; entirely walled off – or elsewhere non-existent – frontier demarcations; uncertainly feasible and fiercely opposed democratic-state building projects; pervasive border-straddling tribal affiliations and hostilities, immiserating cultures and predicaments of underdevelopment, paralysing corruption, persistent, widely popular revanchism or even eliminationism, strategic kidnapping of individuals for prisoner exchange or public online decapitation; endemic social, inter-communal, or military intimidation; and dependence of local elites on outside donors, military allies, international terrorists, drug dealers, or self-interested third-party would-be puppet master states and their quasi-autonomous intelligence services.

As one critic put it, in a review of the Quinlan and Guthrie book, the Just War tradition is less a road-map of any kind at all, than 'a road-side billboard saying "Beware! Hazards Ahead!" '[33] Analogously, the credibility of International Humanitarian Law is under significant challenge as a result of constant pressures

---

[33]   Alasdair Palmer, 'The Lawfare of Warfare', *Daily Telegraph*, (1 Nov 2007).

to create convenient legal interpretations. Developing military technologies may improve discrimination and proportionate use of force, but will not overcome the intrinsic disputability of the circumstances in which they are used.

Some Implications

The point of this discussion has not been to dissuade moral critics from commitment to one or other side in these situations, but to insist that they should be clearer, and more honest, about which aspects of conflict they are entitled to feel enraged.

For Philosophers, Theologians, and Jurists

There is a lack of internationally cogent arguments addressing the relative claims of conflicting communities and the moral balance sheet from the totality of their past engagements with each other, or their sufferings at the hands of third parties. The Holy Grail of a multiculturally convincing set of criteria may never be attained, but remains worth pursuing, if only slightly to moderate the confusion and embittered self-righteousness of current disputes.

For Politicians, Generals, Theorists of Radicalisation and Information Warriors

It is important to realise how Just War principles are breaking down in their application to complex conflicts – and, unless they can develop to meet contemporary circumstances (which I have called here the 4GW Condition) how selectively, ingeniously and explosively the fragments will be mixed and taken up in a divisive trans-global dispute which itself becomes a major theatre of war.

If Just War theory cannot convincingly evolve to address today's complexities, we expect widespread effective reversion to one of the two classic default moral alternatives: pacifism (the avoidance and condemnation of all violence) or realism (the justification of most actions regarded as necessary for the security or survival of a specific side, nation, or religion). But it seems improbable that, in today's emotional and deliberately media charged circumstances, pacifism will become the preferred choice.

A Final Paradoxical Conclusion

If the 4GW theorists are right, there is little chance of these arguments being widely accepted. The partisan advantage from arguing passionately on all moral and legal fronts that favoured causes are convincingly supported by Just War theory will be too tempting a strategic benefit to give up.

Chapter 12

Countering the Threat of Nuclear Terrorism

Dr. Nick Ritchie

Introduction

The spread of weapons of mass destruction (WMD) to state and non-state actors is considered a profound threat to national security by many governments.[1] The potential for acts of terrorism using weapons of mass destruction has been a feature of international security for several decades.[2] Since the attacks of 9/11 the spectre of WMD terrorism, in particular nuclear terrorism, has seized academics, parliamentarians and policy-makers and galvanised detailed analysis of how to prevent it.

The term 'weapons of mass destruction' is a generic label assigned to highly lethal and indiscriminate nuclear, biological and chemical weaponry. Conflating these three types of 'unconventional' munitions is misleading, however, since nuclear weapons by most measures belong in a category of their own.[3] Indeed the most potent and for many the most terrifying form of mass casualty WMD terrorist attack is a 'nuclear 9/11': the detonation of stolen nuclear weapon or an improvised nuclear device (IND) in a major city.

In keeping with the theme of this book this chapter explores the potential for non-military means of countering the threat of WMD terrorism, specifically nuclear terrorism in this instance. The chapter begins by establishing the potential for acts of nuclear terrorism before exploring non-military means of countering the threat and the possible role and implications of exercising a military option.

First, it is necessary to define what we mean by nuclear terrorism. A standard typology generally constitutes four categories: detonation of a stolen nuclear weapon; detonation of an improvised nuclear device; destruction of a nuclear power reactor or high-level radioactive waste storage facility; and detonation of a radiological dispersal device, or 'dirty bomb', designed to spread radioactive material such as cobalt-

---

[1]   None more so than the United States. See *National Strategy to Combat Weapons of Mass Destruction*, The White House, (December 2002). Available at <http://www.state.gov/documents/organization/16092.pdf >.

[2]   See Paul Leventhal and Yonah Alexander (eds), *Preventing Nuclear Terrorism: The Report and Papers of the International Task Force on the Prevention of Nuclear Terrorism* (Lexington, MA, 1987).

[3]   Biological weapons do, however, have the potential to kill 100,000s. See Malcolm Dando, *Bioterror and Biowarfare: A Beginner's Guide* (Oxford, 2006).

60 or cesium-137 by means of conventional explosive.[4] The first two categories are potentially the most deadly and constitute true acts of nuclear terrorism. The second two can more appropriately be labelled radiological terrorism designed to release radiation and cause injury, panic and social and economic disruption. This chapter focuses on acts of nuclear, as opposed to radiological, terrorism.

Access to Fissile Material

Analysis of the threat of nuclear terrorism cannot focus solely on terrorist groups. An act of nuclear terrorism will require the use of either an intact state-manufactured nuclear weapon or state-manufactured fissile material that can be used to generate a nuclear explosion. Weapon-usable fissile material comes in two forms: highly-enriched uranium (HEU) and weapon-usable plutonium. HEU refers to uranium that has been enriched in the isotope uranium-235 (U^{235}) to 20 per cent or more from a naturally occurring 0.7 per cent. Low enriched uranium (LEU) enriched to 3–5 per cent in U^{235} is used as nuclear reactor fuel. Weapon-grade uranium is typically enriched to above 90 per cent in U^{235}. The higher the level of enrichment the easier it is to use the material to create a nuclear explosion.[5] Enriching uranium is a major industrial process that can only be undertaken by states.

Plutonium is produced by irradiating uranium fuel in a nuclear reactor. The uranium undergoes chemical changes and plutonium is produced within the fuel rods. The plutonium in the spent fuel can be separated from unused uranium and other radioactive by-products through a process called reprocessing. Different isotopes of plutonium accumulate in the fuel rods. Weapon-grade plutonium is around 94 per cent plutonium-239 (Pu^{239}). If uranium fuel is irradiated for a longer period, as is usual in nuclear power reactors, the amount of Pu^{239} is reduced to around 60 per cent and higher concentrations of other plutonium isotopes are produced. Nevertheless, this 'reactor-grade' plutonium can still be used to make nuclear weapons.[6] Chemical reprocessing of spent fuel to produce weapon-usable plutonium is also deemed to be beyond the scope of terrorist groups.

Pure weapon-grade HEU metal is the material of choice for a terrorist group. A simple HEU weapon based on a 'gun-type' design involves firing a HEU projectile of sub-critical mass towards a second sub-critical mass of HEU to create a supercritical mass resulting in a nuclear explosion. About 50–60 kg of HEU metal might be needed (the 'bare critical mass' of weapon-grade HEU is 52 kg). The bomb detonated over Hiroshima in 1945 employed a gun-type design using 60 kg of HEU enriched to 80 per cent.[7]

---

[4]   Charles Ferguson and William Potter, *The Four Faces of Nuclear Terrorism* (London, 2005), p. 3.

[5]   Ferguson and Potter, *Four Faces*, p. 108.

[6]   Ibid., p. 108.

[7]   Michael Levi, *On Nuclear Terrorism* (Cambridge, MA, 2007), p. 65.

Plutonium-based weapons require a more complex 'implosion-type' design in which a sub-critical sphere of plutonium is surrounded by shaped high explosive charges that are detonated simultaneously to produce a uniform compression wave that compacts the spherical plutonium mass to supercritical density resulting in a nuclear explosion. The 'bare critical mass' for weapon-grade plutonium metal is 10 kg and around 13 kg for reactor-grade plutonium.[8] Modern nuclear weapons can be designed to use as little as 4 kg.[9] The bomb that destroyed Nagasaki used an implosion design with 6 kg of weapon-grade plutonium. HEU can also be used in an implosion device and would require around 25 kg.[10]

Nuclear Terrorism

Evidence suggests that terrorist groups have both the intent and potential capability to undertake a nuclear attack. First, terrorist groups have expressed a clear interest in conducting a nuclear attack, in particular the apocalyptic Japanese cult Aum Shinrikyo and Al-Qaʿida. In the early 1990s the well-financed Aum group began recruiting scientists and engineers to try and acquire chemical, biological, and nuclear weapons. Members of the cult made a number of ultimately unsuccessful trips to Russia to try and procure nuclear weapon expertise and nuclear weapons, reportedly for the sum of $15million.[11] The group later focused on building rather than purchasing a nuclear weapon and bought a sheep farm in Australia in 1993 to test chemical weapons and mine uranium, but with little success. The group abandoned its nuclear effort and in 1995 conducted a sarin gas attack on the Tokyo subway killing 12 and injuring over 1,000.[12]

Al-Qaʿida has also attempted to procure nuclear weapons and fissile material.[13] In Sudan in the mid-1990s the group attempted to purchase uranium for a weapon but fell victim to a scam in which it reportedly paid $1.5million for radiological waste. The group may also have attempted to purchase nuclear weapons from

---

[8]   Richard Garwin, 'Reactor-Grade Plutonium Can be Used to Make Powerful and Reliable Nuclear Weapons: Separated plutonium in the fuel cycle must be protected as if it were nuclear weapons', August 26, 1998. Available at <http://www.fas.org/rlg/980826-pu.htm>.

[9]   See International Panel on Fissile Materials, 'Fissile Materials and Nuclear Weapons', at <http://www.fissilematerials.org/ipfm/pages_us_en/fissile/fissile/fissile.php>.

[10]   Ferguson and Potter, *Four Faces*, pp. 132–135.

[11]   Sara Daly, John Parachini, William Rosenau, *Aum Shinrikyo, Al Qaeda, and the Kinshasa Reactor Implications of Three Case Studies for Combating Nuclear Terrorism*, RAND (Arlington, VA, 2005), p. 13.

[12]   Daly *et al*, *Aum Shinrikyo*, pp. 16–18.

[13]   See David Albright, *Al Qaeda's Nuclear Program: Through the Window of Seized Documents*, Nautilus Institute Special Forum 47, November 6, 2002. Available at <http://www.nautilus.org/archives/fora/Special-Policy-Forum/47_Albright.html>.

Russia and other former Soviet republics in the early 1990s.[14] Documents uncovered after the invasion of Afghanistan in 2001 strongly suggest that Al-Qaʻida was studying nuclear weapon design, effects and properties and procurement of fissile material. It is also reported that in August 2001 Osama bin Laden met with two senior former officials from Pakistan's nuclear weapons programme to discuss biological, chemical and nuclear weapons.[15] Nevertheless, the group appears to have made little progress in terms of acquiring a weapon or fissile material, or designing and fabricating a workable nuclear device.[16] Concern has also abounded about the security of Pakistan's nuclear arsenal and potential appropriation by Taliban forces.[17]

Second, a number of reports suggest that building a primitive nuclear explosive device does not present insurmountable technical or scientific challenges to a determined terrorist group. If a group has sufficient financial resources, weapon-usable fissile material, laboratory facilities and highly-trained scientists and technicians there is enough publicly available information to enable them to construct a workable nuclear weapon. In 1977, for example, a Princeton undergraduate demonstrated that a detailed workable nuclear weapon design could be achieved from publicly available information. His thesis was assessed by nuclear weapon scientists and immediately classified by the US government.[18] Nevertheless, as Robin Frost points out, putting a design into practice would still be extremely challenging with a high chance of failure.[19]

Third, there is a black market in fissile material, equipment that could be used to make a nuclear explosive device, and information on the construction of nuclear weapons exists. According to the International Atomic Energy Agency (IAEA) there were 18 confirmed cases of HEU and plutonium trafficking between 1993 and 2007 involving a total of 8.35 kg of HEU and 374 g of plutonium (much less than that required for a nuclear weapon).[20] There have also been a number of incidents in which theft of more significant quantities of fissile material has been thwarted. In 1998, for example, the Russian Federal Security Service (FSB) foiled

---

[14]   Daly *et al, Aum Shinrikyo*, p. vii. See also 'Al-Qa'ida's WMD Activities', Center for Nonproliferation Studies, May 13, 2005. Available at <http://cns.miis.edu/pubs/other/sjm_cht.htm>.

[15]   Ferguson and Potter, *Four Faces*, p. 116; Graham Allison, *Nuclear Terrorism: The Risks and Consequences of the Ultimate Disaster* (London, 2006), p. 20.

[16]   Daly et al., *Aum Shinrikyo*, p. 39.

[17]   Shaun Gregory, 'The Terrorist Threat to Pakistan's Nuclear Weapons', *CTC Sentinel*, 2:7, (July 2009).

[18]   Allison, *Nuclear Terrorism*, p. 89.

[19]   Robin Frost, *Nuclear Terrorism after 9/11* (London, 2005), pp. 27–30; Levi, *On Nuclear Terrorism*, pp. 67, 81–82.

[20]   'IAEA Illicit Trafficking Database Fact Sheet', IAEA, Vienna,

        available at <http://www-ns.iaea.org/downloads/security/ITDB_Fact_Sheet_2007.pdf>.

an attempt by employees at a nuclear weapons plant in Chelyabinsk province to steal 18.5 kg of HEU.[21]

There are also extensive clandestine state-to-state nuclear smuggling networks that may have operated and continue to operate beyond the control of central governments. The primary nuclear smuggling network was established by A. Q. Khan, so-called 'father' of Pakistan's nuclear weapon programme. Between 1989 and 2003 the Khan network exported highly sensitive information and materiel for nuclear programmes in Libya, Iran and North Korea and offered the same to Iraq in the early 1990s in exchange for cash, oil and ballistic missile technology. This included a nuclear warhead design, design and equipment for advanced uranium enrichment centrifuges, and uranium hexafluoride gas (the feedstock for a uranium enrichment process based on centrifuge technology) all apparently unsupervised by Pakistani government authorities.[22] The Khan network was exposed and dismantled in 2003 but a comparable network could emerge again.[23]

North Korea has also developed extensive international smuggling networks involving organised crime syndicates and a domestic infrastructure to export drugs, counterfeit currency and other illicit goods. It has also sold ballistic missile technology to Iraq, Iran, Pakistan and Yemen and may sell nuclear assistance and material in the future.[24] Some of these covert smuggling operations are not directly controlled by the North Korean state leadership.[25]

Fourth, significant amounts of weapon-usable fissile material remain unsafeguarded around the world. According to the International Panel on Fissile Materials there were 1,670+/- 300 metric tons (1,000 kg) of HEU in the world in mid-2008. Most of the uncertainty in this figure is due to Russia having not declared how much HEU it produced during the Cold War.[26] In 2003 the US Department of Energy reported that Russia possessed around 600 metric tons of weapon-usable plutonium and HEU outside of its nuclear weapons at more than 50 military and

---

[21]   Rensselaer Lee, 'Nuclear Smuggling: Patterns and Responses', *Parameters*, Spring 2003, p. 101.

[22]   *Nuclear Black Markets: Pakistan, A. Q. Khan and the Rise of Proliferation Networks*, IISS Strategic Dossier (London, 2007), Chapter 3, A.Q. 'Khan and Onward Proliferation from Pakistan'; Ferguson and Potter, *Four Faces*, p. 56; Ian Traynor, 'Blueprint for Nuclear Warhead Found on Smugglers' Computers', *The Guardian*, 16 June 2008.

[23]   David Albright and Corey Hinderstein, 'Unraveling the A. Q. Khan and Future Proliferation Networks', *The Washington Quarterly*, 28:2, Spring 2005.

[24]   Allison, *Nuclear Terrorism*, p. 68; Jonathan Medalia, 'Nuclear Terrorism: A Brief Review of Threats and Responses', *CRS Report for Congress*, Congressional Research Service, February 2005, p, 3.

[25]   Sheen Chestnut, 'Illicit Activity and Proliferation: North Korean Smuggling Networks', *International Security*, 32:1, Summer 2007, p. 81.

[26]   *Global Fissile Material Report 2008*, International Panel on Fissile Materials, 2008, p. 7. Available at <http://www.fissilematerials.org/ipfm/site_down/gfmr08.pdf>, p. 10.

civilian sites, some of which remain poorly protected.[27] The vast majority of HEU is located in Russia and the US as part of their military programmes, but some 10 tons of the global HEU stockpile can be found in approximately 130 civil research reactors in 40 countries, some of which are in unsafeguarded locations such as university departments.[28]

The global stockpile of separated plutonium amounts to roughly 500, all of which is weapon-usable. Approximately half of this is military but the other half is found in civilian nuclear programmes and continues to grow at around five tons per year.[29] A major problem here is that the IAEA cannot guarantee the timely detection of the deliberate diversion of weapon-usable plutonium from reprocessing facilities.[30] This is due in part to the limited ability of the IAEA to maintain constant surveillance at all possible locations for weapon-usable fissile material diversion, and partly because the accounting measures that are used are stymied by the nature of nuclear-fuel plant operations. The problem is most acute for industrial plutonium-reprocessing plants in which significant amounts of material can be lost during the production process such that the amount of feedstock that enters the plant does not tally exactly with amount of plutonium produced. This 'material unaccounted for' or MUF can be substantial, perhaps up to 5 per cent of plutonium throughout amounting to many weapons worth.[31] For example 29.6 kg of separated plutonium were deemed MUF at the Sellafield plant in the UK in 2005 and 69 kg of separated plutonium were unaccounted for after six years of operation at the Tokai-mura Plutonium Fuel Production Facility in Japan.[32]

Finally, there is some evidence for legitimate concern about the fate of the Soviet Union's vast arsenal of 22,000 tactical nuclear weapons. When the Soviet Union collapsed in 1991 the Russian Federation embarked on a massive logistical effort to remove tactical nuclear weapons from the territory of the newly independent republics and consolidate them all on Russian soil. Concern was prevalent throughout the 1990s that not all of these weapons could be accounted for and that poor security at nuclear-warhead storage facilities and lack of pay for soldiers protecting the sites increased the risk of theft by criminal and terrorist groups.[33] In perhaps the most notorious case Russian President Boris Yeltsin's

---

[27]   Ferguson and Potter, *Four Faces*, p. 143.

[28]   Ibid., p. 155.

[29]   *Global Fissile Material Report 2008*, p. 7

[30]   Henry Sokolski, 'Rethinking Nuclear Terrorism', The Nonproliferation Policy Education Center, Washington, D.C., presentation in before the Roundtable of the Hanns-Seidel Stiftung, Wildbad/Kreuth, Germany, 24–25 January 2006.

[31]   'Secure energy: options for a safer world: Effective Safeguards?', Fact Sheet 2, Oxford Research Group, November 2005. Available at <http://www.oxfordresearchgroup. org.uk/publications/briefing_papers/pdf/factsheets1–2.pdf>.

[32]   Sokolski, 'Rethinking Nuclear Terrorism'.

[33]   Ferguson and Potter, *Four Faces*, p. 59.

assistant for national security affairs, General Alexander Lebed, claimed in 1997 that 84 of 132 Soviet-era 'suitcase' battlefield nuclear demolition munitions with explosive yields of between 0.1 and 1 kiloton could not be accounted for. The Russian government strongly refuted Lebed's claim.[34]

A Network of Prevention

The potential for a terrorist group to conduct a nuclear attack cannot be dismissed, even if judgements vary as to the possibility and probability of such an event. How, then, can such acts be prevented and can or should military force be sidelined as a component of a counter-nuclear terrorism strategy?

A terrorist group committed to a nuclear attack will have to acquire either a complete nuclear weapon or weapon-usable fissile material from a state programme. The immediate orientation of a counter-nuclear terrorism strategy must therefore focus on denying nihilistic terrorist groups access to nuclear weapons and fissile material by securing existing stockpiles of weapons and weapon-usable HEU and plutonium.

Over the longer-term a counter-nuclear-terrorism strategy must focus on halting the further spread of nuclear weapons to countries that currently do not possess them and limiting the spread of uranium enrichment and plutonium reprocessing capabilities as part of a global civil nuclear power renaissance. It must be noted that the operation of uranium enrichment and plutonium reprocessing facilities is a legitimate enterprise for a state with a civil nuclear power programme since both processes can be used to manufacture nuclear reactor fuel for domestic energy production. The problem lies in the potential for weapon-grade or weapon-usable material to be produced in these facilities and diverted to a military nuclear programme or acquired by a terrorist group.

Michael Levi presents a comprehensive and compelling case for a preventive 'layered defence' approach based on a range of non-military measures to thwart, constrain and divert a terrorist group at every step of a nuclear plot in order to increase the risk, cost and probability of failure. He argues that if the odds of success are insufficient to warrant the risk and expense of attempting a nuclear attack in the face of mounting preventive obstacles or if the resources and capabilities required to mount a nuclear attack are judged beyond the means of the group then they may be deterred from attempting a nuclear attack in the first place.[35]

In this context it is worth spending a moment to elaborate some of the complexities involved in a nuclear terrorist plot.[36] First, a nuclear attack plot will

---

[34]   Allison, *Nuclear Terrorism*, pp. 10, 43–45.

[35]   Levi, *On Nuclear Terrorism*, p. 2.

[36]   These steps draw on material in Frost, *Nuclear Terrorism*; Ferguson and Potter, *Four Faces*; Levi, *On Nuclear Terrorism*; Jeffrey Lewis, 'The Economics of Nuclear Terrorism', Fund for Peace Threat Convergence New Pathways to Proliferation? Expert

require a well-organised international network of agents to locate and acquire fissile material or a nuclear weapon. Second, it will require accumulation and movement of major financial resources to purchase either a weapon or fissile material, bribe security officials, and procure essential equipment, materials and expertise.

Third, the group may need to recruit inside collaboration at a targeted nuclear weapon or fissile material storage site or negotiate a sale with middle-men who may be state law enforcement officers engaged in a sting operation or part of a scam to sell fissile material that cannot be used for a nuclear weapon, such as depleted uranium. Alternatively, they may have to attempt an armed raid on a nuclear facility and risk immediate detection and pursuit. Fourth, they will need to transport the weapon or fissile material from point of acquisition to a secure facility without detection and capture.

Fifth, they will probably need to test the fissile material to ensure it is suitable for weapon purposes. If they have acquired a nuclear weapon they may have to run diagnostic tests, overcome electronic locks to prevent unauthorised firing without disabling the weapon, and be confident that radioactive decay of the weapon's fissile material and degradation of other ageing components has not affected the weapon's integrity.

Sixth, construction of an IND using stolen fissile material will require a secure site and specialised laboratory equipment to conduct the required fabrication, assembly and testing of the weapon components. Seventh, they will require a small but highly trained group of scientists and technicians with expertise in physics, chemistry, metallurgy, computation, electronic engineering, nuclear radiation effects, metal casting and precision machining, weapon design testing and assembly, and arming and firing a nuclear weapon including technology concerning high explosives and chemical propellants.

Eighth, they will need successfully to fabricate all the necessary component parts. This may include converting the fissile material from powder form to pure metal (HEU and plutonium are often found in powder forms as uranium oxide (UO_2) and plutonium oxide (PuO_2)) and casting it into an appropriate size and shape (casting plutonium can be particularly difficult as it undergoes extreme density changes at different temperature ranges). Ninth, they will need to transport the weapon without detection and without inadvertent pre-initiation to the desired destination for detonation and finally, tenth, they will have to successfully arm and fire the weapon and generate a nuclear explosion.

Measures can be, and have been, established to stymie successive stages of a nuclear terrorist plot. Some of these are generic counter-terrorist measures designed to deny their freedom of movement, access to financial resources, and a secure location for training and operational planning. A more targeted network of preventive measures is also in place to keep nuclear weapons and fissile material out of terrorist hands. This involves US–Russian bilateral programmes

Series, available at <http://www.fundforpeace.org/web/images/pdf/lewis.pdf>; and Rensselaer Lee, 'Nuclear Smuggling: Patterns and Responses', *Parameters*, Spring 2003.

and multilateral international programmes, none of which are perfect, but together constitute the foundations of a layered defence.

US–Russian programmes generally fall under the umbrella of the US Cooperative Threat Reduction (CTR) programme established in 1991 to commit US financial resources and expertise to secure the sprawling Soviet nuclear weapons stockpile and infrastructure. They include a substantial Materials Protection Control and Accounting (MPC&A) programme to improve security and accounting mechanisms at facilities with fissile materials; a Nuclear Weapons Storage Security (NWSS) programme to enhance security systems at nuclear weapons storage sites; a Nuclear Weapons Transportation Security (NWTS) programme to increase the security and safety of nuclear weapons during shipment; construction of the Mayak Fissile Materials Storage Facility to secure 50 tons of weapon-grade plutonium and HEU; an HEU Purchase Agreement to purchase and down-blend 500 tons of weapon-grade Russian HEU to be sold as commercial nuclear reactor fuel; and a plutonium disposition programme to use 34 tons of weapon-origin plutonium in nuclear reactor fuel.[37]

Following 9/11 the US expanded the cooperative threat reduction concept beyond Russia and the former Soviet states and worked with other governments on new international initiatives to create a network of preventive measures to mitigate the threat of nuclear terrorism. In June 2002, for example, the G-8 established a Global Partnership Against the Spread of Weapons and Materials of Mass Destruction that committed $20 billion over 10 years to secure WMD materials worldwide and prevent terrorists, or those that harbour them, from gaining access to weapons or materials of mass destruction – effectively a global multilateral expansion of the US CTR programme.[38]

In 2004 the US Department of Energy announced a new Global Threat Reduction Initiative to repatriate all US and Soviet/Russian-origin HEU reactor fuels in other countries back to Russia and the United States, and work with those countries to convert HEU-fuelled reactors to low-enriched fuel.[39] For example, in August 2002 the US removed 48 kg of HEU from a research reactor site at the

---

[37] Ferguson and Potter, *Four Faces*, p. 148; Amy Woolf, 'Nunn-Lugar Cooperative Threat Reduction. Programs: Issues for Congress', CRS Report for Congress, Congressional Research Service, Washington, D.C., March 2001.

[38] 'Statement by G8 Leaders: The G8 Global Partnership Against the Spread of Weapons and Materials of Mass Destruction', G8 Kananaskis Summit, 27 June 2002. Available at: <http://www.g7.utoronto.ca/summit/2002kananaskis/arms.html>.

[39] Ferguson, 'Preventing Catastrophic Nuclear terrorism', pp.19–20; 'Global Cleanout of Highly Enriched Uranium', International Panel on Fissile Materials. Available at:

    <http://www.fissilematerials.org/ipfm/pages_us_en/projects/global_cleanout/global_cleanout.php>.

Vinca Nuclear Institute near Belgrade and in 2008 removed 74 kg of HEU from Kazakhstan.[40]

At the United Nations the Security Council adopted Resolution 1540 in 2004 that commits all states to refrain from supporting by any means terrorist groups attempting to acquire, use or transfer WMD and to establish domestic law to that effect.[41] It amended the 1980 Convention on the Physical Protection of Nuclear Materials in 2005 to make it legally binding for signatory states to protect nuclear facilities and material in civil domestic use, storage and transport,[42] and in 2005 the UN General Assembly adopted the International Convention on the Suppression of Acts of Nuclear Terrorism to provide a legal basis for international co-operation in the investigation, prosecution and extradition of those involved in the preparation or execution of nuclear terrorism. The convention laid the legal foundation for greater cooperation between the US and Russia resulting in the 2006 US–Russian Global Initiative to Combat Nuclear Terrorism to prevent acquisition of nuclear weapons or materials and hostile action against nuclear facilities.[43]

Finally, in 2005 and 2006 IAEA Director General Mohammed El Baradei set out a plan for an international nuclear fuel bank to be administered by the IAEA. The objective reflects the 2006 US Global Nuclear Energy Partnership to create an international reserve of nuclear reactor fuel and provide an assured supply for nuclear power reactors on a non-discriminatory, non-political basis in order to reduce incentives for countries to develop indigenous uranium enrichment and plutonium reprocessing technologies as part of an expanding civil nuclear power programme.[44] The IAEA reported in 2009 that 50–60 countries were in talks with the agency about constructing new nuclear power plants, some of which are planning to develop enrichment and reprocessing facilities for a complete nuclear fuel cycle to ensure energy independence.[45]

---

[40]   Ferguson and Potter, *Four Faces*, p. 157; 'U.S. removes Highly Enriched Uranium from Kazakhstan', *Global Security Newswire*, 19 May 2009.

[41]   UN Security Council press release SC/8076, 'Security Council decides all states shall act to prevent proliferation of mass destruction weapons', 28 April 2004. Available at <http://www.un.org/News/Press/docs/2004/sc8076.doc.htm>.

[42]   International Atomic Energy Agency, 'Convention on the Physical Protection of Nuclear Material'. Available at <http://www.iaea.org/Publications/Documents/Conventions/cppnm.html>.

[43]   'Statement of Principles for the Global Initiative to Combat Nuclear Terrorism', US State Department, 20 November 2006. Available at <http://www.state.gov/t/isn/rls/other/76358.htm>.

[44]   Frank Barnaby, 'The Nuclear Renaissance: Nuclear Weapons Proliferation and Terrorism', Institute for Public Policy Research, March 2009, p. 6. Available at: <http://www.ippr.org.uk/publicationsandreports/publication.asp?id=650>; Mark Holt, 'Nuclear Energy Policy', CRS report for Congress, Congressional Research Service, Washington, D.C., September 2008.

[45]   'Over 50 nations want to build nuclear plants: report', *Space Daily*, 16 April 2009. Available at <http://www.nuclearpowerdaily.com/reports/Over_50_nations_want_

Looking to the Future

Despite the existence of this network of preventive measures there is growing concern that the threat of nuclear terrorism will rise if: 1) the amount of weapon-usable fissile material and nuclear know-how continues to grow with an expansion of civil and military nuclear programmes; 2) if new and expanding nuclear programmes are subject to poor security, material control and accounting; 3) if a state's nuclear cadre is populated by people who have an ideological affinity to extremist groups; and 4) if more intrusive controls on civil nuclear programmes are not agreed and enforced.

This last point is crucial in that it relates to nuclear disarmament and the 1968 Nuclear Non-Proliferation Treaty (NPT). The NPT represents the keystone of the international nuclear order. It is often presented as a 'grand bargain' between the five recognised nuclear weapon states (NWS)[46] and the rest of the world in which the nuclear weapon states agreed to work towards nuclear disarmament, not provide nuclear weapons or weapon materials or technology to other countries and to assist non-nuclear weapon states (NNWS) with the peaceful uses of nuclear technology. Non-nuclear weapon states in return agreed not to acquire or develop nuclear weapons and to accept international safeguards on their civil nuclear power programmes monitored by the IAEA. Evidence suggests a strong sentiment among the NNWS that the NWS have not made sufficient progress towards nuclear disarmament and a deep reluctance to negotiate and accept more stringent controls on civil nuclear programmes until they do so.

This concern captured global attention in January 2007 when four influential American statesmen (former Secretaries of State Henry Kissinger and George Shultz, former Secretary of Defense William Perry and former Senator Sam Nunn) urged the international community to work towards a world free of nuclear weapons.[47] These four 'Cold Warriors' sought to rekindle President Ronald Reagan's vision of a nuclear weapons-free world because of two pressing issues: the attacks of 9/11 that raised the spectre of a devastating act of nuclear terrorism; and the revival of global interest in nuclear power generation as part of the solution to climate change and energy security demands that could lead to a proliferation of uranium enrichment and plutonium reprocessing capabilities. Their underlying concern is that the only way to halt nuclear proliferation, impose much greater

---

to_build_nuclear_plants_report_999.html>. See also Appendix C 'Countries Considering Nuclear Energy' in *Proliferation Implications of the Global Expansion of Civil Nuclear Power*, International Security Advisory Board, US State Department, April 2008.

[46] Defined as those that had 'manufactured and exploded a nuclear weapon or other nuclear explosive device prior to January 1, 1967', namely the United States, the Soviet Union (now the Russian Federation), Britain, France and China. Pakistan, India, Israel and North Korea also have nuclear weapons but remain outside the treaty.

[47] George Shultz, William Perry, Henry Kissinger and Sam Nunn, 'A World Free of Nuclear Weapons', *Wall Street Journal*, 7 January 2007.

controls on civil nuclear power programmes, and reduce the risk of nuclear terrorism is to move forward decisively towards nuclear disarmament.[48]

Many challenges lie ahead not only in securing current weapon-usable fissile material and nuclear weapons but in limiting the further spread of nuclear weapons and enrichment and reprocessing capabilities. There is still more that can and should be done, for example, to further consolidate, secure and reduce HEU worldwide, especially in Russia, Pakistan and unsecured research reactors; to promote strict nuclear materials safety and accounting standards; to negotiate a global Fissile Material Cut-off Treaty to end the production of fissile materials for use in nuclear weapons; to establish viable international nuclear fuel centres to limit proliferation of uranium enrichment and plutonium reprocessing facilities; and to dramatically cut global stockpiles of nuclear weapons.[49]

Military Force

The use of military force, or planning for the use of force, in the context of nuclear terrorism could take several forms. The first could involve very limited employment of the military instrument for targeted covert or overt operations or as an adjunct to law enforcement operations against a terrorist cell if a state had unambiguous, multiple and actionable intelligence that an act of nuclear terrorism was imminent or underway. In such circumstances the proportionate use of force against the would-be terrorist perpetrators would generally be considered a legitimate act of self-defence to pre-empt a devastating attack.

The use of military force beyond a counter-terrorist operation to thwart an imminent attack becomes much more complex and is likely to involve conflict between states rather than between a state and a non-state actor. The unavoidable direct or indirect, intentional or unintentional, involvement of states in acts of nuclear terrorism is a double-edged sword. Whilst it raises barriers to such acts by undermining the capacity for wholly indigenous terrorist nuclear attacks, it creates greater potential for inter-state conflict because a state will necessarily be implicated in any actual or suspected nuclear attack or plot by a terrorist group – the nuclear weapon or fissile material used has to originate from somewhere.

Furthermore, targeting the nuclear infrastructure and leadership of a state suspected of supporting a nuclear terrorist attack or plot may be tactically, strategically and perhaps politically more attractive than attempting to eliminate the terrorist group itself and may accomplish a number of other goals besides mitigating

---

[48]   See Nick Ritchie, 'A Regime on the Edge? How Replacing Trident Undermines the Nuclear Non-Proliferation Treaty', Department of Peace Studies Research Report, University of Bradford, November 2008. Available at <http://www.brad.ac.uk/acad/bdrc/nuclear/trident/Regime_on_the_edge.pdf>.

[49]   For a detailed analysis see Matthew Bunn, *Securing the Bomb 2008* (Cambridge, MA., 2008).

the threat of nuclear terrorism or retaliating against a successful or thwarted nuclear terrorist attack. This may include degrading the state's nuclear infrastructure to undermine its capacity to wield nuclear threats, removing a hostile regime deemed a threat to allies and 'vital interests', or other context-specific motivations.

The risk of inter-state conflict in the context of nuclear terrorism is particularly salient with regard to so-called 'rogue' states known to possess or suspected of developing nuclear weapons. Fear that a 'rogue' state leadership may be sufficiently motivated by ideology, money or desperation to directly or indirectly support a terrorist nuclear attack through provision of a nuclear weapon, fissile material or a safe haven for planning an attack is widespread within the post-9/11 US and wider Western international security discourse.

Use of military force in this context has generally taken two forms: 'nip it in the bud' selective attacks against a country's embryonic nuclear programme and with it the potential for the state to directly or indirectly support a nuclear terrorist attack; and a broader conflict to comprehensively destroy a state's nuclear infrastructure and wider war-fighting capacity and perhaps remove the leadership from power.

Examples of the former include: Israel's air strike against Iraq's Osiraq nuclear reactor in June 1981 destroying it before it became operational, which David Fisher discusses in Chapter 7;[50] evidence of an Israeli approach to India in 1982 for support for air strikes to destroy Pakistan's Kahuta reactor to terminate development of an 'Islamic bomb';[51] US planning for airstrikes against North Korea's Yongbyon nuclear complex in 1994;[52] the four-day US–UK Operation Desert Fox bombing campaign in December 1998 against 100 suspected WMD facilities in Iraq;[53] and Israel's air strike in September 2007 against a suspected North Korean-built nuclear reactor at Al Kibar in Syria.[54]

Attacks on a state's nuclear and other WMD facilities have also been undertaken as part of a wider conflict to degrade or even eliminate the state's future capacity for producing nuclear, chemical or biological weapons. In April 1945 the US bombing of Tokyo destroyed Japan's most advanced nuclear weapons research

---

[50] Barry Schneider, *Radical Responses to Radical Regimes: Evaluating Preemptive Counter-Proliferation*, McNair Paper Number 41 (Washington, D.C., May 1995), p. 12; David Albright and Khidir Hamza, 'Iraq's Reconstitution of its Nuclear Weapons Program', *Arms Control Today*, October 1998.

[51] Schneider, *Radical Responses*, p. 15.

[52] William Perry and Ashton Carter, *Preventive Defense: A New Security Strategy for America* (Washington, D.C., 1999), p. 128.

[53] William Cohen, *DoD News Briefing*, US Department of Defense, 21 December 1998. Available at <http://www.defenselink.mil/transcripts/1998/t12211998_t1221fox. html>.

[54] Seymour Hersh, 'A Strike in the Dark: What did Israel Bomb in Syria?', *The New Yorker*, 11 February 2008. Available at <http://www.newyorker.com/reporting/2008/02/11/ 080211fa_fact_hersh>.

laboratory during the Second World War.[55] During the Iran-Iraq war Iran launched an unsuccessful attack on the Iraq's Osiraq nuclear reactor in September 1980 at the start of the conflict and Iraqi forces conducted seven air strikes against Iran's nuclear reactor at Bushehr between 1984 and 1988, ultimately destroying it.[56] In 1991 the US-led coalition attempted to destroy Iraq's nuclear, biological and chemical weapon programmes and Scud missiles during the 1991 Gulf War with 970 airstrikes against WMD and ballistic-missile targets.[57] In 2003 the US invaded Iraq to remove Saddam Hussein from power ostensibly due to the implacable WMD threat his regime posed.[58] Finally, in 2006 and 2007 it was widely reported that the US had developed detailed plans for a prolonged air campaign against Iranian nuclear infrastructure and other suspected WMD facilities.[59]

The attacks listed here have not been conducted or planned to prevent nuclear terrorism but to prevent the acquisition of nuclear weapons by 'rogue' states. Nevertheless, the association of 'rogue' states with terrorist activities, the purportedly illicit nature of their nuclear programmes and the oft-stated potential for a nuclear-armed 'rogue' state to aid and abet an act of nuclear terrorism have been used in part to sanction actual or planned military attacks against a state's nuclear infrastructure.

This trend accelerated after 9/11 with the Bush administration's post-9/11 national security paradigm that placed a nexus of WMD, 'rogue' states and terrorism at the heart of US national security strategy.[60] The post-Cold War focus on 'rogue' states characterised as 'outlaw regimes' with large militaries, hostile to the US, developing chemical, biological and above all nuclear weapons, opposed to the spread of democracy and a threat to US allies emerged as a central focus of US national security strategy in the very early 1990s as the Cold War ended.[61] By early 1990 Pentagon officials began to substitute the Soviet threat with the threat of rising Third World powers 'armed with 'First world' weapons' and nuclear proliferation in their statements on global security.[62] President George H. W. Bush, for example, stated in May 1991 that 'As superpower polarization

---

[55]   Schneider, *Radical Responses*, p. 11.

[56]   Ibid., pp. 11, 15.

[57]   Ibid., p. 17.

[58]   See Nick Ritchie and Paul Rogers, *The Political Road to War with Iraq* (Abingdon, 2007).

[59]   Seymour Hersh, 'The Iran Plans', *The New Yorker*, 17 April 2006; 'US 'Iran attack plans' revealed', *BBC News*, 20 February 2007. Available at <http://news.bbc.co.uk/1/hi/6376639.stm>.

[60]   Set out explicitly in the Bush administration's 2002 National Security Strategy, 2002 National Strategy to Combat Weapons of Mass Destruction and 2004 National Military Strategy.

[61]   See Michael Klare, *Rogue States and Nuclear Outlaws* (Hill and Wang, 1995).

[62]   Statement by Admiral Carlisle A.H. Trost before the House Appropriations Committee, Washington, D.C., 22 February 1990, p. 4.

and conflict melt, military thinkers must focus on more volatile regimes, regimes packed with modern weapons and seething with ancient ambitions'[63] and Senator John Kerry, later Democratic Presidential Candidate in 2004, remarked in 1992 that a new containment policy was needed 'directed not against a particular nation or ideology, but against a more diffuse and intensifying danger – the danger that nuclear, chemical and biological weapons, and ballistic missiles to propel them, could pass into the hands of rogue-states or terrorists'.[64] The 'rogue' state doctrine was adopted wholesale by the Clinton administration in the 1990s.

After the attacks of 9/11 the Bush administration adapted this 'rogue state doctrine' to the new 'war on terror'. Having initially focused its response to the attacks on attacking and eradicating Al-Qaʻida in Afghanistan, the 'war on terror' doctrine eventually settled its sights at the end of 2001 on states with WMD programmes, links to international terrorism and a history of hostility towards the US – in other words 'rogue' states that may have some connection to Al-Qaʻida or other perpetrators of international terrorism.[65] This was fully expressed by President Bush in his 2002 State of the Union address four months after 9/11 that singled out the three familiar 'rogues' of Iran, Iraq and North Korea for opprobirum. 'States like these, and their terrorist allies', he argued, 'constitute an axis of evil, arming to threaten the peace of the world. By seeking weapons of mass destruction, these regimes pose a grave and growing danger. They could provide these arms to terrorists, giving them the means to match their hatred. They could attack our allies or attempt to blackmail the United States. In any of these cases, the price of indifference would be catastrophic.'[66] National Security Advisor Condoleezza Rice succinctly encapsulated the amalgamation of the 'rogue' state doctrine and 'war on terror' in April 2002: 'The world's most dangerous people simply cannot be permitted to obtain the world's most dangerous weapons. And it is a stubborn and extremely troubling fact that the list of states that sponsor terror and the lists of states that are seeking to acquire weapons of mass destruction overlap substantially.'[67]

Iraq was placed at the centre of the post-9/11 threat nexus of 'rogue' states, WMD and terrorism and the threat of nuclear terrorism formed an important part of the Bush administration's rationale for invading Iraq and overthrowing Saddam

---

[63] George H. W. Bush, 'Remarks at the United States Air Force Academy Commencement Ceremony in Colorado Springs, Colorado, 29 May 1991, *Public Papers of the Presidents George Bush – 1992 Volume 1*, US Government Printing Office.

[64] Senator John Kerry, 'American Agenda for the New World Order: A. Cementing the Democratic Foundation; B. Forging a New Strategy of Containment', Congressional Record (Senate), 30 June 1992, p. S9177.

[65] Ritchie and Rogers, *The Political Road to War*.

[66] George W. Bush, 'President Delivers State of the Union Address', White House, 29 January 2002.

[67] Condoleezza Rice, 'Remarks by National Security Advisor Condoleezza Rice on Terrorism and Foreign Policy', The White House, 29 April 2002.

Hussein's regime. Bush, for example, declared in September 2002 that 'The regime is seeking a nuclear bomb, and with fissile material, could build one within a year. Each passing day could be the one on which the Iraqi regime gives anthrax or VX – nerve gas – or some day a nuclear weapon to a terrorist ally.'[68] Defense Secretary Donald Rumsfeld argued that Iraq was a 'classic example of the nexus between a terrorist state and well advanced weapons of mass destruction programs and relationships with terrorists'[69] whilst his deputy, Paul Wolfowitz, warned that 'the more time passes the more time Saddam Hussein has to develop his deadly weapons and to acquire more. The more time he has to plant sleeper agents in the United States and other friendly countries or to supply deadly weapons to terrorists he can then disown, the greater the danger. We cannot afford to wait until Saddam Hussein or some terrorist supplied by him attacks us with a chemical or biological or, worst of all, a nuclear weapon, to recognize the danger that we face.'[70] Similar justifications have appeared with regard to Iran and North Korea.[71]

Utility of Force

History suggests that use of military force to combat nuclear terrorism would in all likelihood be part of a wider attack designed first and foremost to reduce a perceived threat of nuclear attack from a proven or potential state sponsor, either in retaliation for supporting a terrorist nuclear attack or more controversially as a preventive operation to degrade the potential for nuclear attack by the state or possible terrorist surrogates. Historical experience suggests that the key variable affecting the use of force is the perceived hostility of the targeted state towards the West in general and the US in particular. A state already branded a 'rogue'

---

[68] George W. Bush, 'Remarks by the President on Iraq', The White House, 26 September 2002.

[69] Transcript, 'Secretary Rumsfeld Interview with *The Sunday Times* London', US Department of Defense, 21 September 2002.

[70] Paul Wolfowitz, 'Remarks by Deputy Secretary of Defense Paul Wolfowitz, Fletcher Conference, Ronald Reagan Building and International Trade Center, Washington', US Department of Defense, 16 October 2002. For further analysis see Ritchie and Rogers, *Political Road to War*.

[71] On Iran see R. Nicholas Burns, Under Secretary for Political Affairs, US State Department, 'United States Policy Toward Iran', opening statement before the House International Relations Committee, Washington, D.C., 8 March 2006 and Robert Joseph, Under Secretary for Arms Control and International Security, US State Department, 'Countering the Iranian Nuclear Threat', Remarks at the Annual Dinner of the Greater Washington Area Council for the American-Israeli Public Affairs Committee, Washington, D.C.,1 February 2006. On North Korea see Bill Gertz, 'N. Korean Threatens to Export Nukes', *The Washington Times*, 7 May 2003 and speech by Under Secretary of State John Bolton, 'Dictatorship at the Crossroads', East–West Institute, Seoul, South Korea, 31 July 2003.

and suspected of supporting terrorist groups and developing nuclear weapons would likely face a significant military assault in retaliation for a terrorist nuclear attack or plot and would be considered guilty until proven innocent. If a state on relatively good terms with the US, such as Pakistan, or a particularly powerful and influential state, such as Russia, were implicated, the response would likely be more measured, targeted and cooperative.

Use of military force for selective 'nip it in the bud' attacks has many attractions. Historically the consequences for the attacker have been minimal and international condemnation for an aggressive breach of the peace and transgression of the attacked state's sovereignty has undoubtedly covered tacit support behind closed doors in a number of capitals. But selective attacks may not, and perhaps cannot, hope to nip the nuclear or other WMD programme in question in the bud. The best prognosis is a significant delay in the WMD programme by a number of years rather than its termination for a number of reasons.[72] First, such an attack is unlikely to successfully locate and destroy all key aspects of a WMD programme: Israel's 1981 Osiraq raid left Iraq's reprocessing plant and fuel fabrication plant intact and the US and its allies failed to locate and destroy all of Iraq's nuclear weapons programme infrastructure during the 1991 Gulf War, the full extent of which was only revealed through UN inspections after the conflict. Second, the likely response to a limited attack will be a redoubling of efforts to develop a WMD programme and drive it underground both literally to protect against attack in hardened facilities and figuratively to shield more skilfully from the prying eyes of foreign intelligence agencies.

The limited use of military force to terminate the potential threat from a 'rogue' state's nuclear programme and concomitant potential threat of nuclear terrorism is no silver bullet. The use of military force for a much wider attack to try and eliminate a terrorist group, a 'rogue' state leadership, and its actual or suspected nuclear weapon infrastructure and other possible WMD capabilities is a far more onerous undertaking fraught with uncertainty and danger.

The decision to invade Iraq, for example, has been disastrous for the US. Estimates suggest it has cost the American exchequer $3 trillion[73], the lives of over 4,300 US soldiers and a further 300 allied troops with over 30,000 injured,[74] at least 92,000 documented Iraqi civilian deaths and undoubtedly thousands more and tens of thousands of casualties.[75] Many international leaders opposed the invasion and thought the US cure to Saddam Hussein was worse than the disease. The war

---

[72]   Richard Haass, 'Regime Change and its Limits', *Foreign Affairs*, July/August 2005, p. 71.

[73]   Linda Bilmes and Joseph Stiglitz and 'The Iraq War will cost us More than $3 Trillion, and Much More', *Washington Post*, 9 March 2008.

[74]   See 'Global War on Terrorism – Operation Iraqi Freedom: By Casualty Category within Service, March 19, 2003 through February 28, 2009', US Department of Defense. Available at: <http://siadapp.dmdc.osd.mil/personnel/CASUALTY/OIF-Total.pdf>.

[75]   See www.iraqbodycount.org.

has caused widespread regional instability, is widely regarded as an illegal act that has set a dangerous precedent for the future, has demolished America's moral authority in international affairs, fuelled anti-Americanism in the Middle East for a generation, caused antagonism between the West and Muslim worlds, weakened the United Nations and spurred the growth of terrorism in reaction to US actions.[76]

The same applies in North Korea and Iran. Serious and enduring concerns about each country's nuclear programme and potential for state sponsorship of nuclear terrorism may be real, but the cure of military force would likely be far worse than the disease given the relatively robust and growing network of non-military measures in place.

In North Korea Washington could destroy North Korea's nuclear and missile facilities and weapons but it may struggle to locate and destroy them all. The US would then have to contend with retaliation by North Korea's one million-strong army that could decimate Seoul, the South Korean capital that lies just 30 miles south of the Demilitarised Zone separating it from the North, with long-range artillery and missiles. North Korea has an estimated 500–600 Scud missiles that could strike targets throughout South Korea and around 100 No-dong missiles capable of striking Japan, perhaps with chemical or even one or two nuclear warheads. It was estimated in 1993 that US and South Korean military forces could suffer 300,000–500,000 casualties in the first 90 days of a conflict, with 100,000s of civilian casualties even though the US would eventually defeat North Korean forces. Civilian and military casualties would probably number more than a million and the reconstruction costs would be phenomenal.[77]

In Iran an air attack could destroy the country's nuclear and missile infrastructure, air defence capabilities and wider war-waging capabilities but Iran would have many means of retaliation. It could disrupt of Gulf oil production and exports; expand its support for insurgents in Iraq, Hezbollah and Hamas to attack Israel and US assets in the Middle East; launch ballistic missile attacks on Israel and US forces in the Gulf, possibly armed with chemical or biological warheads; reconstruct a nuclear programme in dispersed and duplicated underground facilities and develop it rapidly into a nuclear weapons capability with the full support of the population who would undoubtedly unite behind a hardline government.[78]

---

[76] See, for example, Brent Scowcroft's warning in, 'Don't Attack Saddam', *Wall Street Journal*, 15 August 2002.

[77] See General Gary Luck, testimony before the Senate Armed Services Committee, 26 January 1995; Colin Robinson and Stephen Baker, 'Stand-off with North Korea; War Scenarios and Consequences', Center for Defense Information, Washington, D.C., May 2003. Available at <http://www.cdi.org/north-korea/north-korea-crisis.pdf>; Vernon Loeb and Peter Slevin, 'Overcoming North Korea's Tyranny o Proximity', *Washington Post*, 20 January 2003.

[78] See Paul Rogers, 'Iran: Consequences of a War', Oxford Research Group, February 2006 and Patrick Clawson and Michael Eisenstadt 'Halting Iran's Nuclear Programme: The Military Option', *Survival*, 50:5 2008.

Occupation would likely meet fierce resistance. As Richard Haass argues, Iran 'is nearly the size of Alaska and has 70 million people, roughly three times as many as Iraq – more than enough to make any occupation costly, miserable, and futile for the United States.'[79]

The US is currently engaged in diplomatic processes with both countries. The US and North Korea's neighbours (China, Japan, Russia and South Korea) have been involved in a difficult 15 year process with the leadership in Pyongyang of negotiation, compromise, agreements, threats, sanctions and confrontation in an effort to persuade the regime of North Korean leader Kim Jong-Il and previously his father Kim Il-Sung to abandon their quest for a nuclear capability. An agreement to freeze and eventually eliminate the North's nuclear weapons programme in exchange for a series of incentives was brokered in 2007 between the US, North Korea, China, Japan, Russia and South Korea through the Six Party Talks process that began in 2003. The process broke down once again at the start of 2009 following Pyongyang's test of a long range ballistic missile/satellite launch vehicle and a second nuclear test in what has become a familiar pattern of two-steps forward one-step back. The prospects for a lasting diplomatic solution currently look bleak.[80]

In Iran the diplomatic process is equally troubled but perhaps less intense than on the Korean peninsula. Concern about Iran's suspected nuclear weapons programme became a major issue in 2002 when undisclosed Iranian nuclear activities at a number of sites unknown to Western intelligence were exposed, including the Natanz site where uranium enrichment was taking place and the Arak site where facilities were being built to support a nuclear reactor of the type that very efficiently produces weapon-grade plutonium. There followed a long period of diplomatic negotiation first between the EU-3 (France, Britain and Germany) and Iran and later between the P5+1 (the permanent members of the UN Security Council Britain, France, China, USA and Russia plus Germany) to reach an agreement to halt Iran's uranium enrichment programme in exchange for a range of incentives. No agreement has been reached but diplomatic efforts continue albeit with the implicit threat of military action by the US or Israel if negotiations ultimately fail.[81]

---

[79]   Haass, 'Regime Change and its Limits', p. 73.

[80]   See Mitchell Reiss, 'A Nuclear-Armed North Korea: Accepting the 'Unacceptable'?', *Survival*, 48:4, December 2006, Victor Cha 'Hawk Engagement and Preventive Defense on the Korean Peninsula', *International Security*, 27:1, 2003, and Roland Bleiker 'A Rogue is a Rogue is a Rogue: US Foreign Policy and the Korean Nuclear Crisis', *International Affairs*, 79:4, 2003.

[81]   See Robert S. Litwak, 'Living with Ambiguity: Nuclear Deals with Iran and North Korea', *Survival* 50:1, 2008, David Dunn, "Real Men want to go to Tehran': Bush, Pre-emption and the Iranian Nuclear Challenge', *International Affairs* 83:1, 2007, and Michael McFaul, Abbas Milani and Larry Diamond, 'A Win-Win U.S. Strategy for Dealing with Iran', *The Washington Quarterly* 30:1, Winter 2006–07.

The long, inconclusive and challenging nature of these diplomatic negotiations can lend military options an attractive, if perhaps illusory, aura of decisiveness despite dire predictions about the consequences of using military force to terminate or at least substantially degrade the nuclear weapon programmes of either country. Advocates of military force often paint both leaderships as implacable, irrational and undeterrable and insist that diplomatic negotiations to freeze or verifiably eliminate the nuclear programmes of either state will never work. The issue is often reduced to the question of how states should deal with a 'nuclear Hitler' in their midst, that is, a nuclear-armed state leadership bent on military aggression and expansion with close links to terrorist groups? US policy-makers and members of Congress frequently demonised Saddam Hussein as a modern-day unstoppable Hitler in the build-up to the 2003 invasion.[82]

In *Radical Response to Radical Regimes* Barry Schneider urges policy-makers to consider whether such an adversary is truly undeterrable, to determine clearly the extent to which US vital interests are directly threatened, whether key enemy targets are precisely located and vulnerable to attack, whether the US has a first strike capability to destroy the adversary's WMD in a surprise attack with high confidence, whether the US or its allies could be face retaliatory use of WMD; whether all other non-military options had been truly exhausted; and whether clear objectives have been set and all appropriate means identified and mobilised.[83]

Added to this list should be whether the benefits of a major preventive attack outweigh the long-term costs that will surely follow, in particular from the perceived legitimacy or illegitimacy of an attack. Preventive attacks are seen by some as legitimate operations under certain conditions to delay acquisition of nuclear weapons or other WMD by a 'rogue' state and buy time for a long term political solution. Others may interpret legitimacy quite differently. This chapter has focused on potential use of force by Western governments against 'rogue' states developing nuclear capabilities that could be used in a terrorist attack. Use of force by Western states, however, is unlikely to be deemed legitimate if the perceived purpose is to maintain Western control to serve Western power and interests justified by a Western security paradigm. It is instead likely to be associated with 'illegitimate' images of Western hegemony, neo-imperialism and hypocrisy. This is certainly the case in the vast swathes of the Middle East with respect to the US-led invasion of Iraq and it can bring important costs in terms of popular and elite resentment towards the attacking state, sympathy and support for the attacked party, wider resistance to the policies and strategies of the attacking state, and a loss of prestige, influence and authority.

Schneider concludes that if the answer to all these questions is 'yes', then the US might, perhaps, be wise to intervene with military force to prevent a hostile

---

[82] See, for example, Representative Howard Cable, 'Authorization of the Use of United States Armed Forces against Iraq', *Congressional Record Online (House)*, vol. 148, no. 131, 8 October 2002, p. H7209.

[83] Schneider, *Radical Responses*, pp. 23–27.

'rogue' state from acquiring or using WMD. If 'no' or 'maybe' then it 'should decide against military intervention ... decision-makers would do very well to proceed with extra caution when the preemptive decision they are tempted to make is based on many large uncertainties accompanied by huge costs for failure.'[84]

The answer must then be containment and engagement from a position of considerable conventional military, diplomatic and economic strength, such as the dual isolation and engagement of North Korea from the early 1990s. Containment and engagement strategies can be tailored to restrict a state's freedom of action, deter the use of military force including nuclear weapons, and deter any consideration of support for a terrorist nuclear attack whilst holding out the prospect of a negotiated solution to the confrontation.[85] This succeeded with the Soviet Union after many long and at times dangerous decades and more recently with Libya.[86]

Conclusion

This analysis generates a number of conclusions. First, the potential for nuclear terrorism is real, and deep concern about countering it is valid. Second, the consequences of a successful attack would be enormous but the probability is low given the many difficulties faced in procuring weapon-usable fissile material or stealing a weapon and then activating and firing a stolen weapon or IND. Third, a preventive layered defence strategy is the most appropriate approach but the network of measures already in place needs bolstering and streamlining to reduce risks from proliferation of nuclear weapons and uranium enrichment and plutonium reprocessing facilities. It may be appropriate for governments to consider consolidating the plethora of national, bi-lateral and multi-national measures currently in place in order to minimise operational and bureaucratic duplication and identify and address gaps in the layered network of prevention.

Fourth, countering nuclear terrorism by non-state actors and countering nuclear proliferation to states are intertwined. A number of the preventive initiatives outlined above are designed first and foremost to restrict the nuclear weapon programmes of states with mitigation of nuclear terrorism a second order effect. Similarly, many of the selective 'nip it in the bud' attacks and broader conflicts targeting WMD programmes described were planned or undertaken to prevent

---

[84] Ibid., p. 27.

[85] See 'Non-Nuclear Strategic Deterrence of State and Non-State Adversaries', DFI International for Defense Threat Reduction Agency (Fort Belvoir, VA, October 2001).

[86] See Sharon Squassoni, 'Disarming Libya; Weapons of Mass Destruction', CRS Report for Congress, Congressional research Service, Washington, D.C., September 2006, Wyn Bowen, *Libya and Nuclear Proliferation: Stepping Back from the Brink* (London, 2006), and Bruce Jentleson and Christopher Whytock, 'Who 'Won' Libya?', *International Security* 30:3, Winter 2005.

acquisition of nuclear weapons by a 'rogue' state rather than to prevent nuclear terrorism, although the effect is comparable.

Fifth, the use of force may be legitimate in countering a specific and imminent nuclear terrorist plot, but wider use of the military instrument is fraught with danger. Selective 'nip it in the bud' attacks have served to delay nuclear weapon programmes but they have failed to eliminate them, instead pushing them underground and severely restricting international access. Sixth, wider use of military force is unlikely to be employed in the name of preventing nuclear terrorism alone but as part of a wider strategy of confronting WMD-armed 'rogue' states that reside at the centre of US and wider Western international security discourse.

Large-scale military attacks to degrade a state's nuclear and other WMD programmes and support infrastructure may be attractive in the face of seemingly intractable and futile diplomatic negotiations, but use of force would likely be deeply counterproductive to national, regional and global security goals. Preventive diplomatic tools based on the network of US-Russian, US-led multilateral and international programmes, conventions and treaties and generic counter-terrorism operations and programmes to target the financial resources of terrorists, their ability to travel freely and to improve intelligence gathering and analysis capacity offer the best long term prospect of reducing the threat of nuclear terrorism. This must be combined with sustained diplomatic negotiations with countries like North Korea, Iran and previously Libya based on regional containment and engagement that ultimately seeks regime evolution rather than threatening regime change, however politically and morally unpalatable it may be for some of those involved. Over the longer term the nuclear weapon states will have to commit seriously to nuclear disarmament to ensure effective and intrusive controls on civil nuclear power programmes by an enhanced IAEA. Nuclear terrorism may be the 'ultimate preventable catastrophe', as Graham Allison argues, but long-term prevention will require substantial diplomatic cooperation and compromise with very limited scope for the use of military force.

PART FOUR
Afterword:
Concluding Reflections

Chapter 13

A Re-emphasis more than a Reply

Philip Bobbitt

It is an exceptional honour to have been invited to contribute to this volume, and even more so to be the subject of such thoughtful commentary by such distinguished analysts and scholars. It is therefore difficult to decline the opportunity – itself also generous and flattering – to respond to these critics. As any lawyer knows, the chance to have both the first and the last word is a priceless rhetorical position.

But who among us has not been bored by the letter to a journal of an outraged author following the publication of an adverse book review? And then the reply of the reviewer? And then, sometimes, an even further exchange as the ambit of the whirlpool of claims and counterclaims becomes narrower and faster and more tedious.

Therefore, I hope the editors of this volume will not think me ungracious if I simply confine myself to a few general remarks devoted to some subjects as to which my own clumsiness has apparently misled many commentators.

Market States and Sovereignty

Market states are not markets, they are states. As the most recent candidate for the mantle of a legitimate constitutional order, they stand in a long line of modern states since the Renaissance – princely states, kingly states, colonial territorial states, imperial state-nations, and industrial nation states. Because all these constitutional orders characterize states, they unite both the juridical ability to promulgate and enforce law, and the strategic aim of serving a unique claim to legitimacy. Neither role characterizes markets.

Thus, though market states may resemble multinational corporations in their organizational structure, such corporations are not states. Nor would an international order dominated by market states be run as a global market. It would be run as a society of states, as was the case when earlier constitutional forms achieved international pre-eminence.

Nor is it the case – on my view – that market states will emerge because they are transparent states of consent. On the contrary: (1) Market states can be states of consent, or states of terror, or mixtures of both elements that might be called, in Michael Howard's felicitous phrase in Chapter 5, 'states of acquiescence.' Indeed, I suggest that if the wars on terror should someday become epochal wars – wars that turn 'constitutional' by implicating the very legitimacy of the rules by which states govern – it will be to determine whether the order of market states is dominated by systems of consent or terror. This does not mean, however, that opposition to the order of market states of consent translates into support for the order of market states of terror anymore than it meant that states in the twentieth century that witnessed the struggle to define the industrial nation state as communist, fascist or parliamentarian all fell neatly within these three categories. (2) Transparency is not a common element that characterizes states of consent. Rather it is a characteristic of sovereignty, being distinguished from opaque sovereignty, and translucent sovereignty.

In *Terror and Consent*, I describe three current views of state sovereignty that contend within the society of states: *opaque* sovereignty, a classical concept that holds that events within a state's borders are entirely internal matters, beyond the purview of other states; *translucent* sovereignty, an outgrowth of European integration and the campaign for human rights, which holds that authoritative agencies like the UN Security Council can declare a state in violation of fundamental international norms – against genocide, for example – and forfeit or compromise the perpetrator's sovereignty; and, a more recent result of the human rights movement, *transparent* sovereignty, which holds that because a regime's sovereignty arises from its compact with its people as well as with the society of states, sovereignty can be penetrated when a state commits widespread acts of violence against its own people, or acquires weapons of mass destruction in violation of its international agreements, or supports global terrorists who threaten the civilians of other states. At present, critical states holding some version of these paradigmatic positions are, for example, China and Israel (opaque), France and Germany (translucent) and the US (transparent).

It should follow from this description that while market states have global interests that transcend their borders, they are by no means non-territorial. My suggestion that Al-Qaʿida might be a virtual state – a characterization I declined to rely upon in making my argument about Al-Qaʿida as a subject of warfare – should not be taken to suggest that all states will become virtual.

Anticipatory Warfare and Legitimacy

The use of the term 'pre-emption' in the US National Security Strategy and elsewhere has befogged rather than clarified the debate about the lawfulness of anticipatory warfare. In my book *Terror and Consent*, I suggested that the following distinctions would be helpful.[1]

Pre-emption occurs when a state uses force in the context of an imminent attack on itself. This anticipatory act of self-defence is lawful under international law but is carefully limited. As stated in Webster's famous paper, pre-emption is only lawful as a matter of self-defence when the 'necessity of that self-defence

---

[1]   Philip Bobbitt, *Terror and Consent* (London and New York, 2008).

is instant, overwhelming, and leaving no choice of means, and no moment of deliberation.'

Preventative war is a very different matter. This kind of anticipatory use of force occurs when a state is persuaded that armed conflict – though not imminent – is inevitable and that the balance of forces is shifting against that state such that any postponement of hostilities will tend to disadvantage that state. When Cato the Elder ended his speeches with something like '*Carthago delenda est*' preventative war (not merely total war, as is usually inferred) was what he had in mind. In the twentieth century – the century, by the way, of modern total war – preventative war has been considered illicit. A notorious example of preventative war is the Japanese attack on Pearl Harbor or the Nazi attack on Soviet Russia.

Preclusive war is easy to confuse with both pre-emption and preventative war. The grounds for preclusion, however, do not lie in the imminence of an anticipated threat to the state (pre-emption) nor are they limited to an anticipated change, for the worse, in the correlation of forces with a threatening adversary (preventative war). When the North Atlantic Council voted to intervene against Serbia in order to prevent its campaign of ethnic cleansing in Kosovo, the NATO countries did not claim that they faced the threat of an imminent Serbian attack on themselves. Nor when Tony Blair defended the UK/US invasion of Iraq on the grounds that it would prevent the Iraqi acquisition of weapons of mass destruction did he do so solely on the grounds of an increasing threat to the UK. Rather, there was a further and absolutely indispensable claim that had to be made, namely, that Iraq had fatally compromised its own sovereignty by its acts against its own people, in defiance of UN resolutions, and in its abrogation of the armistice agreement. Preclusion, which has elements of both pre-emption and preventative war, is quite different from both because the legal grounds for preclusive intervention are not entirely up to the judgment of the intervener. It is only when the state against whom preclusive intervention is to be taken has compromised its sovereignty – for example, by providing terrorists with weapons of mass destruction or conducting a campaign of genocide and ethnic cleansing against its own people, or supporting mass slavery, all of which have been recognized in international law as delicts – that such a state can be the subject of legitimate preclusive intervention.

This important requirement can be satisfied by a recognition by an international body of state actions that render that state vulnerable to intervention. Unilateral claims by the intervening state will not supply a sufficient legal rationale, without more. But what is 'more'? Doubtless, action by the UN Security Council is sufficient. Perhaps also recognition by regional security organizations would suffice. But what do we say when a single state acts without such recognition, as for example occurred when Tanzania invaded Uganda to preclude further atrocities by the Idi Amin regime or when Vietnam invaded Cambodia to halt its mass killings?

We must develop international legal standards for preclusive intervention; otherwise not only will we be ensnared by confusing this concept with pre-emption and preventative war, but we will never be able to ground legitimately those acts of preclusion necessary for the international system. It cannot be enough that the intervening state simply charges the target state with aggression or genocide; recall that Japan invaded Manchuria based on allegations of Chinese aggression and Hitler threatened Czechoslovakia with false charges of anti-German persecution.

In the postscript to the American (but not the British) paperback edition of *Terror and Consent*, I concluded that:

> Developing legal standards for preclusive intervention is an urgent matter because the war aim in the war against terror is not the acquisition of territory or the forced adoption of any ideology or the rejection of any religion – it is the protection of civilians. The growing potential threat to civilians posed by armed groups and states that turn on their neighbours or their own people has given a new urgency to preclusive measures, including theatre missile defences, strengthened alliances, robust international legal institutions, extended deterrence, and regional denuclearization. It is this threat to civilians (and the war aim to protect them) that links intervention on humanitarian grounds, intervention to prevent the deployment of nuclear weapons and intervention to deny sanctuaries to terrorists.[2]

Wars on Terror

I have misled my readers if they believe that my claim that the transformation of the State and the commodification of WMD and terrorism this transformation has brought about is so profound that it is now appropriate to reify the activities of groups like Al-Qaʻida as 'Terror' and thus as an appropriate object of war because this seems to equate terrorism with terror. I believe rather that it is terror, not simply terrorism, which we must fight. By that I mean that it is terror that de-stabilizes states and leads them either to be seized by terrorists (as is their object in the ongoing wars in Iraq and Afghanistan) or tempts the publics of well-established democracies to demand repressive measures in their own societies. That is why I – bewilderingly to many of my readers – insist that hurricanes, climate change, epidemics and infrastructure failures pose a threat on a par with terrorists and the proliferation of WMD. Thus, I have often made the point that if every Islamist became a Presbyterian we would still face the threats I attempted to illuminate in *Terror and Consent*, because they arise from a historic change in the nature of the leading states which is itself in part, but only in part, a reaction to these threats

In many quarters it has been urged that there is a sharp distinction between policing and war-fighting and that because combating terror successfully involves policing, it is a task ill-suited to war. However attractive such a distinction might have been in the past, I believe the events of the last seven years should have disabused us. When General Tommy Franks announced the end of major combat

---

2   Philip Bobbitt, *Terror and Consent* (New York, 2009), p. 551.

operations, Coalition forces had lost 146 men. Since then, we have lost more than an additional 4,000. The reason General Franks made this mistake is because he had a certain view of warfare. He thought: we have captured the enemy's capital, we have removed the enemy's political leadership, the enemy army has surrendered – it's over. Had he realized that warfare is changing he would have insisted on precisely that combination of constabulary and conventional military forces that we are only now achieving in Iraq. This change is not captured simply by new doctrine; rather it is a change in the war aim. The war aim of a war on terror is not the seizure of territory or the conversion of hearts and minds but the protection of civilians. That is what is distinctive about such a war.

Moreover, I would urge that the whole concept of legitimacy crucially depends on recognizing this change in the nature of warfare. To refuse to recognize this leads us to ignore the application of the Geneva Conventions, and to steadily erode the influence of international law and the laws of war.

It is also the reason such a war can be won. If victory is the achievement of the war aim, the victory in a war against terror – a war to protect civilians from that intimidation that would prevent them from doing what they have a lawful right to do – is by no means a fanciful objective. That is why it is important to remember we are fighting not just terrorists but terror – the awful sense that one dare not act on one's conscience for fear of violence. It is the potential of terror thus to disrupt the political operations of states of consent, which depend upon countless acts of conscience.

Both because a novel form of terrorism is becoming more warlike – able to threaten the stability of great states – and because war is becoming more a matter of terror – intimidating civilians rather than holding ground – I think it is imperative that we call these conflicts wars. Perhaps I am wrong. There are many good reasons, as Michael Howard notes in Chapter 5, why it is costly to use this inflammatory term. But it is unlikely that I will be persuaded so long as my critics simply assume away the problem.

But now I see that I am slipping into the aggrieved author role I wished to avoid, and so I will end my Reply here with my warm thanks for being asked to contribute, and my pleasure that such thoughtful and reflective persons should bother to comment on my work.

Chapter 14

Countering Terrorism Justly – Reflections Nine Years After 9/11

David Fisher and Brian Wicker

The attacks on New York and Washington on 11 September 2001 were as unexpected as they were devastating. They were followed by further devastating assaults in Bali (October 2002), Madrid (March 2004) and London (July 2005). Intelligence analysts, having failed to predict the 9/11 attack, tended in its immediate aftermath – perhaps understandably – to commit the opposite error of portraying Al-Qaʿida as if it were ten feet tall. Indeed, the very rhetoric of 'a global war on terror' had the effect, however unintended, of talking up the terrorist organisation's capability. For only against a truly global threat, such as that as had once been posed by the Nazi *Wehrmacht*, would a global war be required.

Nine years on, the threat posed by Al-Qaʿida and its associated groups remains deadly, serious and global. But we can now perceive more clearly some of the limitations and weaknesses of the organisation. It is also salutary to recall, as Audrey Kurth Cronin has recently reminded us, that, '*All* movements that use terrorism as a tactic end, and although they can cause appalling damage both to their targets and their own constituencies, they rarely achieve their strategic aims.'[1] Indeed, most terrorist campaigns end in failure, often amid in-fighting and fractionalisation, as the very tactic of terror becomes increasingly unpopular.

A first and fundamental weakness – as it has been one of the main aims of this book to expose – is that the ideology of Al-Qaʿida is not shared by the overwhelming majority of Muslims. Al-Qaʿida seeks to establish – by a regime of violence and terror – a borderless universal Muslim *umma*, ruled by an absolute caliph, regulated by sharia law and firmly eschewing democratic principles and practice. Even those Muslims who might share elements of that vision do not, in the main, support the use of violence to bring it about, while many Muslims would also eschew its anti-democratic bias. This would include the 190 million Muslim citizens of Indonesia, a flourishing democracy and country with the largest Muslim population in the world.

Moreover, Al-Qaʿida's ideology is not shared even by a fellow terrorist organisation such as Hamas. The goal of Hamas is the establishment of a Palestinian state, not a universal caliphate. They have not imposed sharia law in Gaza. They

---

[1]   Audrey Kurth Cronin, *How Terrorism Ends – Understanding the Decline and Demise of Terrorist Campaigns* (Princeton and Oxford, 2009), p. 168.

were prepared to participate in elections for the Palestinian legislative council in January 2006. For all of these actions, Hamas has been fiercely condemned by Al-Qa'ida and accused of following the 'infidel religion of democracy'.[2] Hamas may thus stand reproved. But for Al-Qa'ida the consequences are more serious. For its dispute with Hamas has severely weakened its ability to exercise any influence over what for Muslims is the core issue of international security – the future of Palestine.[3]

Most importantly, the commitment of Al-Qa'ida to violence against civilians as both an end (smashing the infidel civilisation) and a means (destabilising its governments) is not shared by other Muslims. Attacks on civilians are as great an affront to the Islamic moral code, as they are to the Christian, as Ahmad Achtar clearly demonstrates in Chapter 3.

Such violence has also proved decidedly counter-productive. Al-Qa'ida may have hoped that they could pursue a tactic of maximising civilian casualties without risking loss of support from their own constituency. But that hope has proved illusory, particularly since the casualties have included many Muslims. The violent attacks of Al Zarqawi against civilians and Shiite holy shrines in Iraq, together with the bombing of three hotels in Amman, Jordan, on 9 November 2005, alienated the Sunni population in Iraq. The attacks on civilians were widely morally condemned. They provoked a violent counter-reaction against Sunnis from Shiites in Iraq. This in turn led to the Sunni Awakening, in which Sunni tribesmen aligned themselves alongside US coalition forces to fight against the Al-Qa'ida insurgents in Iraq. Al Zarqawi's tactics even led, belatedly, to a rebuke from Osama bin Laden.[4] More significantly, the attacks by Al-Qa'ida on civilians, including Muslims, have proved extremely unpopular throughout the Muslim world. Bin Laden's Egyptian deputy, Ayman al-Zawahiri, was fiercely barracked at an on-line 'town hall' session by fellow Muslims, one questioner demanding to know, 'what is it that makes legitimate the spilling of the blood of even one Muslim?'[5]

Doubts have also arisen over the extent of Al-Qa'ida's global reach and capability. Its global reach has been achieved by outsourcing its operations to local groups and individuals. This tactic has proved very effective. But its disadvantage is that the local groups have their own agenda and priorities, which may be at odds with those of the central command of Al-Qa'ida. This was illustrated by Al Zarqawi's vicious murders of Shiite Muslims in Iraq. A divergence of aims has also been apparent elsewhere. Al-Qa'ida's affiliate in Indonesia – Jema'a Islamiya – staged the bombing in Bali in 2002. But, with key personnel detained or killed

---

[2]   Abu Yahya al-Libi, 'Palestine, Warning Call and Cautioning Cry', 29 April 2007. (Translations, here and elsewhere, except where indicated otherwise, by Open Source Center).

[3]   As argued by Barak Mendelsohn, 'Al-Qaeda's Palestinian Problem', *Survival*, vol. 51, no. 4, (August–September 2009).

[4]   Osama bin Laden, 'A Message to Our People in Iraq', (23 October 2007).

[5]   Ayman al-Zawahiri, 'Open Interview – Part One', (3 April 2008).

by the Indonesian security forces, they have subsequently renounced violence in their homeland.

The effectiveness of Al-Qaʿida's operations has been curtailed by the success of security operations undertaken against them. They have lost much of their leadership, particularly in the middle layers, not least to unmanned predator drone attacks by US forces on their bases in the Pakistani borderlands and elsewhere. Their communications are severely disrupted by electronic countermeasures. Patient intelligence gathering and police work have also been successful in forestalling attempted terrorist attacks, such as the liquid bomb or 'lucozade' plot to blow up seven transatlantic airliners in August 2006. That date could have had as chilling – or even a more chilling – resonance to it as that of 9/11. The fact that it does not is a tribute to the success of the security operation mounted by the British police and intelligence services.

Thus nine years on, Al-Qaʿida no longer wields the force and influence it once did. Its narrative still, however, has appeal, and its capability remains deadly, as even the failed attempt to blow up a transatlantic flight to Detroit on Christmas Day 2009 reminds us. Vigilance remains, therefore, essential to ensure the threat remains muted. Governments combating terrorism need to be successful all the time if they are to protect their civilian populations. For a terrorist group, only one success may be enough to revive their fortunes. Only one suicide bomber needs to get through to cause immense carnage and suffering.

Amongst the governments combating terrorism, a significant change since 9/11 has been in the US Administration itself, with President Obama replacing President Bush. Under Obama, the rhetoric of 'a war on terror' has been replaced by talk of 'The Long War.' Most importantly, the coercive interrogation techniques employed at Guantanamo Bay and elsewhere – including the notorious practice of water-boarding or simulated drowning of interrogatees – have been banned. The new US Administration has not repudiated the doctrine of pre-emption and has, indeed, explicitly retained a right to use pre-emptive military force. But its overall approach to countering terrorism, as to international relations generally, is more multilateralist and accords higher priority to diplomacy and non-military options than did its predecessor. President Obama reaffirmed the commitment of his administration to multilateralism in his address to the UN General Assembly on 23 September 2009.

These changes in the US approach are important. But the underlying challenges posed to governments by the new terrorist threat still remain. The US may no longer be at war with terror but its forces are still at war with terrorists in both Iraq and Afghanistan. So what lessons have been learnt in seeking to counter the terrorist threat in the last nine years?

A first lesson has been that military force, while it may be an essential weapon in the armoury to be deployed against terrorists, is only one weapon, to be wielded with care and only as a last resort. One of the main objections to the rhetoric of a 'war on terror' was that it appeared, by contrast, to prejudge the appropriate response to terrorism always in favour of military action. Military force may, indeed, on occasion, be necessary. But often old-fashioned police and intelligence-gathering may furnish the most effective counter. There is no better illustration of this than the successful foiling by the British security services of the 'lucozade' plot in August 2006, for which the ringleaders were sentenced on 14 September 2009 to terms of life imprisonment of up to 40 years.

Crucial lessons have been learnt about both when and how the military option should be exercised. The failure to uncover Saddam's non-existent weapons of mass destruction, concern over which had furnished a main ground for the 2003 invasion of Iraq, underlined how difficult it may be to acquire the degree of assured foreknowledge of the future that alone could justify pre-emptive military action. The authorised use of coercive interrogation techniques by US military and CIA personnel was plainly unjustifiable in its own right and in breach of just war principles. But it also appears to have encouraged the use of unauthorised – and even more extreme – measures elsewhere by US forces, notably in the abuse of Iraqi civilian detainees in the autumn of 2003 at Abu Ghraib. There were also cases of ill treatment of detainees by UK forces in Basra. The unlawful death in custody of Baha Mousa is currently the subject of a public enquiry in the UK.

Such abuse ran counter to the just war principle of non-combatant immunity, as well as the Geneva conventions on handling detainees and the prohibition of torture. But such moral failings at the tactical level also had adverse repercussions at the strategic level by casting doubt on the proclaimed humanitarian objectives of the campaign. How could coalition leaders claim to be helping the Iraqi people if their forces were engaged in ill-treating them?

A further lesson that had to be painfully learnt in both Iraq and Afghanistan – as military operations in those countries shifted from conventional operations to those required to counter a growing insurgency – is how to conduct a successful counterinsurgency campaign. For this – as Hugh Beach traces in Chapter 10 – a new counterinsurgency strategy and doctrine has had to be developed and implemented. A crucial insight of this new doctrine is that seeking out and killing terrorists is not always the overriding priority. For what is of fundamental importance is the protection of the civilian population, on whose support the success of a counterinsurgency operation depends.

A common thread running through all the lessons learnt has thus been a rediscovery of the importance of morality even amidst and, indeed, particularly amidst the pressures and passions of conflict. This was underlined by Sarah Sewall in her introduction to the new *US Army Counterinsurgency Field Manual*:

> The doctrine's most important insight is that even – perhaps most especially – in counterinsurgency, America must align its ethical principles with the nation's strategic requirements.[6]

---

[6]   Sarah Sewall, Introduction to the University of Chicago Edition of *The US Army and Marine Corps Counterinsurgency Field Manual* (Chicago and London, 2007), p. xxii.

There are, however, two qualifications to be made to this observation. First, the importance of ethical restraint applies not just to counterinsurgency operations but to all our endeavours to counter terrorism. Hence the wisdom of President Obama's decision to ban coercive interrogation. Second, Sewall appears, whether deliberately or inadvertently, to have got the alignment the wrong way round. It is not ethical principles that need to be aligned with a nation's strategic requirements. Moral principles are not to be twisted and shaped to accord with military strategy. It is rather – and crucially – the strategic requirements that need to be aligned, and, if necessary, changed, to accord with our ethical principles.

For the fundamental lesson that has had to be learnt is that, when confronted with a terrorist threat – however menacing it may appear – it remains vital that any community and, in particular, a liberal democracy, in seeking to defend its own values, should not lose them. Among the values being defended are the principles of the just war tradition. These principles are echoed within both Christian and Islamic thinking about war but are also of appeal to people of reason anywhere. That tradition insists that to fight well is to fight justly, to fight in accordance with the constraints of morality.

Bibliography

Abou El fadl, Khaled, *And God Knows the Soldiers: The Authoritative and Authoritarian in Islamic Discourses* (University Press of America, 2001).

— *Rebellion and Violence in Islamic Law* (Cambridge: Cambridge University Press, 2001).

Abu-Nimer, Mohammed, 'A Framework for Nonviolence and Peacebuilding in Islam', *Journal of Law and Religion*, 15, (2000–01).

Ahmed, Rumee. 'Rescuing the Wretched: Between Universal and Particular Readings of Q. 4:75', *Journal of Scriptural Reasoning*, 8, (2009).

Akhtar, Shabbir, *The Final Imperative: an Islamic theology of liberation* (London: Bellew, 1992).

Albright, David, A*l Qaeda's Nuclear Program: Through the Window of Seized Documents* (San Francisco, CA: Nautilus Institute Special Forum 47, 6 November 2002).

Albright, D., and Hamza, K.,'Iraq's Reconstitution of Its Nuclear Weapons Program', *Arms Control Today*, (October 1998).

Albright, D., and Hinderstein, C., 'Unraveling the A.Q. Khan and Future Proliferation Networks', *The Washington Quarterly*, 28.2, (Spring 2005).

Al-Qa'ida's WMD Activities (Washington DC: Center for Nonproliferation Studies, 13 May 2005).

Allison, Graham, *Nuclear Terrorism: The Risks and Consequences of the Ultimate Disaster* (London: Constable, 2006).

Anheier, H., Kaldor, M., and Glasius, M. (eds), *Global Civil Society 2006/7* (London: Sage Publications, 2006).

Anscombe, G.E.M., 'Modern Moral Philosophy', *Philosophy*, 33, (1958) reprinted in Anscombe, *Collected Philosophical Papers* (Oxford: Basil Blackwell, 1981), iii, pp. 26–42.

Aquinas, Thomas, *Summa Theologiae* (London: Eyre and Spottiswode; New York: McGraw-Hill).

Arendt, Hannah, *Eichmann in Jerusalem* (2nd Edition, New York: Viking Press, 1965).

Assman, Jan., *Moses the Egyptian: the memory of Egypt in Western monotheism* (Cambridge and London: Harvard University Press, 1997).

Augustine, *City of God against the Pagans*, ed. R.W.Dyson (Cambridge: Cambridge University Press, 1998).

Ayoob, Mohammed, 'Political Islam: Image and Reality', *World Policy Journal*, vol. 21, issue 3, (Fall 2004).

Ayoob, Mohammed, *The Many Faces of Political Islam: Religion and Politics in the Muslim World*, (Ann Arbor: University of Michigan Press, 2008).

Bacevich, Andrew J., 'The Petraeus Doctrine', *The Atlantic Online*, (October 2008).

Barlas, Asma, *Believing Women in Islam: Unreading Patriarchal Interpretations of the Qur'an*, (Austin: University of Texas Press, 2002).

Barnaby, Frank, 'The Nuclear Renaissance: Nuclear Weapons Proliferation and Terrorism', *Institute for Public Policy Research*, (March 2009).

Bentham, Jeremy, *The Panopticon* (Dublin: Thomas Byrne, 1791).

Bernstein, Richard J., *The Abuse of Evil: The Corruption of Politics and Religion since 9/11*, (Cambridge: Polity, 2005).

Bettenson, H. (transl.), *City of God* (London: Penguin, 2003).

Biggar, N., 'Just War Thinking in Recent Religious Debate' in Charles Reed and David Ryall (eds), *The Price of Peace* (Cambridge: Cambridge University Press, 2007).

Bleiker, Roland, 'A Rogue is a Rogue is a Rogue: US Foreign Policy and the Korean Nuclear Crisis', *International Affairs*, vol. 79:4, (2003).

Bobbitt, Philip, *The Shield of Achilles: War, Peace and the Course of History* (London and New York: Allen Lane, 2002).

— *Terror and Consent – The Wars for the Twenty-First Century* (London and New York: Allen Lane, 2008; New York: Anchor Books, 2009, pbk).

Booker, C., 'Our Army failed its test in Iraq', *The Sunday Telegraph,* (4 January 2009).

Bottoms, Major J.B., 'When Close Doesn't Count: An analysis of Israel's jus ad bellum and jus in bello in the 2006 Israel–Lebanon War', *The Army Lawyer*, (Charlottesville VA: 2009).

Bowen, Wyn, *Libya and Nuclear Proliferation: Stepping Back from the Brink* (London: IISS Adelphi Paper 380, 2006).

Bull, Hedley, *The Anarchical Society* (New York: Columbia University Press, 1977).

Bunn, Matthew, *Securing the Bomb 2008* (Cambridge, MA. and Washington, DC: Harvard University, 2008).

Burrell, David, *Freedom and Creation in Three Traditions* (Notre Dame: University of Notre Press, 1993).

Bush, President George W., 'President Bush Calls for Action on the Economy and Energy', (Washington, DC, 26 October, 2001).

— 'President's Remarks to the Nation', (Ellis Island: 11 September 2002).

— 'The National Security Strategy of the United States of America', (Washington: The White House, 17 September 2002).

— 'President's Address to the Nation', (Washington, 11 September 2006).

The Butler Report, *The Review of Intelligence on Weapons of Mass Destruction*, London: House of Commons: HC 898, (14 July 2004).

Cameron, J.M., *On the Idea of a University* (Toronto: University of Toronto Press, 1978).

Camilleri, Joseph A. and Falk, Jim, *The End of Sovereignty?* (Aldershot: Edward Elgar, 1992).

Campbell, Alastair, 'The Nature of Practical Theology' in James Woodward and Stephen Pattison (eds), *The Blackwell Reader in Pastoral and Practical Theology* (Cambridge: Cambridge University Press, 1994).

Cavanaugh, William T., *Torture and Eucharist: Theology, Politics and the Body of Christ* (Oxford: Blackwell, 1998).

— *The Myth of Religious Violence* (Oxford: Oxford University Press, 2009).

Cha,Victor, 'Hawk Engagement and Preventive Defense on the Korean Peninsula', *International Security*, 27:1, (2003).

Chestnut, Sheena, 'Illicit Activity and Proliferation: North Korean Smuggling Networks', *International Security*, 32:1, (Summer 2007).

Clark, Ian, *The Post Cold War Order: The Spoils of Peace* (Oxford: Oxford University Press, 2001).

Clarke, Michael, 'Does my bomb look big in this? Britain's nuclear choices after Trident', *International Affairs*, vol. 80, (2004).

Clawson, Patrick and Eisenstadt, Michael, 'Halting Iran's Nuclear Programme: The Military Option', *Survival*, 50(5), (2008).

Cole, David, *Justice at War* (New York: New York Review of Books, 2008).

Commager, Henry Steele (ed.), *Documents of American History* (New York: Prentice Hall, 1946).

— *The Comprehensive Approach: Joint Discussion Note 4/05* (Swindon, Wilts: Joint Doctrine and Concepts Centre, Ministry of Defence, 2006).

Convention against Torture and Other Cruel, Inhuman or Degrading Treatment or Punishment, Dec 10, 1984, 1465 U.N.T.S 85.

Counter-Terrorism Strategy (CONTEST 2), UK Government Cm 7547, (London: Home Office, 24 March 2009).

— *Countries Considering Nuclear Energy* in Appendix C of *Proliferation Implications of the Global Expansion of Civil Nuclear Power*, International Security Advisory Board (Washington DC: US State Department, April 2008).

Cragg, Kenneth, *The Lively Credentials of God* (London: Darton, Longman and Todd, 1995).

— Semitism: *The Whence and the Where. 'How Dear Are your Counsels'* (Brighton and Portland: Sussex Academic Press, 2005).

Cronin, Audrey Kurth, *How Terrorism Ends – Understanding the Decline and Demise of Terrorist Campaigns* (Princeton and Oxford: University of Princeton Press, 2009).

Dalacoura, K., *Islam, Liberalism and Human Rights: Implications for International Relations* (London: I.B. Tauris, 1998).

Daly, S., Parachini, J., Rosenau, W., Aum Shinrikyo, *Al Qaeda, and the Kinshasa Reactor Implications of Three Case Studies for Combating Nuclear Terrorism* (Arlington, VA: RAND, 2005).

Dando, Malcolm, *Bioterror and Biowarfare: A Beginner's Guide* (Oxford: Oneworld Publications, 2006).

Daulatzai, Anila, 'The Discursive Occupation of Afghanistan', *British Journal of Middle Eastern Studies*, vol. 35:3, (2008).

Davis, Charles, *Religion and the Making of Society: Essays in Social Theology* (Cambridge: Cambridge University Press, 1994).

Day Lewis, Cecil, 'Where Are The War Poets?' in John Lehmann and Roy Fuller (eds), *Penguin New Writing 1940–50* (London: Penguin New Writing 1940–50, 1985).

Devlin, Patrick, *Too Proud to Fight: Woodrow Wilson's Neutrality* (Oxford: Oxford University Press, 1974).

Donner, Frederick, *The Early Islamic Conquests* (Princeton: Princeton University Press, 1981).

— 'Sources of Islamic Conceptions of War', in Kelsay and Johnson, *Just War and Jihad*.

Dunn, D., 'Real Men Want to Go to Tehran: Bush, Pre-emption and the Iranian Nuclear Challenge', *International Affairs*, 83.1, (2007).

Durward, R. and Marsden, L. (eds.), *Religion, Conflict and Military Intervention* (Aldershot: Ashgate, 2009).

Elshtain, Jean Bethke, *Just War Against Terror* (New York: Basic Books, 2003).

Esposito, J.L., *Islam: The Straight Path* (Oxford: Oxford University Press, 2005).

Esposito, John, and Mogahed, Dalia, *Who Speaks for Islam: What a Billion Muslims Really Think* (New York: Gallup Press, 2008).

Euben, Roxanne L., 'Killing (For) Politics: Jihad, Martyrdom and Political Action', *Political Theory*, 30, (2002).

Evans, M. (ed.), *Just War Theory: A Reappraisal* (Edinburgh: Edinburgh University Press, 2005).

Ezzat, Heba Raouf, and Kaldor, Mary, 'Not Even a Tree: delegitimising violence and the prospects for preemptive civility' in Helmut Anheier, Mary Kaldor, and Marlies Glasius (eds), *Global Civil Society 2006/7* (London: Sage Publications, 2006).

Faraj, Abd al-Salām, *Al-farīḍa al-ghā'iba*, translated by Johannes J.G. Jansen as *The Neglected Duty: The Creed of Sadat's Assassins and Islamic Resurgence in the Middle East* (USA : Macmillan, 1986).

Farley, Edward, 'Interpreting Situations: An Inquiry into the Nature of Practical Theology', in Woodward and Pattison (eds), *Blackwell Reader in Pastoral and Practical Theology*.

Farr, Charles, Director General of the Office for Security and Counter-Terrorism in the Home Office, *Colin Cramphorn Memorial Lecture* (London: Policy Exchange, April 2009).

Ferguson, Charles, and Potter, William, *The Four Faces of Nuclear Terrorism* (London: Routledge: 2005).

Ford, D., *A Muscat Manifesto: Seeking Inter-faith Wisdom* (Cambridge: Cambridge Inter-Faith Programme, and Dubai: Kalam Research and Media, 2009).

Foss, Michael, *People of the First Crusade* (London: Michael O'Mara, 1997).

Foucault, Michel, *Discipline and Punish: the Birth of the Modern Prison* (Paris: Gallimard, 1975; London: Vintage Books, 1995).

— 'Truth and Power' in *Power: Essential Works of Foucault 1954–1984* (vol. 3, London: Penguin, 2001).

Friedmann, Yohanan, *Tolerance and Coercion in Islam: Interfaith Relations in the Muslim Tradition* (Cambridge: Cambridge University Press, 2003).

Frost, Robin, *Nuclear Terrorism After 9/11*, Adelphi Paper 378 (Abingdon: Routledge for the IISS, 2005).

— *Nuclear Terrorism*, IAEA Illicit Trafficking Database Fact Sheet (London: 2004).

Fukuyama, F. (ed), *Nation-Building: Beyond Afghanistan and Iraq* (Baltimore: John Hopkins University Press, 2006).

Galula, D., *Counterinsurgency Warfare: Theory and Practice* (Westport CT: Praeger, 1964).

Gentile, Gian P., 'Misreading the Surge Threatens US Army's Conventional Capabilities', *World Politics Review*, (4 March 2008).

Gesink, Indira., *Islamic Reform and Conservatism: Al-Azhar and the Evolution of Modern Sunni Islam* (London: I.B. Tauris, 2009).

Gilkey, Langdon, *On Niebuhr: A Theological Study* (Chicago: University of Chicago Press, 2001).

Goldstone, R. et al., *Human Rights in Palestine and Other Occupied Arab Territories: Report of the United Nations Fact-Finding Mission on the Gaza Conflict* (New York: UN Human Rights Council, September 2009).

Gregory, Shaun, 'The Terrorist Threat to Pakistan's Nuclear Weapons', *CTC Sentinel*, 2(7), (July 2009).

Grotius, Hugo, *On The Law of War and Peace*, in Reichberg, Syse and Bagby (eds), *Ethics of War*.

Guillaume, Alfred, *Islam* (London: Cassell, 1956).

Guthrie, Charles, and Quinlan, Michael, *Just War – The Just War Tradition: Ethics in Modern Warfare* (London: Bloomsbury, 2007).

Haass, Richard, 'Regime Change and its Limits', *Foreign Affairs*, (July/August 2005).

Haleem, H., Ramsbotham, O., Risaluddin, S., and Wicker, B. (eds), *The Crescent and the Cross – Muslim and Christian Approaches to War and Peace* (Basingstoke: Macmillan, New York: St. Martin's Press, 1998).

Hamidullah, Muhammad, *Muslim Conduct of State, being a treatise of Muslim public international law, consisting of the laws of peace, war and neutrality, together with precedents from orthodox practice and preceded by a historical and general introduction* (3rd Edition, Lahore: Muhammad Ashraf, 1953).

Ibn Ḥanbal, Aḥmad, *al-Musnad* (Cairo: al-Maymaniyya, 1313AH).

Hashmi, Sohail H., 'Saving and Taking Life in War: Three Modern Muslim Views', *The Muslim World*, vol. 89, no. 2, (April, 1999).

Hauerwas, Stanley, *A Community of Character: Towards a Constructive Christian Social Ethic* (Notre Dame, ID: University of Notre Dame, 1981).

— 'A Story-Formed Community: Reflections on *Watership Down*' in *The Hauerwas Reader* (North Carolina: Duke University Press, 2001).

— *With The Grain of the Universe: The Church's Witness and Natural Theology* (London: SCM. 2002).

Hersh, Seymour, 'The Iran Plans', *The New Yorker*, (17 April 2006).

— 'A Strike in the Dark: What did Israel Bomb in Syria?', *The New Yorker*, (11 February 2008).

Hobbes, Thomas, *Leviathan* (London: J.M. Dent, 1962).

Hodgson, P. and King, R. (eds), *Christian Theology: An Introduction to Its Traditions and Tasks* (London: SPCK, 1983).

Holt, Mark, *'Nuclear Energy Policy'* (Washington DC: Congressional Research Service, September 2008).

Honderich, Ted, *Humanity, Terrorism, Terrorist War: Palestine, 9/11, 7/7 ...* (London and New York: Continuum, 2006).

Howard, Michael, 'Review of The Making of Strategy: Rulers, States and War' in Williamson Murray, Macgregor Knox, and Alvin Bernstein (eds.), *War in History*, vol. 4, no. 1, (1997).

— 'Are we at war?' *Survival*, vol. 50, no.4, (August-September 2008).

Human Rights Watch, 'Open Letter to Attorney-General Albert Gonzales', 5 April 2006.

Samuel Huntington, 'The clash of civilisations?' *Foreign Affairs*, 72 (3), (Summer 1993): pp. 22–49.

Innes, M. (ed.), *Denial of Sanctuary: Understanding Terrorist Safehavens* (Westport Connecticut/London: Praeger Security International, 2007).

Iraq Survey Group Final Report, (New York: UN, 30 September 2004), vol. I.

Jackson, Sherman, 'Domestic Terrorism in the Islamic Legal Tradition', *The Muslim World*, 91, (2001).

Jentleson, Bruce and Whytock, Christopher, 'Who "Won" Libya?', *International Security*, 30:3, (Winter 2005).

Johnson, J.T., *The Holy War Idea in Western and Islamic Traditions* (University Park PA: Pennsylvania State University Press, 1997).

Jones, R.V., *Reflections on Secret Intelligence* (London: Mandarin, 1989).

Kaplan, Esther, *With God on Their Side: George W. Bush and the Christian Right* (New York: The New Press, 2005).

Kelsay, John, 'Sources of Islamic Conceptions of War', in Kelsay and Johnson, *Just War and Jihad* (1991).

— *Islam and War: a study in comparative ethics* (Westminster: John Knox Press, 1993).

— 'Arguments Concerning Resistance in Contemporary Islam' in Sorabji and Rodin (eds.), *Ethics of War* (2006).

— *Arguing the Just War in Islam* (Cambridge MA: Harvard University Press, 2007).

Kelsay, John, and Johnson, James Turner (eds), *Just War and Jihad: Historical and Theoretical Perspectives on War and Peace in Western and Islamic Traditions* (New York, Westport and London: Greenwood Press, 1991).

Keown, Damien. *The Nature of Buddhist Ethics* (Basingstoke: Palgrave, 1992).

Kilcullen, David, 'Counterinsurgency *Redux*', *Survival*, 48/4, (Winter 2006–7).

Kimmage, Daniel, and Ridolfo, Kathleen, *Iraqi Insurgent Media: the war of images and ideas* (Washington DC: Radio Free Europe/Radio Liberty, 2007).

Kitson, Frank, *Low intensity Operations: Subversion, Insurgency and Peacekeeping* (London: Faber and Faber, 1971).

Klare, M., *Rogue States and Nuclear Outlaws* (New York: Hill and Wang, 1995).

Kung, Hans, *The Church* (London: Burns and Oates, 1967).

Kurzman, Charles, 'Bin Laden and other thoroughly modern Muslims', *Contexts: Understanding People in their Social Worlds*, 2 Fall-Winter, (University of California, 2002).

Landon, Harold R. (ed.), *Reinhold Niebuhr: A Prophetic Voice in Our Time* (Greenwich, CT: Seabury Press, 1962).

Lawrence, Bruce (ed.), *Messages to the World: The Statements of Osama Bin Laden* (New York: Verso, 2005).

Lawrence, T.E., *Seven Pillars of Wisdom: a Triumph* (New York: Anchor, 1991).

Lehmann, J., and Fuller, R. (eds.), *Penguin New Writing 1940–50* (London: Penguin New Writing 1940–50, 1985).

Leventhal, Paul, and Yonah, Alexander (eds), *Preventing Nuclear Terrorism: The Report and Papers of the International Task Force on the Prevention of Nuclear Terrorism* (Lexington MA: Lexington Books: 1987).

Levi, Michael, *On Nuclear Terrorism* (Cambridge, MA: Harvard University Press, 2007).

Lewis, Bernard, 'The roots of Muslim rage', *Atlantic Monthly*, 266, (September 1990): p. 60.

Liddell Hart, Basil, *Strategy* (2nd Revised Edition, London: Faber and Faber, 1954/67).

Lieven, Anatol, and Hulsman, John, *Ethical Realism: A Vision for America's Role in the World* (New York: Pantheon, 2006).

Lind W.S., Nightengale, K., Schmitt, J., Sutton, J., and Wilson, G.I., 'The Changing Face of War Into the Fourth Generation', in *Military Review*, 69/9, (1989).

Lindbeck, George A., *The Nature of Doctrine: Religion and Theology in a Postliberal Age* (London: SPCK, 1984).

Litwak, R., 'Living With Ambiguity: Nuclear Deals With Iran and North Korea', *Survival*, 50.1, (2008).

Lovatt, Mark F.W., *Confronting the Will to Power: A Reconsideration of the Theology of Reinhold Niebuhr* (Carlisle: Paternoster Press, 2001).

Lovin, Robin W., *Reinhold Niebuhr and Christian Realism* (Cambridge: Cambridge University Press, 1995).

Mansfield, Stephen, *The Faith of Barack Obama* (Nashville: Thomas Nelson, 2008).

Al-Māwardī, *Al-Aḥkām al-Sulṭāniyya* edited by Aḥmad Mubārak al-Baghdādī (Kuwait: Dar Ibn Qutayba, 1989).

Martin, Richard, 'The Religious Foundations of War, Peace and Statecraft in Islam', in Kelsay and Johnson, *Just War and Jihad*.

Mayer, Jane, 'The Predator War', *The New Yorker*, (26 October 2009).

McCabe, Herbert, *God Matters* (London: Geoffrey Chapman, 1987).

McChrystal, General Stanley A., 'Lecture to the International Institute of Strategic Studies' (London, IISS, 1 October 2009).

McCullough, David, *Truman* (New York: Simon & Schuster, 1992).

McFaul, M., Milani, A., and Diamond, L., 'A Win-Win US Strategy for Deal With Iran', *The Washington Quarterly*, 30.1, (Winter 2006–7).

McMahan, Jeff, 'Preventive War and the Killing of the Innocent' in Sorabji and Rodin (eds), *Ethics of War*.

Medalia, Jonathan, '*Nuclear Terrorism: A Brief Review of Threats and Responses*', CRS Report for Congress, (Washington DC: Congressional Research Service, February 2005).

Mendelsohn, Barak, 'Al-Qaeda's Palestinian Problem', *Survival*, vol. 51, no.4, (August–September 2009).

Meyer, Ann, 'War and Peace in the Islamic Tradition and International Law', in Kelsay and Johnson, *Just War and Jihad*.

The Military Balance 2009 (Abingdon: Routledge Journals for the IISS, 2009).

Moinuddin, Hasan, *The Charter of the Islamic Conference and the Legal Framework of Economic Co-operation among its Member States* (Oxford: Clarendon Press, 1987).

Monroe, James A., *Hellfire Nation: The Politics of Sin in American History* (New Haven: Yale University Press, 2003).

Moore, John Bassett (ed.), *A Digest of International Law* (vol. 2, Washington, DC: 1906*)*.

A more secure world: Our shared responsibility, Report of the Secretary-General's High Level Panel on Threats, Challenges and Change (United Nations, 2004).

Morgenthau, Hans J., 'The Influence of Reinhold Niebuhr in American Political Life and Thought', in Harold R. Landon (ed.), *Reinhold Niebuhr: A Prophetic Voice in Our Time* (Greenwich, CT: Seabury Press, 1962).

Murad, Abdal Hakim, *Bombing without Moonlight: the origins of suicidal terrorism* (Bristol: Amal Press, 2008).

Murray, Williamson, Knox, Macgregor, and Bernstein, Alvin (eds), *War in History*, vol. 4, (1997).

Muslim ibn al-Ḥajjāj, *al-Jāmi' al-Ṣaḥīḥ* (Vaduz: Thesaurus Islamicus Foundation, 2000).

Nagl, John A., *Learning to Eat Soup with a Knife: Counterinsurgency Lessons from Malaya and Vietnam* (Chicago: University of Chicago Press, 2005).

The National Security Strategy of the United States of America, President George W. Bush, The White House, 17 September 2002, at www.whitehouse.gov/nsc/nss.pdf.

National Strategy to Combat Weapons of Mass Destruction, Dec.2002, at: www. state.gov/documents/organization/16092.pdf

Niebuhr, Reinhold, *The Nature and Destiny of Man, Vol. 1. Human Nature* (London: Nisbet, 1941).

— *The Nature and Destiny of Man, Vol 2. Human Destiny* (London: Nisbet, 1943).

— *The Children of Light and the Children of Darkness* (New York: Charles Scribner, 1944).

— *The Irony of American History* (London: Nisbet and Co., 1952).

— *Christian Realism and Political Problems* (London: Faber and Faber, 1954).

Niebuhr, Reinhold, and Heimart, Alan, *A Nation So Conceived: Reflections On the History of America from Its Early Visions to Its Present Power* (London: Faber and Faber, 1963).

Non-Nuclear Strategic Deterrence of State and Non-State Adversaries, DFI International for Defense Threat Reducation Agency (DTRA: Fort Belvoir, VA: October 2001).

Nuclear Black Markets: Pakistan, A.Q. Khan and the Rise of Proliferation Networks, IISS Strategic Dossier (London: IISS, 2007).

Obama, Barack, *The Audacity of Hope* (Edinburgh: Cannongate, 2007).

— *Dreams from My Father* (Edinburgh: Cannongate, 2008)

— *Change We Can Believe In* (Edinburgh: Cannongate, 2009).

O'Connell, M.E., *Unlawful Killing with Combat Drones, A Case Study of Pakistan, 2004–2009* (Notre Dame, Indiana: Notre Dame Law School, Legal Studies Research Paper No. 09–43, 2009).

Omand, David, 'Ethical guidelines in using secret intelligence for public security', *The Cambridge Review of International Affairs*, vol. 19: 4 (2006).

— *Securing the State* (London: Hurst, 2010).

Osama bin Laden, 'Conversation with Terror', interview by Rahimilla Yusufzai in *Time*, (11 January 1999).

Partner, Peter, *God of Battles: Holy Wars of Christianity and Islam* (London: HarperCollins, 1997).

Patterson, Eric (ed.), *The Christian Realists: Reassessing the Contributions of Niebuhr and His Contemporaries* (Lanham, MD: University Press of America, 2003).

— 'Niebuhr and His Critics: Realistic Optimism in World Politics' in *The Christian Realists*.

Pattison, Stephen, 'Some Straw for the Bricks: A Basic Introduction to Theological Reflection', in James Woodward and Stephen Pattison (eds), *The Blackwell Reader in Pastoral and Practical Theology* (Oxford: Blackwell, 2000).

Perry, W., and Carter, A., *Preventive Defense: A New Security Strategy for America* (Washington DC: Brookings Institution Press, 1999).

Popovski, Vesselin, and Turner, Nicholas, *World Religions and Norms of War* (New York: United Nations University Press, 2009).

al-Qadi, Wadad, 'The Primordial Covenant and Human History in the Qur'an', *Proceedings of the American Philosophical Society*, 147, (2003).

Quinlan, Michael, 'Just Intelligence: Prologomena to an Ethical Theory', in *Intelligence and National Security*, vol. 22, no. 1, (Feb 2007).

Quinlan, Michael, and Guthrie, Charles, *Just War* (London: Bloomsbury, 2007).

Al-Rasheed, M., *Contesting the Saudi State: Islamic Voices from a New Generation* (Cambridge: Cambridge University Press, 2007).

Rasmussen, Larry (ed.), *Reinhold Niebuhr: Theologian of Public Life – Selected Writings* (London: Collins, 1989).

Reed, C., and Ryall, D. (eds), *The Price of Peace* (Cambridge, Cambridge University Press, 2007).

Reed, C., *Changing Society and the Churches: Just War?* (London: SPCK, 2004).

Reichberg, G., Syse, H., Bagby, E. (eds), *The Ethics of War – Classical and Contemporary Readings* (Oxford: Basil Blackwell, 2006).

Reiss, Mitchell, 'A Nuclear-Armed North Korea: Accepting the "Unacceptable"?', *Survival*, 48:4, (December 2006).

Rensselaer Lee, 'Nuclear Smuggling: Patterns and Responses' in *Parameters* (Carlisle PA: Spring 2003).

— *Responsibility to Protect: Report of the International Commission on Intervention and State Sovereignty* (Ottawa: International Development Research Centre, 2001).

Ricks, Thomas E., *Fiasco: the American Military Adventure in Iraq* (London: Penguin, 2006).

Ricoeur, P., *The Conflict of Interpretations: Essays in Hermeneutics* (London: Athlone Press, 1989).

Rigby, Andrew (2005), 'Forgiveness and Reconciliation in Jus Post Bellum', in Mark Evans, *Just War Theory*.

Ritchie, Nick, 'A Regime on the Edge? How Replacing Trident Undermines the Nuclear Non-Proliferation Treaty', *Bradford University Department of Peace Studies*, (November 2008).

Ritchie, N., and Rogers, P., *The Political Road to War With Iraq* (Abingdon: Routledge, 2007).

Robertson, D.B. (ed.), *Love and Justice: Selections from the Shorter Writings of Reinhold Niebuhr* (New York: World Publishing, 1957).

Robinson, P. (ed.), *Just War in Comparative Perspective* (Aldershot: Ashgate, 2003).

Rogers, Paul, *Iran: Consequences of a War* (Oxford: Oxford Research Group, February 2006).

Roy, Olivier, *The Failure of Political Islam* (London: I.B.Tauris, 1994).

Rūmī, Jalāl al-Dīn, *The Mathnawī*, edited and translated by R.A. Nicholson (London: E.J.W. Gibb Memorial, 1925–40).

Saeed, A., Trends in Contemporary Islam: A Preliminary Attempt at a Classification, *The Muslim World*, vol. 97, (July 2007): pp. 395–404.

Sanger, David E. and Baker, Peter, 'Obama to accelerate deployment of troops', *International Herald Tribune*, 2 December 2009.

Sayyid, S., *A Fundamental Fear: Eurocentrism and the Emergence of Islam* (London/New York: Zed Books, 2003).

Schlesinger, Arthur M. Jr., *War and the American Presidency* (New York: W.W. Norton and Co., 2005).

Schneider, Barry, *Radical Responses to Radical Regimes: Evaluating Preemptive Counter-Proliferation* (Washington DC: National Defense University, McNair Paper Number 41, May 1995).

Shepard, W., 'The Diversity of Islamic Thought: Towards a Typology', in Suha Taji-Farouki and Basheer M. Nafi (eds), *Islamic Thought in the Twentieth Century* (London:I.B. Tauris, 2004).

Shue, Henry, and Rodin, David (eds), *Preemption: military action and moral justification* (Oxford: Oxford University Press, 2007).

Shultz, George, Perry, William, Kissinger, Henry, and Nunn, Sam, 'A World Free of Nuclear Weapons', *Wall Street Journal*, (7 January 2007).

Al-Shybānī, *The Islamic law of Nations* (trans. by Majid Khadduri, Baltimore: The John Hopkins Press, 1966).

'Secure energy: options for a safer world: Effective Safeguards?' (Oxford: Oxford Research Group, Fact Sheet 2, November 2005).

Sewall, Sarah, Introduction to *The US Army and Marine Corps Counterinsurgency Field Manual* (Chicago and London, Chicago University Press, 2007).

Shaikh, Naveed S., *The New Politics of Islam: Pan-Islamic foreign policy in a world of states* (London: RoutledgeCurzon, 2003).

Shihadeh, Ayman, *The Teleological Ethics of Fakhr al-Dīn al- Rāzī* (Leiden: E.J.W. Brill, 2006).

Shinn, Roger L., 'Christian Realists in a Pluralistic Society: Interactions between Niebuhr and Morgenthau, Kennan, and Schlesinger' in Patterson (ed.), *Christian Realists*.

— *Silence is Violence: End the abuse of women in Afghanistan* (UN Assistance Mission for Afghanistan (UNAMA) and Office of the High Commissioner for Human Rights (OHCHR, July 2009).

Singer, Peter, *The President of Good and Evil: Taking George W. Bush Seriously* (London: Granta Books, 2004).

Smith, Gary Scott, *Faith and the Presidency: From George Washington to George W. Bush* (Oxford: Oxford University Press, 2006).

Smith, Jane Idleman, and Haddad, Yvonne Yazbeck, *The Islamic Understanding of Death and Resurrection* (Albany: State University of New York Press, 1981).

Smith, General R., *The Utility of Force: The Art of War in the Modern World* (London: Penguin Books, 2006).

Sokolski, Henry, *Rethinking Nuclear Terrorism* (Washington DC: The Nonproliferation Policy Education Center, January 2006).

Solomon, Norman, 'The Ethics of War in Judaism', in Sorabji and Rodin (eds.), *Ethics of War*.

Sorabji, Richard and Rodin, David (eds.), *The Ethics of War – Shared Problems in Different Traditions* (Aldershot: Ashgate, 2006).

Stirrup, Air Chief Marshal Sir Jock, *Defence Daily Update*, 5 January 2009.

Stone, Ronald H., *Prophetic Realism: Beyond Militarism and Pacifism in an Age of Terror* (London: T&T Clark, 2005).

Sykes, Stephen, *Power and Christian Theology* (London: Continuum, 2006).

Ibn Taymiyya, *al-Siyāsa al-Shar'iyya fī iṣlāḥ al-rā'ī wa al-ra'iyya*, edited by 'Alī b. Muḥammad al-'Imrān (Saudi Arabia: Dar 'ālam al-Fawa'id, 2008).

— *Muslims under Non-Muslim rule* (trans. by Yahya Michot, Oxford: Interface Publications, 2006).

Terriff, T. and Karp, A. and R. (eds.), *Global Insurgency and the Future of Armed Conflict; Debating Fourth Generation Warfare* (London: Routledge, 2007).

Thompson, Robert, *Defeating Communist Insurgency: Experiences from Malaya and Vietnam* (St Petersburg: F.L. Hailer, 2005).

UK Agencies and Rendition (Intelligence and Security Committee, London: Cabinet Office, July 2007).

US Army Marine Corps Counterinsurgency Field Manual FM 3–24 (Chicago: University of Chicago Press, 2007).

US National War College Guide to Security Issues (Carlisle PA: US Strategic Studies Institute, 2008).

Walzer, Michael, *Just and Unjust Wars* (New York: Basic Books, 1977).

— 'Just and Unjust Occupations', Foundation for the Study of Independent Social Ideas, *Dissent magazine* (New York, Winter 2004).

— 'War Fair', *The New Republic*, (July 31 2006).

Wasserstein, Bernard, *Divided Jerusalem: The Struggle for the Holy City* (Yale and London: Yale University Press, 2001).

Westbrook, Robert B., *Democratic Hope: Pragmatism and the Politics of Truth* (Ithaca: Cornell University Press, 2005).

Wiley, Tatha, *Original Sin: Origins, Developments, Contemporary Meanings* (New York: Paulist Press, 2002).

Williams, B.G., 'Death from the Skies: An Overview of the CIA's Drone Campaign in Pakistan', *Jamestown Foundation Terrorism Monitor*, vol. 7, (2009).

Williams, Robert R., 'Sin and Evil' in Hodgson and King (eds), *Christian Theology: An Introduction to Its Traditions and Tasks*.

Williams, Shirley, *God and Caesar* (London: Continuum, 2003).

Windass, Stanley, *Christianity Versus Violence* (London: Sheed and Ward, 1964).

Winter, Tim. 'The last trump card: Islam and the supersession of other faiths', *Studies in Interreligious Dialogue*, 9, (Leuven, 1999).

Woodward, James and Pattison, Stephen (eds.), *The Blackwell Reader in Pastoral and Practical Theology* (Oxford: Blackwell, 2000).

Woolf, Amy, *Nunn-Lugar Cooperative Threat Reduction Programs: Issues for Congress* (Washington DC: Congressional Research Service, March 2001).

Yusuf Ali, Abdullah, (trans.) *The Holy Qur'an* (Hertfordshire, UK: Wordsworth Editions, 2000).

Zawati, Hilmi M., *Is Jihad a Just War? War, Peace, and Human Rights under Islamic and Public International Law* (Lewiston and Lampeter: Edwin Mellen Press, 2001).

Index